YARMOUTH CASTLE BURNING

YARMOUTH CASTLE BURNING

THE DEADLIEST PASSENGER SHIP DISASTER OFF THE COAST OF THE UNITED STATES SINCE 1934

ERIC TAKAKJIAN & RANDALL PEFFER

SCHIFFER PUBLISHING

4880 Lower Valley Road • Atglen, PA 19310

Other books by the authors

Eric Takakjian and Randall Peffer: *Dangerous Shallows: In Search of the Ghost Ships of Cape Cod*

Randall Peffer's nonfiction: *Watermen*; *Logs of the Dead Pirates Society*; *Where Divers Dare*; *Never to Return* (with Robert Nersasian); *Windward Passage*

Randall Peffer's Cape Island novels: *Killing Neptune's Daughter*; *Provincetown Follies, Bangkok Blues*; *Old School Bones*; *Bangkok Dragons, Cape Cod Tears*; *Listen to the Dead*; *Screams & Whispers*; *Forever Barcelona*

Randall Peffer's Civil War at Sea novels: *Southern Seahawk*; *Seahawk Hunting*; *Seahawk Burning*; *The Blockade Runner*

Library of Congress Control Number: 2025930115

Designed by Jack Chappell
Cover design by Jack Chappell
Type set in Le Havre/Mrs. Eaves/Times New Roman

ISBN: 978-0-7643-6987-2
ePub: 978-1-5073-0582-9
Printed in China
10 9 8 7 6 5 4 3 2 1

FSC
www.fsc.org
MIX
Paper | Supporting responsible forestry
FSC® C104723

Published by Schiffer Publishing, Ltd.
4880 Lower Valley Road
Atglen, PA 19310
Phone: (610) 593-1777; Fax: (610) 593-2002
Email: Info@schifferbooks.com
Web: www.schifferbooks.com

CONTENTS

AUTHORS' NOTE

The events, the actions of individuals, and the dialogue in this book have been carefully reconstructed from the stories of the people involved, their families, eyewitnesses, and seafarers from the era. Extensive newspaper accounts from 1965, as well as thousands of pages of testimony given in the United States Coast Guard's accident investigation, add depth with their vivid recollections of the disaster that struck the SS *Yarmouth Castle*. Where firsthand accounts fall short, we have relied on an extensive collection of relevant books, websites, and historical records to supplement the narrative. The text also roots in established protocols of operation and communication aboard mid-twentieth-century cruise ships. As with almost all events with multiple witnesses, sometimes the stories about what happened diverge. When such discrepancies arose during our research, we have gone with the story for which there exists the most corroborating firsthand testimony and evidence, or we have presented the diverging accounts.

TIMELINE

1700 hours, Friday, November 12, 1965

The *Yarmouth Castle* departs Miami for a weekend holiday cruise to Nassau.

2000 hours, Friday, November 12

It is dinner aboard the liners *Yarmouth Castle* and *Bahama Star* as they cross the Gulf Stream for the Bahamas.

2030 hours, Friday, November 12

While Captain Carl Brown on the *Bahama Star* hosts passengers at a festive dinner aboard his ship, Captain Byron Voutsinas on the *Yarmouth Castle* is feeling the weight of command and takes his dinner alone in his cabin.

2300 hours, Friday, November 12

As the evening activities wind down aboard the two liners, most of the passengers and crew head to their cabins. Only the diehard partyers and gamblers are populating the lounges once the floor show ends.

0030 hours, Saturday, November 13

A fire ignites in storage cabin #610 on the *Castle*, but the night watchman on his rounds skips the corridor with #610. The fire goes undetected.

0040 hours, Saturday, November 13

Crewmen in the *Castle*'s engine room smell smoke coming through the ventilation system. A steward and a few passengers smell it too. The chief engineer and others start searching the ship for the source of the smoke.

0050 hours, Saturday, November 13

The chief finds the fire in #610. It is raging and cannot be doused with fire extinguishers. The fire hoses lack pressure.

0055 hours, Saturday, November 13

The ship's ventilation system spreads flames throughout the central part of the ship via the airspace beneath the false ceiling in the cabins.

0110 hours, Saturday, November 13

The engine room alerts the bridge about the fire, and the captain is called. The fire has already spread to other cabins.

0120 hours, Saturday, November 13

A woman in burned clothing stumbles into the passenger lounge and screams, "Fire!" In the cabins adjacent, and especially on the decks above #610, trapped passengers are already burning to death or succumb to smoke inhalation as they try to flee.

0130 hours, Saturday, November 13

The smoke and flames have spread to the radio room and the bridge.

0140 hours, Saturday, November 13

The captain and a few crewmen launch the #3 boat and abandon the *Castle*.

0145 hours, Saturday, November 13

The ship is an inferno from the bridge back to the stack. Aboard the freighter *Finnpulp* to the east, her captain has seen the fire and is charging back to the west to give aid.

0205 hours, Saturday, November 13

Captain Carl Brown on the *Bahama Star* sees the fire. He is racing toward the *Castle* as he lays out a rescue plan with his officers and crew.

0225 hours, Saturday, November 13

Carl Brown brings his ship to within 100 yards of the burning *Castle* and begins deploying his lifeboats.

0230 hours, Saturday, November 13

The *Finnpulp* launches a motor lifeboat and directs it toward the people on the bow of the *Castle*. Captain Voutsinas of the *Yarmouth Castle* and his lifeboat arrive at the *Finnpulp*. Captain Lehto, on the freighter, shouts that Voutsinas must go back to his ship, do his duty, and save lives.

0250 hours, Saturday, November 13

Fourteen lifeboats from the *Star* and two from the *Finnpulp* are picking up hundreds of passengers and crew from the water.

0330 hours, Saturday, November 13

Coast Guard aircraft and helicopters begin arriving on the scene.

0415 hours, Saturday, November 13

The last of the survivors are rescued. *Bahama Star* has saved 240 passengers and 133 crew. The *Finnpulp* has taken fifty-one passengers and forty-one crew aboard. Eighty-eight passengers and two crew members will never come home.

0603 hours, Saturday, November 13

SS *Yarmouth Castle* sinks.

November 22, 1965

The US Coast Guard convenes three weeks of hearings in Miami at a Marine Board of Inquiry about the accident.

February 1966

The US Coast Guard releases its Commandant's Action Report on the SS *Yarmouth Castle* disaster.

CAST OF CHARACTERS

SS *Yarmouth Castle*

Crew

Byron Voutsinas, captain
George Vazeos, chief engineer
Francisco Argilagos, chief mate
José Ramos de Leon, second mate
Virgilio Quiñones, third mate
Pamagiotis Menegatos, staff captain
José Pinder Gozan, chief boatswain
Steve Arampatzis, port engineer
Edwin Stephan, general manager, Yarmouth Cruise Lines
José Martinez, cruise director
Ruth Wright, hostess
Charles Agero, gift shop operator
Ann Fonda, assistant gift shop operator
Winston Roy Drysdale, waiter/entertainer
José Arcadio, night watchman
Charles Whyley, night cleaner
Guy Leslie, bellman

Passengers

Carl and Wilhelmina Apuzzo
Nathan and Betty Barkin

Mr. and Mrs. Murray Bell
Mr. and Mrs. Thomas Kneeland
Lloyd Lamn
Margaret Masters
Charles and Edna Matias
Bernice Shestack
Adele Simister
Mabel Straub
Joan K. Reynolds

SS *Bahama Star*

Carl Gray Netherland-Brown, captain
William Dagner, chief engineer

SS *Finnpulp*

Johan Lehto, captain
Paava Laavikka, second mate
Rauno Suominen, radio operator
Valter Mattias Toikka, chief engineer

PREFACE

Brushes with Death

Captain Eric Takakjian

Wednesday, October 18, 1978, was a bright fall day on the lower Chesapeake Bay, with a light northwest wind blowing. Visibility was unrestricted. I was among the students enrolled in the boatswain's mate / port security (BM/PS) class of '78. We were aboard the US Coast Guard cutter *Cuyahoga* for our first underway training exercise on the ship. Each of the twelve of us students took turns steering the ship, taking radar fixes, and plotting courses and positions on the chart "Chesapeake Bay Entrance." As midday approached, the class gathered on the foredeck for an anchoring drill. The plan was to anchor the ship and then have lunch. The *Cuyahoga* was equipped with a horizontal windlass with two wildcats, one for each anchor and two gypsy heads. This would be the first time any of us had anchored a ship.

Our class gathered aft of the windlass, many of us standing on the crew's quarters escape hatches, which sat on raised coamings aft of the windlass. The ship's superstructure and bridge were farther aft. Our instructor, a chief boatswain's mate, went over the procedures for anchoring in detail, ensuring that we all understood before the evolution took place. Splitting into two groups, half on the bridge and half on the foredeck, we maneuvered the ship into our preselected anchoring position and dropped the hook. After lunch, our groups traded places. Following procedures as described by our chief boatswain's mate, we heaved anchor and got the ship underway. We spent the remainder of the afternoon conducting seamanship and navigation exercises in the lower bay and York River. Before we all knew it, it was time to return to the pier at Yorktown and moor the ship for the night.

After we put the ship to bed, we all headed for the base chow hall and dinner. Over the past few months, all of us had become friends with the permanent crew of the *Cuyahoga*. Often, we would play volleyball together after dinner on the sports field. But on this night of dinner and volleyball, we could not imagine the tragedy that lay just two days ahead.

The next day, Thursday was routine, with everyone on the base attending classes and going about the day-to-day operations. Running simultaneously with our BM/PS class was a group of officer candidates. All the officer candidates were folks who had gone to college and then decided to join the Coast Guard, or they were Coast Guard petty officers who enrolled in the program. OCS (Officer Candidate School) was designed to indoctrinate those students into military life as well as give them the basic training they would need as junior Coast Guard officers. Upon completion of the OCS program, candidates would graduate with a commission as an ensign, the entry-level officer position for both the CG and Navy.

The Coast Guard cutter *Cuyahoga* was an Active-class cutter built during the height of Prohibition in 1927. Originally intended to chase rumrunners, she served many roles during her fifty-year-plus career. But nearing the end of her career in the fall of 1978, she was serving the Coast Guard Reserve Training Center Yorktown, Virginia, as a training ship. RTC Yorktown, as it was known, functioned as a major specialized training center both for enlisted petty officers and officer candidates.

Active-class cutters such as the *Cuyahoga* were small, not particularly fast, but highly maneuverable in capable hands. Displacing 320 tons, the 125-foot ships were powered by twin diesels and capable of 12 knots. The ship's bridge was located one deck above the main deck, at the forward end of the superstructure. Short bridge wings extended out on either side. The ship's single stack and single mast were on the centerline aft of the bridge. Visibility for the helmsman and conning officer was generally very good. The one limitation on the Active-class cutters was the physical size of the bridge. The bridge itself was very small, perhaps 10 feet wide and 6 feet fore and aft. Doors to port and starboard led to each bridge wing. A door in the aft bridge bulkhead led to a chart room, which contained a chart table, the radar unit, and a radio direction finder. With the large helm, compass binnacle, gyro repeater, and engine order telegraph, not much room was left for a bridge team. Three was ideal, four to five doable. Anything more? Well, overcrowded.

For an instructor teaching the art of ship handling and navigation in pilot waters, the stress level can be enormous. The less experienced the instructor, the higher the level of stress. If the instructor is not completely comfortable with his or her own skills and abilities, this will tend to magnify the situation. Adding to the level of stress are distractions in many forms—alarms, incidental ships business such as calls from crew members with various announcements or questions, and the presence of additional people on the bridge.

Physical and environmental constraints come into play as well. An overly crowded bridge may hinder visibility and hearing. Darkness, background lights, and unfamiliarity with equipment and surroundings can add to the confusion. Tragically, all these factors came into play on a Friday night in October 1978 on the lower Chesapeake Bay.

At 1515 hours, Friday afternoon, October 20, 1978, the *Cuyahoga* departed RTC Yorktown on a weekend training cruise. In addition to my friends among the ship's crew of fourteen, the entire OCS class of sixteen students was on board as well. The plan was to depart the mouth of the York River, proceed north in the Chesapeake Bay as far as Smith Point Light, and then turn into the Potomac River and head toward an anchorage for the night. The following day the ship was to proceed to Baltimore.

By 2045 hours it was fully dark on Chesapeake Bay. *Cuyahoga* was steering 014 degrees true, directly abeam Smith Point Light, just below the entrance to the Potomac River, when she sighted the freighter *Santa Cruz II* on her port bow.

Santa Cruz II was a 521-foot bulk cargo ship. Loaded with 19,000 tons of coal, *Santa Cruz II* had departed Port Covington pier in Baltimore at 1420 hours for sea that afternoon. At approximately 2047 hours, Maryland state pilot Hamill, aboard the *Santa Cruz II*, was proceeding toward the Smith Point fairway buoy. At this time, pilot Hamill observed a northbound vessel on the radar. Pilot Hamill observed a red sidelight and a single white mast light. Seeing this, pilot Hamill assumed there would be a normal port-to-port passing. The ships were about 8 miles apart and did not exchange whistle signals or speak on the VHF radio to make passing arrangements.

Aboard the *Cuyahoga*, her skipper, Chief Warrant Officer Donald K. Robinson, a Coast Guard veteran of twenty-six years, was on the bridge along with seven members of the OCS class. Various OCS students were performing roles as officer of the deck, navigator, lookout, and helmsman. Others observed. Three minutes later, at 2048 hours, after passing Smith Point Light, *Cuyahoga* altered course to port to 338 degrees true. This was the course for the northbound section of the fairway above Smith Point.

Santa Cruise II was on a nearly reciprocal course, making 14.4 knots with a fair tide. *Cuyahoga* was making 11.8 knots for a relative closing speed of 26.2 knots. If both ships maintained course and speed, they would pass each other port to port at a distance of roughly a half mile. The OCS student acting as officer of the watch spotted the *Santa Cruz II* and advised CWO Robinson. Both the student and Robinson observed the ship through binoculars and could see the port sidelight and mast lights.

CWO Robinson stepped to the chart room and observed the southbound ship in the radar scope at a range of 15,700 yards, just under 8 miles. Robinson formed the opinion that the radar contact was a small vessel bound into the Potomac River. Nothing could have been further from the case. The course into the Potomac River from that location would have been more like 300 degrees, not 163 degrees, which was what the *Santa Cruz II* was steering.

Aboard the *Santa Cruz II*, pilot Hamill, the chief mate, and the ship's master all observed the northbound *Cuyahoga*. At 2104 hours, pilot Hamill observed the lights on the *Cuyahoga* change. The green and red sidelights became visible, and then just the green sidelight and mast light. This indicated that the *Cuyahoga* had turned to port across the bow of the oncoming *Santa Cruz II*. Pilot Hamill made a quick check of the radar and observed the *Cuyahoga* to be at a distance of approximately 1 mile. The chief mate stood by the port side of the bridge, and the master, the starboard side, all observing the *Cuyahoga*'s approach. At 2105 hours, pilot Hamill sounded one short blast on the ship's whistle, indicating his intent to maintain course and speed and pass port to port. No reaction was noted on the *Cuyahoga*. At 2106 hours, pilot Hamill again sounded one blast on the ship's whistle. After this, the pilot ordered the engine stopped, the rudder hard to port, and the sounding of the danger signal, five short blasts of the horn.

Shortly before 2100 hours, aboard the *Cuyahoga*, OCS students were rotating through various positions on the bridge. CWO Robinson had stepped into the bridge to quiz the oncoming OCS student who would act as officer of the deck, or OOD. Robinson then proceeded to the port bridge wing to take bearings on Smith Point Light. Shortly after this, at approximately 2102 hours, the seaman apprentice lookout on the flying bridge, one deck above the bridge, reported seeing a series of lights ahead. The OOD acknowledged the report. But having been told that CWO Robinson was aware of the vessel, the OOD did not relay the report to Robinson. At 2104.5 hours, Robinson entered the bridge and ordered the helmsman to come left to 303 degrees true toward the mouth of the Potomac River, a course directly across the path of the *Santa Cruz II*. A minute later, at 2105.5 hours, a single whistle blast was heard. Robinson went to the starboard bridge wing to investigate. At this point, Robinson still believed that the other ship was a small vessel bound into the Potomac on nearly the same course as he. Returning to the bridge, he told the OOD, "We are going to return that with one blast, and I advise you to change course to 290 true." The OOD went to the chart room to advise the quartermaster of the watch of the course change. At this point the two ships were less than 1,200 yards apart. The lookout on the flying bridge now realized that the lights he saw were another ship, not a small vessel, and was about to make another report when Robinson blew one blast on the ship's whistle. Robinson then returned to the starboard bridge wing to take bearings on the other ship.

Thirty seconds later, another short blast was heard from the *Santa Cruz II*. Robinson then stepped into the bridge, put the engine order telegraph to all stop for both shafts, and returned to the starboard door. At this time the ship's executive officer, Boatswain's Mate First Class Roger Wilde, came running up the starboard bridge wing steps and said, "Oh my god, captain, she's going to hit us." Everyone heard the *Santa Cruz II*'s danger signal. The ships were 200 yards and twenty seconds apart. Robinson rang full astern both engines on the telegraph, but it was too little, too late. The *Santa Cruz II* plowed into the starboard side of the *Cuyahoga* at almost right angles just aft of the bridge.

The time was 2107 hours, roughly twenty-two minutes after the *Cuyahoga* first sighted the *Santa Cruz II*, a vessel CWO Robinson mistook to be a small craft entering the Potomac River to the northwest.

Pushed sideways at nearly 13 knots, with her portside deck submerged, *Cuyahoga* heeled nearly 50 degrees to port and stayed there for almost a minute. She then slid around the bow of the bulk carrier and down the starboard side, sinking two minutes after impact. Inside the ship, crew members were thrown around like rag dolls. Ships fittings and equipment broke loose, violently being slammed around. Electrical power was lost immediately, plunging the ship into darkness.

My friends who were above deck at the time of the collision stood a chance, but those below did not. Some of those on deck were thrown overboard by the impact. Others were able to claw their way clear. *Cuyahoga* came to rest in 58 feet of water. Eighteen men found themselves in the water and separated from each other. Shortly after the sinking, the cutter's Boston Whaler workboat, which had been lashed in chocks on the stern deck, broke free and surfaced. Roger Wilde swam to it and made it ready for use in mustering survivors. The injured, including CWO Robinson (who was going into shock), were placed inside the whaler. Others hung on around the outside.

Santa Cruz II circled back to the scene, using her searchlights to spot people in the water. Lowering her motor lifeboat, with the chief mate in charge and the ship's nurse on board, the freighter's crew made their way to the whaler and picked up the survivors. *Santa Cruz II* remained on scene until the following morning, searching for further survivors. Those rescued from the whaler were taken to nearby Patuxent River Naval Air Station by Coast Guard helicopters and boats.

Coast Guard divers reached the wreck the following day, hoping to find survivors trapped inside. Sadly, it was not to be. Eleven people died that night. It was a tragic accident that was completely avoidable.

At the time, the Coast Guard had no formal procedures for training deck watch officers, and no formal standards for selection of cutter commanding officers. Concepts of bridge resource management (BRM) and structured formal training were completely foreign to the Coast Guard in 1978.

Days later, I was a pallbearer at four of my friends' funerals. For me at the time, knowing a number of the men who were lost, the accident came as a shock and a wake-up call for better training and safety procedures at sea. The *Cuyahoga* accident underscored my lifelong obsession with deconstructing events leading to seaborne disasters as a way of learning from the mistakes of others and preventing future accidents and loss of life at sea. After a long, deep dive into the story of the SS *Yarmouth Castle* disaster, I believe that her story has much to teach us as a cautionary tale about unsafe practices in seafaring vessels. On a human level, it offers an uncommon and dramatic narrative about personal vigilance, the will to survive the unthinkable, compassion, heroism, and the triumph of the human spirit.

Captain Randall Peffer

Before I was a professional seafarer, I worked in commercial aviation as a young man during the late 1960s. I had grown up around airplanes. My father was a US Navy pilot and a decorated veteran of multiple World War II combat tours in such places as the Solomon Islands and the Philippines. He had also been on the front line of combat aviation during the Korean Conflict, the Cuban Missile Crisis, and the early days of the Vietnam War. When he wasn't flying for the Navy, he had a side hustle teaching instrument flying to general aviation pilots, and he always had access to a variety of their light aircraft.

I remember taking my first flight strapped to my father's lap at age three or so in a Piper J-3 Cub. When I was six, I sat on two pillows in the copilot seat of a Stinson "Station Wagon" and, with my father backing me up on the controls, made my first takeoff. It was from a lumpy grass field in Pennsylvania, and I still remember that when the Stinson bounced into the air and started climbing above the trees, I felt like the king of the world.

By my late teens I had a private pilot's license and was working my way to commercial, instrument, and multiengine ratings. After finishing high school,

I took a summer job as a "line boy," servicing aircraft, then as a ferry pilot, for an air taxi operation flying passengers and freight daily back and forth from the Jersey Shore to airline hubs in New York, Philadelphia, and Baltimore.

As it turned out, 1968 was a challenging year along the Mid-Atlantic Seaboard for aviation. The weather was hazy, hot, humid, and fraught with thunderstorms. On many days the mornings and evenings featured thick fog. These were what pilots refer to as IMC, instrument meteorological conditions. Simply put, you needed to be a current instrument-rated pilot with a fully instrument-capable aircraft to fly in such weather when you had little or no visual reference to the ground or landmarks. You also needed to file an instrument flight plan with air traffic control and be "released" (approved) for the flight before takeoff and landing. All these things took time.

To complicate matters, federal air traffic controllers that summer were staging a "slowdown" at major airports as they lobbied for better pay and working conditions. What this meant for aircraft approaching airports such as New York's JFK on instrument flight plans was a requirement to "hold" (fly in ovals over a prescribed radio navigation aid outside the airport's control zone) until a controller *slowly* sequenced inbound aircraft into the queue for landing. In such situations, it was not unusual to fly holds for thirty minutes or more.

Holds were not only time consuming and tedious; they also caused the aircraft flying holding patterns to burn a lot of expensive fuel. Flying holding patterns on the perimeter of New York, Philadelphia, or Baltimore for a medium-twin air taxi flight with two to six passengers aboard could easily double the normal time of the flight and turn the expenses for fuel and crew into a profit-draining endeavor. Meanwhile, air taxi passengers began missing their connections with airline flights.

These issues presented a major headache for the operations manager of the air taxi company where I worked. By midsummer, the company was bleeding money, and senior pilots began to fear for their jobs. This is when they started coming up with "creative work-arounds."

Normally, air taxi flights require only a single pilot for a light or medium-twin aircraft. But constant IMC flying in congested airspace involves significant task loads for a single pilot, especially when air traffic control is changing their requirements and routes for traffic separation on a nearly daily basis. My company's solution was to add copilots to our flights to share the tasks in the cockpit. It was, in theory, a good nod to safer flying, and I found myself promoted from an aircraft ferry pilot to a copilot at age twenty. I relished the chance to learn the ins and outs of challenging IMC flying from older, seasoned aviators.

But the reality of these flights was different from what I expected. Unlike today, when the protocols of collaboration and constructive dialogue between pilots in the cockpit on commercial flights have become industry standards, back in the summer of 1968 the pilot in command, like the captain of a ship, was a virtual god. The pilots I flew with that summer were, to a man, exceedingly skilled aviators, autocratic, and full of bravura. They were mavericks, and they were not safe. They were sure the rules of instrument flying didn't apply to them. They had no patience for a lowly copilot who might question their decision or offer to take on an additional task in the cockpit besides maintaining radio navigation, communicating with air traffic control, lowering the landing gear, or sharing snacks and beverages with the passengers.

Even though I saw (on nearly every flight!) sketchy choices the pilots in command made to save time and money, I listened to the counsel of a more senior copilot who told me, "Don't talk unless he [the pilot in command] speaks to you. Don't touch *anything* unless asked."

But among a plethora of "hairball" passenger and air freight flights I copiloted that summer, one scared the actual piss out of me, nearly caused a major air disaster, and forever changed my awareness of safe operations both as an aviator and a professional seafarer.

We left at midmorning with four passengers in a twin-engine Aero Commander from an uncontrolled airfield on the New Jersey coast, bound for JFK in New York.

Mistake 1: The weather was thick fog, and there was no way we should have taken off. But we did take off.

Mistake 2: The pilot in command did not file an instrument flight plan. His "seat of the pants" flight plan was to take off in this terrible weather, climb to a height of 400 feet on an easterly heading, then make a descending left turn until we saw the surf line off the beach. We would follow the beach north to New York Harbor at a height of about 200 feet. This kept us below 500 feet, where air traffic control radar would pick us up as a target. We had a locator transponder aboard, but I was told to turn it off. This was a "dark op" and totally illegal.

Mistake 3: As we approached New York Harbor, the pilot instructed me to scan New York–area approach control radio frequencies to determine weather conditions, altimeter setting, active runways, and traffic volume. He said he planned on flying right into the New York air traffic control zone and "popping up" on their radar when we were so deep into the control airspace that "they will have to get us out of the way [of a steady stream of airliners] and land us."

Mistake 4: I remember seeing the vague silhouette of Sandy Hook Lighthouse pass by at eye level as we started across New York Harbor and entered the control zone. At this point the pilot in command put our aircraft into a steep climb. As we climbed through about 600 feet, he told me to turn on our transponder, set it to a VFR (visual flight rules) code (1200), and tell the controller we were at 3,500 feet (the minimum "floor altitude" to enter the control zone under visual flight rules). We were VFR for landing, requesting radar vectors to runway 14 (the general aviation runway at the time, northeast of the main runways). Jet traffic was landing on runways 13 Left and 13 Right.

At the time, transponders were not required to encode our radar signature with our altitude. The controller had to trust us when we reported 3,500 feet, but we were lying by a vertical distance of almost 2,000 feet. We were also *not* flying under visual flight rules. We were fully IMC in fog and clouds. We knew from terminal weather reports that the top of the cloud deck was slightly above 2,500 feet, so we expected to break into the clear before we had to tangle with any "heavy" (jet) traffic.

Mistake 5: After fielding a radio call from a completely surprised and aggravated Kennedy Approach controller and receiving a heading change, we continued to climb with all our might through the "soup" toward our "reported" altitude of 3,500 feet. Meanwhile, air traffic control was warning us of descending jet traffic on final approach. It was to our left at 3 miles. Of course, we couldn't see the jet, and he told the controller he could not see us. "No joy," as they say in airplane speak. The controller told us to maintain 3,500 feet. The jet descending to land on 13 Right would pass safely below us, said the controller. Collision course.

Still, climbing, I could see the fog outside the cockpit lightening to haze and patches of blue sky opening up overhead. Meanwhile, the approach controller kept informing us of our near-collision course with the jet and told us to immediately climb to 4,000 to maintain vertical separation with the airliner. The controller thought we were above the jet's glide path and still wanted us to climb higher. But we were, actually, *below* the jet's glide path and climbing ever closer to it. Once again, both the jet and I reported "no joy" to the controller. We didn't see each other, and we were only about a mile apart.

At about the same time, we broke out of the clouds at 2,700 feet; both the pilot and I computed in our heads that if we didn't do something fast, we were going to climb right into a collision with the jet.

"Where the hell is he?" The pilot was looking off to his left and up.

I looked straight up above the nose. And right there, descending just hundreds of feet in front of us, was the silver belly of a Delta Airlines DC-8.

I couldn't even speak. I just pointed . . . and peed my pants.

The pilot in command shrugged and continued to climb to reach 4,000 feet, as if to say, "No harm, no foul."

We landed without incident. When I got off the plane to disembark our passengers, I wrapped my flight jacket around my waist to mask the dark spot on my trousers. Then I promised myself I would never fly with this cowboy or any of his brethren again.

Shortly thereafter, I quit my job with the air taxi service and bought my first sailboat. Then I went looking for a job as an oysterman on Chesapeake Bay. Back then, seafaring seemed a safer choice. Within five years of that scary summer of aviation, two of the four pilots in command whom I had flown air taxis with died in aviation accidents of their own making. They came from a dangerous and toxic culture, steeped in rugged individualism, machismo, and a cavalier spirit.

At the time, I thought those pilots were anomalies, but since then, my seafaring experiences, subsequent interludes as a commercial pilot, and this book's deep dive into the causes of the SS *Yarmouth Castle* catastrophe all have underscored for me a chronic problem with crew resource management that raised its ugly head in the aviation and the maritime professions of the mid to late twentieth century. Perhaps this book will add an exclamation point to remind all of us who venture out into the wild blue yonder of something my father told me a long time ago: "There are old pilots, and there are bold pilots. But there are no old, bold pilots!"

He might have been speaking of seafarers as well.

CHAPTER 1

Cruise to Paradise

1530 hours, Friday, November 12, 1965

Margaret Masters felt her cheeks flush. Her blood rushed with excitement for the adventure to come. But there was something nagging at her. If she was being honest, she felt the weight of responsibility as she guided her tour group up the gangway to the SS *Yarmouth Castle*. She was not very superstitious, but she was glad that today was Friday the twelfth. Starting a cruise from Miami to the Bahamas on Friday the thirteenth would not have set well for some of the travelers in her tour. She had led group tours like this before, and she had learned to expect the unexpected. Things rarely went according to plan. You just never knew what might be coming down the pike, so you hoped your lucky stars aligned for good fortune.

Masters was sailing this evening as the hostess to seventy folks from the North Broward Senior Citizens Club; most of them came from Pompano Beach, Florida, but nine were from the Ft. Lauderdale area. The cruise was a repeat of a club fling the previous year that the members were still raving about as a great break from their afternoon canasta and bridge games. This little adventure was sort of a celebration of the end of the brutally muggy fall in Florida, which had included the extremely destructive Hurricane Betsy back in September. They called the cruise "a lark" and "a bargain." Club members paid only $32 apiece (discounted from the regular $59 fare) for a three-night cruise to Nassau.

But there was nothing cut-rate about this weather. The air was soft and warm this afternoon at the old passenger ship terminal at Biscayne Boulevard and 9th Street in downtown Miami. The *Yarmouth Castle* was the first of two cruise ships preparing to depart for Nassau before dinner. The other ship was the SS *Bahama Star*. The two liners gleamed white in the afternoon sun. Masters thought that she and her gang sparkled too. Both the women and the men were dressed in Hawaiian prints. Many wore freshly purchased straw sun hats. The ladies were showing off their jewelry.

Masters was the manager of the Venetian branch of the Pompano Federal Travel Service. At age forty-seven, she felt in the prime of her life, and she loved her job. She liked to call herself a "people person." The travel groups she shepherded remembered her as fit, athletic, and perky. For the next three days, it would be her job as their hostess on the cruise to make sure her gang of seventy let the salt air, calypso rhythms of the islands, Gombay punch, gambling tables, and duty-free shopping cast all their worries to the wind.

Beneath the clipboard that Masters clutched against her right forearm was a paper bag full of rolls of colored streamers. She planned to pass them out to the group to launch from the dockside rail of the ship. Their cue would come when the ship's band ceased playing calypso tunes and struck up a chorus of "Anchors Aweigh." Then the *Yarmouth Castle*'s horn would bellow, the crew would drop the lines, and the ship would pull away from the quay with streamers flying in the breeze. The whole event was a little stagy. After all, the *Yarmouth Castle* was not the RMS *Queen Mary*. The passengers were middle-class Americans, not the Astors, Rockefellers, or Guggenheims of transatlantic steamship legend. But it was fun to pretend. And after everyone found their cabins, and the ship left the jetties at Miami's Government Cut astern, the party would start in earnest as night fell over the Gulf Stream.

In 1965 the SS *Yarmouth Castle* was a thirty-eight-year-old relic of the "Roaring Twenties." She was tired from a constant life at sea. But she had been considered a state-of-the-art coastwise passenger ship when launched.

She had started her life as the SS *Evangeline* in 1927. At 5,002 gross tons and 379 feet in length, she was a small liner. She and her sister ship the SS *Yarmouth* had been built for the Eastern Steamship Lines of Boston, Massachusetts, by the highly respected William Cramp & Son shipyard in Philadelphia, Pennsylvania, at a cost of $900,000. Their hulls were riveted steel, but their superstructure was wood. Originally intended for service between New England and Canada, the ships were also constructed with cruises to Bermuda, the Bahamas, and the Caribbean in mind.

The two ships remained under the United States flag until after World War II. As British passenger ships took on troop-carrying duties in late 1939 and 1940, the Eastern Steamship Lines ships were called upon to service British territories in the Caribbean. In early 1940, *Evangeline* began running between Miami and Havana, Cuba. Later in the year, she took over a Miami-to-Nassau run.

With the US entering the war in late 1941, the United States government requisitioned the *Yarmouth* and *Evangeline* to ferry troops from the States to bases in Bermuda, in the Bahamas, and throughout the Caribbean. The two sister ships spent the remainder of the war as troop carriers. By 1944 they were in the Pacific. For a short time, the *Evangeline* served as a hospital ship.

After the war ended, the United States returned *Yarmouth* and *Evangeline* to Eastern Steamship Lines. The remainder of Eastern's fleet had either been sunk in action or were so modified that the cost of returning them to commercial service was cost prohibitive. But the *Yarmouth* and *Evangeline* still had a bit of life in them, and they went to Bethlehem Steel's shipyard in Quincy, Massachusetts, in 1946 for restoration work. It cost the United States $1,704,170 to renew *Evangeline* for service as a passenger liner for Eastern.

In February 1947, *Yarmouth* started sailing on seven-day cruises from New York to Nassau, Bahamas. *Evangeline* returned to service in June, departing weekly from New York to Bermuda. But after only two months of running to Bermuda, her owners found this cruise unprofitable. Eastern laid up Evangeline in August 1947 at a berth on Manhattan's East Side, known as Luxury Liner Row.

American seamen's union demands for better living conditions along with higher wages gained ground in the late 1940s. Ships running between US ports are subject to the Jones Act, which requires them to be American built, manned, and owned. Foreign-flag ships are not permitted to transport passengers or cargo between US ports. Complying with union demands and the Jones Act proved very costly, particularly in the case of older ships that would need substantial interior modifications. So, in 1954, New England–based Eastern Steamship Lines sold their company name and their two ships to a Jamaican investor. He had a dream that he could turn Miami into a hub for tropical cruises using the *Yarmouth* and the *Evangeline*. In short order they began running regular three-day and four-day cruises from Miami to the Bahamas.

Ten years later the ships were still plying the same route, but the *Evangeline* had a grand, new name, SS *Yarmouth Castle*. When passengers asked the *Castle*'s crew about her history, they mostly smiled and shrugged their shoulders. They didn't know. They were too young and too busy with their jobs to be curious. The best that could be said was the *Castle*/*Evangeline* was a sailing legend, a grand dame from a bygone era. She had carried tens of thousands of passengers safely over a million miles of the deep blue sea.

Lloyd Lamn wasn't taking any chances. He was one of the senior citizens in Margaret Masters' group, and a retired electrician. He had also been a volunteer fireman for eighteen years, and he didn't like what he saw when he came aboard. The first thing that caught his attention was that everything seemed caked with layers of paint. It looked like a lot of the portholes, windows, and machinery for lowering the lifeboats had been painted so many times that they would have difficulty functioning as built. When he peered into a lifeboat, he found that someone had left or stored a collection of dirty tools in there. The swimming pool was strangely empty. It looked like a pit waiting to swallow some passenger in the dark.

Lamn became more concerned when he discovered that his cabin, #634, had no porthole or window at all. The interior of the ship felt like a maze, and some of the interior corridors ran to dead ends. While other members of his tour group were settling into their staterooms or heading off to meet Margaret Masters on the port rail of the promenade deck to toss streamers, he started walking around the ship, cataloging the fire exits, lifeboats, rafts, sprinkler system heads, and fire stations, just in case things went sideways.

As soon as Murray Bell and his wife found their cabin, #534, near the stern on A deck, they knew they could not spend even an extra second in this tiny cubical. If there was air-conditioning, it did not seem to be functioning at the moment. So, like Lloyd Lamn, they headed for the boat deck to catch the cooling breeze and the view of downtown Miami silhouetted against the sun. Like Lamn, Bell noticed the shabby paint job and the tools discarded in a filthy lifeboat. The fire hoses looked in good order. But who knew if they actually worked? If there was no water in the swimming pool, would there be water for the sprinklers and hoses?

It was at this point that Bell and his wife decided to spend as little time as possible belowdecks and headed for the spacious and airy Neptune Bar on the boat deck. A cold beer might help settle their nerves and cheer them up.

Adele Simister and her friend Mabel Straub had similar thoughts after viewing their claustrophobic cabin, #615. Mabel gave a loud laugh at the absurdly small cabin and said the moment called for a beer.

Simister thought her friend was "a card," always the life of the party. This eight-day vacation to Florida had been her idea. The two women were longtime friends, retired from the same trust company in Manhattan. They had been having a blast in sunny Florida with three other widows from New York.

Straub roused her friends and strode out of her cabin and down the hallway. It was Miller (beer) time. The stocky widow led Simister and their companions to the Neptune Bar like the Unsinkable Molly Brown of *Titanic* fame.

As the passengers boarded this afternoon, Ruth Wright had her hands full. She was blond, short in stature, and approaching fifty, but like Margaret Masters, her energy and broad smile belied her age. As *Yarmouth Castle*'s hostess and a floor-show entertainer, her job was to assist the pursers during the boarding phase of the cruise. So now she was helping passengers such as Carl and Wilhelmina Apuzzo from Coral Gables, Florida, find their cabin (#835). She liked their spirit. Carl was a fifty-five-year-old architect who designed high-end condos in South Florida. The Apuzzos had won this cruise at their church raffle.

A lifelong boater and saltwater fisherman, Carl had been keener than his wife, "Willie," to take this cruise. She didn't swim and felt uneasy on the ocean. Willie had put off taking this gift cruise at least once, but finally she had agreed to make the trip. Given his wife's anxiety about this cruise, the architect said nothing alarming to Willie, but now that he was aboard, he was not impressed with the condition of the ship. He counted the number of cabin doors as he walked the hallway from the main lobby to his cabin. It was his way of marking a trail for his mind to follow in case he and Willie needed to escape from their cabin in an emergency. When he saw that the latches on his cabin window were painted shut, he took his pocketknife and scraped away the paint on the latches until they were free. Then he opened the window just in case he and the love of his life needed to make a quick escape and the door was blocked.

This afternoon the hunt for the Apuzzos' cabin felt more than a little ironic to Wright because she had not really found her own. Or, rather, she had, but she discovered that her usual cabin had been converted into a storage closet. Cabin #610 had been hers for each of her sailings over the last six months, but now it seemed that the Yarmouth Cruise Lines' port engineer Steve Arampatzis or someone further up the company food chain had finally taken her complaints about the insufferable heat in #610 to heart. The vents from the galley ovens ran upward alongside the forward cabin wall of #610. There was a huge air vent in the false ceiling, and supposedly air-conditioning, but she could never relax or sleep in there because of the radiating heat until hours after the cooks had shut off their ovens following dinner. She would tell Coast Guard accident investigators that when she got to #610 earlier today with her bags, she found it uninhabitable, packed with "stuff." But she could not imagine that the shabby little cabin would be the source of a catastrophe . . . well, not for another eight hours or so.

Wright was one of the few Americans in the *Castle*'s crew, and sometimes she found herself linguistically or culturally left out of the crew's social scene, since many of her shipmates were from Central America or the Latin Caribbean and spoke Spanish among themselves. Miami was her home, but she had been sailing on cruise ships for the better part of the last eight to ten years. In that time, she had ridden the wave of the swiftly growing, postwar cruise ship industry until she had achieved her current post as hostess and entertainer. And now she had a few good friends on the crew. When she needed sympathy, she could always turn to Charles Agero, who ran the gift shop, or cruise director José Martinez.

There were a couple of the Jamaican waiters too. One of them was Winston "Roy" Drysdale, who doubled as a singer and dancer in the Caribbean-style floor show with her. She could always count on Drysdale and his young friends in the crew to make her laugh with their youthful and carefree banter. But she sensed that beneath Drysdale's bravura lay an essential integrity and grace under pressure. It felt good to call him and his friends shipmates.

In contrast, she found the captain, Byron Voutsinas, handsome but unapproachable. He was aloof in a way that seemed intended to emphasize a class difference between himself and the rest of the crew and passengers. She really hoped that he was, at least, a good and careful mariner.

CHAPTER 2

Cheers

2000 hours, Friday, November 12

The bubbling of laughter and the clinking of silverware on china nearly drowned out the ship's piano, playing songs such as "Fly Me to the Moon." It was the second seating for dinner aboard the liner SS *Bahama Star*. Her captain, Carl Brown, flashed a boyish grin to the passengers assigned to his table and shook their hands. Some people said he had a smile that just beamed with enthusiasm for his passengers, his ship, and his crew. Still smiling, he removed his gold-braided officer's cap, unconsciously straightened the jacket cuffs of his "dress whites," and took his seat at the head table in the dining room.

Opening up this evening's menu and reading, he could not yet decide between two of his favorite entrees, "Roast Young Tom Turkey" with giblet gravy and cranberry sauce or "Broiled fillet of Spanish mackerel with tartar sauce." But he was sure he was going to treat himself with dessert. Getting underway at the start of a new cruise to Nassau was always a bit hectic even on a calm night like this. He was young enough and new enough to the command of this ship (just a few weeks!) to believe that a successful leave taking deserved something festive. While the guests at his table tonight sipped champagne, he would celebrate with a slice of apple pie à la mode. It brought memories of his boyhood in rural Appalachia.

Born in 1936 at McMinn County in the "ridge and valley" area of eastern Tennessee, north of Chattanooga, Brown was the son of an itinerant, evangelical preacher and a free-spirited mother. By the time he was twelve, his parents' marriage had run its course. After the divorce, his mother, Elisabeth Netherland, moved with her only son to Hollywood Beach, Florida, where her sister lived, raised her son as a single mother, and worked as a dental hygienist.

It was here that Brown heard the call of the sea. In his free time, he would go down to the docks in Miami to watch the ships come and go. They seemed magical to him, almost as if they were alive with different quirks and personalities just like people. One day when he was fifteen and hanging around the docks as usual, dreaming of all the adventures that might await just over the horizon, a man asked him how old he was and if he wanted a job. Brown said he was going to be sixteen on August 8.

"That's my birthday too," said the man. "Come back on our birthday, kid, and I will give you a job."

The man was Frank Fraser. He thought his shared birthday with the teenager was an omen, and there was something special about this kid. Fraser owned a large fleet of banana boats at the time, and he had just begun a new business venture, carrying vacationers on cruises out of Miami on a small steamer called the *Nuevo Dominicano*.

The day that Brown reached the legal employment age of sixteen, Fraser hired him to do odd jobs around the docks. It wasn't long before Brown was going to sea as what Fraser called a "cadet" aboard the *Nuevo Dominicano*. Shortly thereafter, Brown served two years in the US Navy as a quartermaster (helmsman) aboard USS *Sierra*, a Dixie-class destroyer.

Following his hitch in the Navy, he returned to work for Fraser as an ordinary seaman, sailing with Eastern Steamship Lines, which Fraser had bought in his efforts to further develop a vacation cruise ship industry in Miami. One of Brown's first cruise ship jobs was aboard the *Evangeline / Yarmouth Castle*. Encouraged by Fraser, Brown began classes at the University of Miami and then in Brooklyn, New York, to prepare him for a career as a merchant marine officer. At the age of twenty-two, he was the third mate on the *Yarmouth* and ascending through the ranks of cruise ship officers. Now, at twenty-nine years old, Brown had taken command of the SS *Bahama Star*. He was the youngest person ever to be promoted to captain for the Eastern Steamship Lines.

This evening, he was just forty-five minutes behind the *Castle* on the run to Nassau. The course would take them northeast across the Gulf Stream, past Bimini Island in the western Bahamas to the lighthouse at Great Isaac Cay. From here, the cruise ships turned southeast through the Northwest Providence Channel. Beyond the lighthouse on Great Stirrup Cay, they would turn farther south, skirting the Berry Islands off their starboard side as they headed at about 14 knots for an arrival at Nassau on New Providence Island shortly after sunrise.

It didn't bother Brown that some of his fellow mariners looked down on his ship as an "old lady," and these 185-mile Miami-to-Nassau cruises as "pretend voyages" or "booze cruises." Brown was proud of his ship and her reputation. Her brochure called her "a very special world of fun and festivity," and her passengers agreed. They found that with her main dining room, Star Lounge, Bahama Salon, the Calypso Club, and a game room (with slot machines and gambling tables), she offered a "hotel experience" from start to finish. *Bahama Star* also got high marks for good food, attentive service, and innovative entertainment.

At 7,114 tons, a length 466 feet, and a beam of 60 feet, the *Bahama Star* was the largest cruise ship sailing year-round from Miami in the early 1960s. When completely booked, she carried 735 passengers in 247 air-conditioned cabins. But her critics were right. The *Star*, like all the Miami cruise ships at the time, was old. Built in 1931, the ship had originally sailed between New York, the Dominican Republic, and Puerto Rico as the *Borinquen*. Later she sailed as a transatlantic liner for the Arosa Line, until the demand for transatlantic ocean voyages dropped off in the late 1950s (with the rise of modern airline service) and Arosa's finances collapsed. Eastern Steamship Lines bought her at a bankruptcy auction to augment their growing cruise ship business between Miami and Nassau and renamed her *Bahama Star*.

Tonight, the *Star* was sailing with over seven hundred passengers and crew, and Brown believed that protecting these people's lives was every bit as important as welcoming them to this ship and showing them a good time. In the young captain's mind, a Gulf Stream crossing was never to be taken for granted. Squalls could pop up out of nowhere, turning the visibility to zero and whipping up high winds and rough seas. The *Star* and the *Yarmouth Castle*, 8 miles in front of her, were, after all, sailing through the dark into the Bermuda Triangle.

So-called "booze cruises" had been around for decades, of course. But before Frank Fraser of Jamaica set up his cruise ship business in Miami, tropical cruises were largely a part-time endeavor, a way for both coastwise and transatlantic ocean liners to stay active and profitable during harsh winter weather. Instead of sticking to their normal routes, the ships would sail south from places such as New York and Boston on vacation cruises to tropical destinations. Such junkets had their origins during the Prohibition era, when going to sea on a liner bound for a foreign port in Bermuda, Cuba, or the Bahamas afforded the opportunity for legal gambling along with the purchase and consumption of alcohol.

Frank Leslie Fraser came from a family who had emigrated from Scotland to Jamaica generations before his birth in 1904. Over the years, the Frasers had built a small empire of banana plantations on the island. They had also assembled their own fleet of banana boats to carry their produce to market, mostly in the US. So, while Frank Fraser did not yet know the business of carrying passengers, he knew a lot about shipping and seafaring in the Caribbean Basin.

Fraser was a visionary. He observed the popularity of a small steamer that carried passengers between Miami and Havana in the years following World War II, and imagined the seeds for a new industry. He saw that if he started tropical vacation cruises from Miami instead of the northeastern coast of the United States, he could eliminate long, rough, and cold ocean passages and give passengers warm weather from the start to the finish of their cruises to the Bahamas and the Caribbean. All he had to do was match the cruise ship sailing schedule with the arrival of the express trains in Miami from the Northeast. He could sell packaged vacations that included an adventure both "by rail and by sail." Because the islands of the Bahamas and the Caribbean were within an overnight's sail of Miami, Fraser could offer shorter, less expensive cruises aimed at the budgets of average Americans eager for curated tropical adventures. He would take the booze cruise to a whole new level. He understood that what he was selling was sunshine and its associated fun.

It was with this business model in mind that Fraser bought his first small passenger ship, the SS *Nuevo Dominicano*, in 1950; over the next four years, the business outgrew the little ship. When he went looking for bigger vessels in 1954, he discovered the struggling Eastern Steamship Lines. In short order, he bought the rights to the company name along with the *Yarmouth* and the *Evangeline*, which he reflagged as Liberian and Panamanian vessels to escape US regulations.

Having foreign-flagged ships allowed Fraser to hire cheap labor, especially from Jamaica, the Bahamas, Cuba, and Honduras. He refitted his ships like floating Las Vegas casinos of the era, complete with gaming tables, live music, floor shows, cheap alcohol, plentiful food (all you can eat!), and air-conditioning. Just to make sure everyone understood that these cruises were about leisure, he added swimming pools and plenty of lounge chairs on deck. One of his brochures claimed that the shipboard atmosphere was "Just like the West Indies afloat."

By 1959, Fraser's reimagined Eastern Steamship Lines was doing so well that it added the *Bahama Star* to the fleet and purchased a luxury liner called the SS *Ariadne*. But while the cruise line thrived, Frank Fraser did not. He had heart disease and died in 1961 at the age of fifty-seven. His investor/partner W. R. Lovett, who had built the Winn-Dixie and Piggly Wiggly food chains, took over Eastern Steamship.

Lovett quickly realized that *Yarmouth* and *Evangeline* were too small and tired to meet the needs of a booming cruise ship company, and he sold them to a Miami-based Panamanian company called Chadade Steamship Corporation, which was hoping to cash in on the burgeoning demand for tropical cruises. Chadade created an international corporate shield so dense that it would take the United States Coast Guard, a legion of personal injury lawyers, and a cadre of investigative journalists weeks to penetrate it and find the actual owner, following the disaster brewing on the night of November 12, 1965.

The mystery man was a Canadian citizen named Jules Sokoloff, and he would have nothing to say to anybody after the disaster. Sokoloff's front man, his general manager of Chadade's subsidiary Yarmouth Cruise Lines, which operated the sister ships, was a decorated Korean War army veteran, thirty-three year-old Edwin Stephan. In one of the ironies surrounding the unfolding catastrophe aboard the *Castle*, Stephan would skirt legal responsibility for the disaster and go on to form the cruise industry juggernaut Royal Caribbean Cruise Lines. But tonight, Ed Stephan wasn't dreaming big. He was back in Miami decompressing after getting the *Castle* on her way to Nassau. He hoped that Capt. Byron Voutsinas and his ship would hold it all together long enough to make some money and pay off a stack of hefty repair and provisioning bills. *Yarmouth Castle* had just emerged from major repairs at a Tampa shipyard after suffering significant dockside damage during Hurricane Betsy.

CHAPTER 3

Fears

2030 hours, Friday, November 12

While Carl Brown was on top of the world this evening, Captain Byron Voutsinas was feeling the weight of command. As his 376 passengers were eating fresh Nassau grouper or leg of lamb in the *Castle*'s vast, pillared dining room, the captain was taking his dinner of red snapper and buttered broccoli alone in his cabin, directly below the bridge. After dropping the harbor pilot and seeing his ship safely offshore and on course for the lighthouse at Great Isaac's Cay, he had left the management of the *Yarmouth Castle* to its chief mate and retired. He needed a break from all the people on his ship.

He wasn't much for socializing, and he was not at all sure he was cut out for this job as master of a passenger ship, where a lot of the job involved managing a large and somewhat transient staff while keeping hordes of passengers happy. Running a cruise ship had not even been faintly in his dreams when he graduated from a maritime training school in Piraeus at the age of nineteen back in Greece. For the better part of the next eleven years, he had worked his way up the ranks of seafarers "through the hawsepipe" (as merchant mariners say) by sailing as an apprentice and officer aboard freighters and tankers. In 1961 he sat for his ten-day Panamanian master's license exams with the Panamanian Maritime Commission in New York City. Previous to this, he held lesser officer licenses issued by the maritime commission of the Republic of Liberia. His first real chance at command had come aboard the tanker SS *Navigator* during 1962–63.

It was not until 1964, when work grew scarce on international freighters and tankers, that he turned to the cruise ship industry for a temporary, two-month posting as an officer aboard the *Bahama Star*. Then, in October 1964, Yarmouth Cruise Lines offered him the job as staff captain on the *Yarmouth Castle*. In April 1965, Yarmouth Cruise Lines general manager Ed Stephan promoted Voutsinas to master aboard the *Yarmouth Castle*. He was thirty-three years old.

Even though he spoke some Spanish, he had found his previous job as staff captain aboard *Yarmouth Castle* challenging. Before this, he had sailed on ships with a crew of fewer than thirty-five. The *Castle* had a crew of 176. Many were Hondurans and Cubans who spoke a Caribbean dialect of Spanish that was hard for Voutsinas to comprehend. His English was not much better than his Spanish, and he also found it difficult to communicate with many of the West Indians in the crew, who came from such places as Jamaica and the Bahamas, with thick, musical accents. Furthermore, although the crew could put on their happy faces for the passengers, morale below the passenger decks on the ship, down in the crew's quarters, and on the bridge was not great. Everyone from the captain to the lowest cabin steward felt that he or she was overworked and underpaid. Many of the crew talked openly about quitting the *Castle* for a job on a better ship like the *Bahama Star* or the *Ariadne*, returning to their home countries, or jumping ship in Miami and taking their chances as undocumented immigrants.

Voutsinas may well have been thinking the same thing when he was the staff captain. Trying to babysit a large, multinational crew—many of them unhappy with their superiors such as Ed Stephan and their staff captain—was not his idea of seafaring in any way, shape, or form. But Voutsinas's last six months as captain had been somewhat better. As the skipper, he had the authority and respect that gave him license to put a buffer between himself and all these other people. He enforced a clear chain of command on the *Castle* that separated him from almost all of his officers, crew, and passengers.

His only equal on the ship was the chief engineer, George Vazeos. The chief was another native of Greece, as was the new staff captain, Pamagiotis Menegatos. But the fact that these three men shared the same native language and culture was not enough to make them close. Sometimes the captain felt a touch of disdain from the chief, who had been serving on the *Castle*/*Evangeline* since 1956 and was old enough to be the captain's grandfather. Menegatos had been aboard less than two weeks. Voutsinas knew little about him, except that people were complaining that the man could barely understand or speak English. Meanwhile, the *Castle*'s other deck officers seemed perturbed by the rigid caste system the captain imposed on their fellow travelers upon what the ancient Greek poet Homer had called the "wine-dark sea."

The captain was off duty until the morning watch for the ship's arrival in Nassau. He would not stand any watches but would be present on the bridge for arrivals and departures. Typically for arrivals and departures, the third mate and boatswain would be on the foredeck, second mate on the aft deck, chief mate and the captain on the bridge. The chief mate would send the engine orders to the engine room. An able seaman would be the helmsman. The pilot would give helm and engine speed commands. The master would observe. In some cases, he might handle the ship into or out of the berth. Then he would leave the moment-to-moment operation of the ship to his crew. So it was that tonight Byron Voutsinas was dining alone and avoiding all those people who made him feel uncomfortable, annoyed, judged, and distracted. He was going to finish his red snapper and a glass of wine, then read a book until he fell asleep.

About 6 miles ahead of the *Yarmouth Castle*, the freighter SS *Finnpulp* was bound for Nassau too. But unlike Byron Voutsinas, the *Finnpulp*'s captain, Johan Lehto, was enjoying his evening and some fellowship. Having left Mobile, Alabama, two days ago with a cargo of cotton, rice, and soybeans, the crew of about two dozen men aboard the freighter had now fully settled into their ship-keeping routines and watch schedule. Tonight, after dinner and off watch, Lehto was puffing on his pipe and continuing his long-standing chess game in his cabin with his chief engineer, Valter Mattias Toikka.

The captain and the chief were proud of their shipmates and their ship. At 415.8 feet in length, the *Finnpulp* was only slightly longer than the *Yarmouth Castle*. But here the similarities ceased. Unlike the *Castle* and the *Bahama Star*, the *Finnpulp* was no antique steamship. Completed in 1953 at Jan Smit Scheepswerf, Alblasserdam, Netherlands, she was a thoroughly modern freighter with a 5,600 bhp diesel engine. She hailed from Helsinki with a dedicated, highly seasoned crew, mostly Finns.

As the dust of World War II had started to settle, Finland emerged from the conflict with only 30 percent of its merchant fleet having survived the war. Much was needed to restart the country's economy, including a means of exporting goods. Enso-Gutzeit, a state-owned timber corporation, needed ships to export Finnish lumber and paper products. As such, they founded the shipping company Merivienti Oy in 1947. Finnlines was the operating subsidiary for Merivienti's ships.

As trade increased during the 1950s, the company made the decision to build seven new motor ships specifically for "liner cargo service." Liner cargo service is regularly scheduled cargo ship service between specific ports on specific dates and times. Of these seven ships, five were built in the Netherlands, one in Finland, and one in Sweden. All the ships had names starting with "Finn" and were delivered from their builders between 1953 and 1958.

Finnlines operated regular liner services from Baltic ports to the US Gulf Coast and East Coast as well as Veracruz, Mexico. Typical westbound cargos consisted mainly of paper, Finnish timber, plywood, and machinery from Sweden. After a last stop in Glasgow or Greenock, Scotland, for cased whiskey, the Finnish ships would cross the Atlantic, calling in Florida, Veracruz, Mexico, Houston, New Orleans, Mobile, and Savannah. In addition to the cotton and rice the *Finnpulp* carried tonight, she and her sister ships regularly carried a cargo of frozen orange juice concentrate, lube oil additives, and oil-drilling equipment. Discharge ports began with Antwerp in Belgium, then Bremen and Hamburg in Germany, Malmö and Helsingborg in Sweden, Helsinki, and, finally, where the ship had started, in Hamina, Finland.

A round-trip voyage took seventy days, which with seven ships provided a ten-day cycle for regularly scheduled service to each port. With the *Finnpulp* and its crew crossing the treacherous North Atlantic once a month, time and again, year after year, in all kinds of weather, Captain Lehto thought that his vessel and shipmates had proven they could handle anything that Ahti, the Finnish sea god, might throw their way. On this calm tropical evening, with pipe in hand and his friend the chief sharing a chess game, Johan Lehto could never have imagined his bizarre meeting with Byron Voutsinas or the challenges and the nightmare that lay just hours ahead.

Captain Voutsinas was not the only person feeling out of sorts aboard the *Yarmouth Castle* tonight. Joan Reynolds was in cabin #536, A deck, port side. Ever since she came aboard this afternoon, she had been having a fight with the air conditioner in her cabin. The damn thing was either not blowing or blowing too cold. She had once been a hostess on the *Castle* and had decided to plunk down $59 for a sentimental journey on her dear, old ship. But she was discovering that no old friends were still working aboard. The ship no longer seemed glamorous. It looked shabby. She really hoped that Ruth Wright's floor show in the lounge would change her mood, because so far this cruise was looking like a bust. Her roast beef with horseradish sauce at dinner was tough and dry.

Charlie and Edna Matias from Berwyn, Illinois, had been glad that #719 was an outside cabin on the starboard side of the promenade deck. It had an actual window with a view, but the window seemed to be painted shut, which did not seem to Charlie like such a good idea if there was ever an emergency and the door was blocked for some reason. He and Edna were also annoyed by the lack of a double bed. They were used to sleeping together after decades of marriage, but now, for the next three nights, Charlie had to haul himself up a steep ladder to an upper bunk. Like Joan Reynolds, the Matiases were really hoping the floor show after dinner would put them in a better mood. They loved calypso music and West Indian dancing.

Twenty-two year old Roy Drysdale had been a championship cricket fastballer back in Jamaica, but he had big dreams of seeing the world, so he left the sport to try his luck as an entertainer on a cruise ship. Now he was one of the stars of the floor show that stirred up the passengers' spirits. *Life* magazine would describe him as a "slim, lithe Jamaican native with a strong resemblance to Harry Belafonte, a flashing wide grin, and a tender warmth for people." At dinner he worked as a waiter, but once the eight o'clock dinner service was over, he changed into a West Indian carnival costume to strut his stuff onstage. He really like turning up the heat, singing "Jump in the Line (Shake, Shake, Senora)" and dancing the limbo under a 14-inch bar. But tonight, he felt tired and depressed. He was planning on telling Ruth Wright to count him out for the floor show. He wanted to go to bed. Something just felt wrong.

CHAPTER 4

In the Heart of the Night

2400 hours, Friday, November 12

The band was "hot and fast," according to *Life* magazine's coverage of that Friday night aboard the *Yarmouth Castle*. In the Neptune Ballroom the dancers were swinging to a tropical beat. At the card tables, "Red Dog" was the game of choice, and serious money was on the table. Charlie, the bartender, was glad the rush for mixed rum concoctions during the floor show was over and the drink orders were now straight-forward calls for beer, scotch, and whiskey. At the bar, a woman of advanced age sat trying to sing the ballad "Show Me the Way to Go Home." Her friends rolled their eyes. The old girl had been overserved.

As is tradition aboard commercial ships the world over, the captains of the *Yarmouth Castle*, the *Finnpulp*, and the *Bahama Star* had long since gone to bed and left their second mates in charge of the bridge on their ships for the midnight-to-0400-hours watch. On the *Castle*, Charles and Edna Matias, Carl and Willie Apuzzo, Mabel Straub, Adele Simister, the Bells, and many others were asleep as well.

The party had not yet ended for passengers such as Margaret Masters and Lloyd Lamn. Lamn had been sticking to his plan to stay away from what he considered a hellhole of a cabin (#634), with its total lack of windows. Since dinner he had been distracting himself with the ship's entertainment offerings. He had first attended the cruise director's lecture. Since no one on the ship had given a safety briefing, Lamn thought that this lecture was where he would learn what to do in case of a fire or the need to abandon ship.

But the cruise director's lecture had not been about safety, and there was no lifeboat drill. The lecture was about sightseeing in Nassau and the port's attractions such as the Straw Market and the duty-free shops on Bay Street selling jewelry, cigars, and liquor. Instead of learning about how to put on a life vest or find and board his assigned lifeboat, Lamn learned about taking horse-drawn surrey rides through colonial Nassau and where he should go to catch a ferry across the harbor. There was a beach over there where scenes for the soon-to-be-released James Bond thriller *Thunderball* had recently been filmed. The beach was on the former Hog Island. Millionaire playboy Huntington Hartford had purchased it in 1959, renamed it Paradise Island, set up a casino called the Ocean Club, and built a cloister from the disassembled stones of a monastery that William Randolph Hearst had stored in Florida.

After the lecture, Lamn had taken a table by himself outside the Neptune Bar, ordered a beer, and settled into a bit of people watching before the floor show started in the ballroom. At around 2030 or 2100, he saw a roaming watchman on his rounds punch his key clock at a station outside the bar. It gave Lamn comfort that the ship had crew roaming the decks with a key clock and regular, appointed rounds, but he thought the watchman looked to be not much more than a teenager. Lamn had to wonder about how professional an operation Yarmouth Cruise Lines was running here. It didn't seem right that a ship based in Miami would have the hailing port of Panama emblazoned on its stern.

Panama was a so-called flag of convenience for the *Castle*. The term carried negative connotations because it referred to a practice whereby a merchant vessel's owners registered their ship in a country other than that of the owners. The practice of registering merchant ships in a foreign country probably dates back to the ancient fleets of the Phoenicians, Greeks, and Romans. It became a popular practice with United States vessels during the War of 1812, when American shipowners registered their vessels in foreign countries to avoid attacks by the British navy. Ships of the Confederate States of America and blockade runners during the American Civil War used flags of convenience to disguise the government they served and their true intentions.

During the 1920s Prohibition era in the United States, American owners of passenger ships registered their ships in Panama in order to legally sell alcohol aboard. Owners of ships sailing under flags of convenience have long been criticized for documenting their vessels in countries that have "open registries," with no residency requirement for the shipowners. Critics claim that flags of convenience allow shipowners to avoid increased safety regulations, labor laws, crew salaries, and higher operating expenses.

Well into the twenty-first century, Filipino mariners on ships flying flags of convenience earn far less than licensed American counterparts on US-registered ships. Flags of convenience have largely priced American seafarers with United States credentials out of the cruise ship jobs in favor of crews from poorer nations who are willing to work for less. It has been the case since the birth of the cruise ship industry. Unlike the *Finnpulp*, with its nearly all-Finnish crew, the *Yarmouth Castle* counted twelve different nationalities among her crew on the night of November 12, 1965. Many of the lowest wage earners were young Jamaicans such as Roy Drysdale and Hondurans such as José Arcadio, who was just reporting for his watch up on the bridge. The crew also included citizens of Austria, the Bahamas, Canada, Colombia, Cuba, the Dominican Republic, Greece, Haiti, and Spain. Americans such as Ruth Wright and Joan Reynolds were the exceptions.

As of 2024, more than half the world's merchant ships are registered in countries to which they have no connection, principally Panama, Liberia, the Marshall Islands, China, and Singapore. The use of flags of convenience is nearly ubiquitous among cruise ships. Back in the 1960s, these same countries also offered crew-credentialing bureaus, which critics alleged were less strict in their oversight than the United States Coast Guard, which controls licensing of American merchant mariners. None of the officers on the *Yarmouth Castle* held American merchant mariner's credentials.

Did Byron Voutsinas's Panamanian and Liberian licenses make him any less qualified for command than the *Bahama Star*'s Carl Brown, who had earned a United States unlimited master's license? It's debatable.

Eventually, Lloyd Lamn cast off his concerns about the ship's safety and hiring practices and moved to a table in the ballroom with Margaret Masters and other folks from the North Broward Senior Citizens Club to watch the floor show. Joan Reynolds was there too, and the former *Yarmouth Castle* hostess was finally beginning to feel better about her choice to make this sentimental journey aboard her old ship. Watching Ruth Wright and Roy Drysdale singing and dancing took her back to her days on that same stage. She swayed to the calypso beat of the bongo drums and sang along with the familiar tunes.

Onstage, Ruth Wright had begun to feel a bit of all right too. She had convinced Roy Drysdale to overcome whatever was bothering him and rally for the passengers. By the time she and Drysdale had finished a rousing rendition of Harry Belafonte's "Banana Boat Song," she felt the buzz of adrenalin that came when the music sparked something in her fellow performers. The audience caught the vibe too. After the show, she gave Drysdale a big hug before he headed for coffee and on to his berth in a section of the crew's quarters known as "the Glory Hole," deep in the bows of the ship. It had been another fourteen-hour workday.

Wright couldn't sleep yet. She was still pumped from being onstage. Like her shipmates from the floor show, she got some coffee from her friend Charles Agero in the gift shop down on the main deck. Then she went back up the lobby staircase to the boat deck and hung around the ballroom and bar for a while, basking in the compliments of passengers, soaking up the last tunes of the dance band, and inhaling the warm, tropical night. She noticed that Margaret Masters was finally in off-duty mode now that most of her tour group had turned in for the night.

Masters was laughing it up at a table in the bar with two other women and the ship's cruise director, José Martinez. He and Masters seemed to be developing a bit of mutual admiration. The stars were out, and a hazy moon glow lit up the calm sea. It was getting a bit chilly, though. Masters asked Martinez if he would mind accompanying her while she went to her cabin to retrieve a pink sweater. Maybe she was hoping for a little alone time with the debonair cruise director. Maybe she was hoping to spark a romance. Sometimes when you were on a cruise ship at night, it all seemed like a fairy tale far from the madding crowds ashore.

By now it was after midnight. Lloyd Lamn's companions at the floor show were wandering off to bed. He guessed it was time to call it a night. But when he got down to his cabin on the main deck, he found his roommate, a man he barely knew, preparing for bed. Lamn decided to give the guy a little privacy and go back up to the Neptune Bar on the boat deck for one last beer. Something seemed to be steering him away from that cabin. On his way through a long hallway from his cabin to the lobby staircase, he thought he smelled smoke and felt a jolt of fear run through his body. But then he told himself that someone had lit a match or was puffing on a pipe.

CHAPTER 5

Fatal Errors

0020–0045 hours, Saturday, November 13

On the bridge, José Arcadio asked the second officer, who was in charge of the bridge, if he could start his watchman's rounds on the ship. Arcadio was one of three ordinary seamen who had just come on duty. They would take turns standing lookout on the bow of the *Castle*, steering the ship according to the direction of the officer in charge, and patrolling the vessel from top to bottom, bow to stern, with a key clock.

Tonight, Arcadio was assigned to be the first of the crewmen on watch to walk the ship and punch his key clock at twenty-one different stations around the ship. He went to the chartroom and picked up the key clock, which he carried on a sling over his shoulder like a Boy Scout's canteen. There was a duty card on the bridge with a map of the ship, highlighting the watchman's route through the ship and each key station he must visit, but Arcadio didn't pay close attention to the duty card. It was written in English, and he could not read English. In fact, he could not read at all.

Like the watchman whom Lloyd Lamn had seen earlier punching his key clock, José Arcadio was young. He was twenty-four years old, and he had left a simple life in the Dominican Republic to seek adventure and opportunity at sea. Since then, he had spent the better part of six years on cruise ships. But the *Castle* was new to him. He was so fresh to the ship, and so unknown, that the staff captain had recorded his first name as "Aicadio" and his last name as "Jose" on the roster of the crew. As a newbie on this trip, he had been assigned to the so-called midwatch (from midnight to 0400 hours), which seasoned crew did not want.

After shouldering his key clock at about half past midnight, Arcadio took a quick look at the duty card on the wall of the bridge. He found the location for all twenty-one key stations and tried to commit them to memory. But he thought it would be easy for him to spot the key stations. They always had a wall-mounted, metal plaque engraved with something like "DETEX WATCH CLOCK STATION." A differently coded key for each station hung on a short chain from the plaque. When Arcadio inserted the key in his watch clock, it recorded the station number and the time on a tape that could be reviewed later to make sure the watchman was completing his rounds thoroughly and in a timely fashion.

Arcadio did not carefully examine the line on the duty card that marked the route he should take through the ship. He had been on bigger ships, so finding his way around the *Castle* from one key station to another hardly seemed like a daunting challenge. He had never walked the watchman's route on the *Castle*, but before coming on duty, another watchman had described the route to him. So off he went down the stairs, from the bridge to the first key station just below the bridge and next to the captain's cabin. His next stop was across the boat deck near cabin #823. From there he moved aft on the boat deck.

He repeated his route on the promenade deck, then down to the main deck. He went to the lower decks, where the crew slept, but he did not check the engine room because a full crew was at work down there and alert to safety concerns. He also checked the now-quiet galley space, looking for anything out of the ordinary, but especially for fire. Nothing caught his attention. Except for the churning of the engine, the *Castle* felt like a ghost ship once he got away from the drinkers and gamblers in the bar area and the folks having coffee at the passengers' lobby gift shop.

After leaving the kitchen, Arcadio walked aft on the main deck through the starboard-side corridor between the passenger cabins. He did not check the portside corridor on the main deck or pass Ruth Wright's old cabin, #610, on that corridor. This was a deviation from the required route on the duty card. If the watchman had followed the instructions on the duty card, he would have passed #610, smelled smoke coming from the cabin, and probably saved the lives of ninety people. Instead, he reappeared back on the bridge, after missing some key stations, at about ten minutes before 0100 hours. He told the Cuban second mate that all was well. Arcadio was eager to ditch the key clock and take his turn steering the great ship. Meanwhile, the fire in #610 had likely been burning for a half hour.

Unlike in 1965, when José Arcadio joined the crew of the *Yarmouth Castle* as a last-minute hire with little vetting and no training for his watchman's job on his new ship, today's seafarers are uniformly trained and vetted. They are hired aboard US ships in one of two ways, either directly or through a seafarer's union. For shipping companies with collective-bargaining agreements, both officers and unlicensed personnel are hired through union halls. There are separate unions in the United States for deck officers, engineering officers, and unlicensed crew members. Some unions such as the Seafarers International Union (SIU) provide both unlicensed crew and limited-tonnage officers. For unlimited tonnage, ships over 1,600 gross tons, the unions are always separate.

In the case of nonunion companies, seafarers are hired directly by the companies. In those cases, seafarers will apply directly to the companies' home offices. In some cases, they may have seen an ad in a trade publication or online. Sometimes seafarers are referred by a colleague or maritime education establishment such as a maritime academy.

With some exceptions in northern Europe and Australia, most foreign shipping companies are nonunion. Union shipping companies both in Europe and Australia follow the same general practices as in the United States. All other shipping companies hire both officers and unlicensed personnel through crewing agencies. These agencies (located in Europe, Asia, and India) supply crew members for all types of ships, all over the world. Shipping-line managers in need of crew contact these agencies when crew members are needed. For a fee, the agency supplies the required mariners and arranges their transportation to the ship, wherever that might be. Some agencies also charge the seafarer as well as the shipping companies for the service of finding them a job. In many cases, shipping lines have long-standing relationships with specific agencies. In the cases of larger parent companies with many lines, such as Carnival (who also owns Cunard), Holland America, Costa, and others, the company may have a financial interest in the agency supplying the seafarers.

Things were different in 1965, when Byron Voutsinas and José Arcadio joined the *Yarmouth Castle*. When Yarmouth Cruise Lines needed crew members for their ships, they turned to a maritime crewing agency both for officers and unlicensed personnel. In the 1960s, pretty much anyone could just sign up with a crewing agency and wait for a job. If someone had credentials of any kind, be it an able seaman's or oiler's "card" (document), radio operator's "ticket," or an officer's license, they made it known to crewing agencies. Credentials in hand, those persons were eligible for any job that might come up. There were minimal to no standards for unlicensed crew members such as José Arcadio. For officers such as Byron Voutsinas, all that was needed was a license and nothing more.

This held true even for US mariners well into the 1970s and 1980s. All that was needed to qualify for a seafaring job was a license and a radar observer's certificate. For able seaman or oilers, all that was required was a year's sea time and a passing grade on an exam. As far as safety competency went, lowering a large, model lifeboat at the Coast Guard's regional exam center was just about the only practical safety test on the US able seaman's exam until the late 1980s.

Crew turnover was high back in the 1960s, and particularly so on the ships that didn't pay as well as others. It was pretty much ensured that after each voyage, the *Yarmouth Castle* and her sister ship the *Yarmouth* would be seeking to replace crew in one department or another. A call placed to a Miami-based crewing agency would fill the slots needed with whoever was available. Unlicensed and entry-level sailors, in particular, generally had minimal experience and little to no training. Carl Brown and Byron Voutsinas never knew who was coming up the gangway for the next voyage or how well they had been trained at seafaring and safety. But seasoned seafarers know that actual competence at sea cannot be measured by a battery of tests, the country of licensing, or the simple accumulation of time afloat. Training, of course, makes a huge difference. But like the heat of battle, crises at sea have a way of making or breaking leaders.

CHAPTER 6

Smoke

0045–0100 hours, Saturday, November 13

After the floor show and dancing aboard the *Yarmouth Castle* ended, Joan Reynolds went to her cabin, #536, on A deck. As she started to undress, she felt a chill. The air-conditioning, which had been a problem in her cabin since she arrived, was now blowing too cold. Later, she would tell Coast Guard investigators that as she tried to turn the air-conditioning down, "hot air was coming in where cold air had been." She suddenly "smelled a metal odor, like a hot appliance." She pulled on slacks under her bathrobe and left her cabin to search for a room steward or someone else in the crew.

Ruth Wright had headed off to bed about a half hour after Reynolds. She was finally coming down off her adrenalin high from her rousing time onstage. Now, all she wanted to do was sleep. She passed #610 but noticed nothing on her way to her newly assigned cabin #616. She changed into pajamas, shut off the air-conditioning, opened her porthole, and slid into bed. As she was about to nod off, she heard footsteps and commotion in the forward stairway but paid no attention. Maybe it was just a few late-night partyers.

Chief Engineer George Vazeos was off watch, and before going to bed he was sipping coffee, as he usually did, at the table in the engineers' mess on D deck, one deck below the main deck. He was in midsip when one of the men from the engine room burst in.

"He say, 'Something smell, chief,'" Vazeos would later recall to Coast Guard investigators.

The messenger said the engine room crew smelled smoke blowing from the natural draft ventilation system. Vazeos left his coffee unfinished. His ship had a problem, maybe a serious problem.

"I was running fast," the engineer testified. He started searching the pantry. Then he sprinted to the main galley, then to the bakeshop, looking for the source of the fire.

"I see nothing. I smell nothing."

Minutes went by as Vazeos charged around D deck in search of smoke and a fire. But he did not alert the bridge or the captain.

When Chief Vazeos ran into the night cleaner, Charles Whyley, he told the "chief" that he smelled smoke in the men's room up on the promenade deck. Both men dashed to the men's room. They smelled smoke but saw no fire. At this point, Vazeos suspected that the fire might be in a cabin down on the main deck, beneath this men's room. As the chief continued searching, Whyley headed for the crew's quarters to wake his shipmates.

"He say get up. The ship is on fire," Roy Drysdale would remember decades later during an interview on CRS Radio Network. "Get up or you going to die."

Whyley ran into Charles Agero at the gift shop and told him of the smoke in the men's room. Agero went up to recheck the men's room. He smelled the smoke. A deck above the men's room, the radio operator also smelled smoke in the radio room and went looking for the source. But like others, he did not report that he smelled smoke to the officers on the bridge or to the captain.

After Lloyd Lamn finished his beer and started toward his cabin via the saloon lobby staircase, he smelled smoke, now for a second time in the last half hour. This time it did not smell like a match or a pipe. He checked an adjacent men's room and smelled more smoke. Then he saw a teenage boy sitting on a stool at the telephone exchange on a phone call. He told the boy he smelled smoke. Something was on fire.

The boy and his friends thought Lamn was joking, and turned back to their ship-to-shore phone call. At this point, Lamn heard urgent voices on the deck above and went to investigate. He was sure the ship was in danger. After eighteen years as a firefighter, no one had to tell him how fast a spark can turn into a bonfire amid a nearly endless supply of dry wood, flammable paint, and unlimited oxygen.

By about ten minutes before 1:00 a.m., the switchboard operator and the chief mate had also smelled smoke and joined the search for the fire along with Whyley, Vazeos, Agero, Lamn, and a growing number of other passengers and members of the crew. Finally, they homed in on #610, on the main deck, and saw smoke billowing from around the door. But, still, Vazeos did not send someone to rally the ship's designated emergency squad. Still, no one alerted the bridge crew, the captain, or the sleeping passengers.

Aboard the *Yarmouth Castle* there were no standardized safety protocols, just as there were no set standards for crew competency. Since those days, what has leveled the playing field as far as safety and competency among seafarers is something called Standards of Training, Certification, and Watchkeeping for Seafarers (STCW). This is an international convention promulgated by the IMO, the International Maritime Organization, which is based in London. Almost all seafaring nations, including the United States, are signatory to the STCW convention.

What STCW has developed are standard levels of competencies for seafarers for each individual level. The level of training and mandatory certifications that are required depend on what credential the mariner holds. All mariners regardless of rank are required to have what is called "basic safety training." This is the first element of STCW. Basic safety training is a weeklong class that includes marine firefighting, survival training, and the use of lifesaving equipment, including the launching of lifeboats and rafts.

Trainees are required to be able to right a capsized life raft while wearing a life jacket or survival suit in the water. They must also extinguish oil fires by using both extinguishers and hoses (while wearing firefighting gear), demonstrate a proficiency in firing distress signals, and more. Under the most-recent amendments of STCW, basic training must be renewed every five years.

As credential levels increase for a mariner, so do the training and certification requirements. Today, masters are required to hold certifications for a myriad of topics, including (but not limited to) ARPA (automatic radar-plotting aids), ECDIS (electronic charting data and information systems), fast rescue craft operations, GMDSS (global marine distress and signal systems), VSO (vessel security officer), bridge resource management, leadership and managerial skills, crowd control, crisis management, and marine firefighting. Similarly, engineering officers have a host of required training under STCW as well.

In addition to specific training in these specialized topics, STCW also standardizes the subject matter that each level of license exam must cover. For example, a third mate's exam in the Philippines will have the same material and required passing grade as that of a third mates' exam in Norway or the United States.

What STCW has for the most part accomplished is to ensure that mariners everywhere are trained to the same level of competency. This has increased maritime safety immeasurably.

The very first STCW convention was drafted in 1978 and became an industry standard in 1984. The convention has been amended eleven times since then. Incrementally, training requirements and skill assessment protocols have been added. The last major revisions were in 2010, referred to as the Manila Amendments, in reference to where the meeting was held. Special requirements for passenger ship crew members were adopted in 1997, including crowd control and crisis management training for senior deck officers.

Previous to STCW training, skill levels of mariners varied widely. Even mariners from the same country could have vastly different skill levels, depending on the ships they staffed and with whom they sailed. So it was aboard the *Yarmouth Castle* an hour after midnight on November 13, 1965.

On the bridge of the liner, none of the seven fire zone lights, triggered by the automatic sprinkler system, had turned red to warn the bridge crew of a fire somewhere on the *Castle*. As Vazeos, Agero, Whyley, and Lamn now knew, cabin #610 harbored the source of an inferno.

The cabin was a tinderbox just waiting for a spark. During the accident inquiry, the captain and a steward would testify that the insulated inner walls, cabinetry, and furnishings in the cabin had been stripped away at the shipyard in Tampa in preparation for a complete makeover. Ruth Wright described the contents of #610, which she had seen earlier in the evening when searching for a replacement mattress with gift shop operator Charles Agero. She would tell Coast Guard investigators that there were "five mattresses, none of which were foam, one roll-away bed, one chair that needed upholstery, and a red bedspread on top of the chair and a vacuum and a sink on the floor. In the corner, going diagonally, was a piece of light cable that usually is inside a lead conduit. To that was spliced a large, perhaps 150-watt light bulb."

Curiously, steward Roderick Smith would tell Coast Guard accident investigators the room was empty except for a mop, vacuum cleaner, and broom. But he was mistaken. Gift shop operator Charles Agero confirmed in his testimony all that Wright had seen. He added that when he went to #610 with her to look for a mattress earlier in the evening, he gave up on getting one, saying, "Let's get out of here" because it was too hot. The heat from the galley stoves had been radiating through the walls. Now those same walls were sheets of fire, and #610 had no automatic sprinkler head to douse the fire, and no temperature sensor to send an alarm to the bridge fire zones monitor.

Meanwhile, José Arcadio continued to hold his course of 102 degrees at the helm, as if all was well. The *Yarmouth Castle* plowed onward at 14 knots into that good night.

CHAPTER 7

Fire

0110 hours, Saturday, November 13

It was not until about ten minutes after one o'clock that the engineer of the watch in the engine room called the bridge to say there was smoke coming into the engine room through the natural ventilation system in ever-thicker clouds. The so-called black gang tending the boilers and engine had begun wearing bandannas over their noses in order to breathe. Second Mate José Ramos de Leon immediately dispatched one of his watchmen to the boat deck and another to the promenade deck to search for a fire. He also called down to the captain via the voice tube from the bridge to the master's cabin, saying the ship was on fire.

Captain Voutsinas told the mate to sound the alarm. He was coming up to the bridge. But passengers never heard an alarm bell. It's likely that fire had already burned out many, if not all, of the alarm bell circuits.

At this point, the fire had been burning for at least three-quarters of an hour. It had spread beyond the contents of #610 and into the men's room on the promenade deck above, and into the ventilation space and false ceiling over the main deck. Flames and smoke were traveling beneath the cabins on the promenade deck, working their way up behind Masonite walls and to the boat deck cabins and the ship's bridge. The dry, teak superstructure, coated in flammable, oil-based paint and varnish, provided unlimited fuel for the fire. The ship's natural ventilation system and air-conditioning ducts supercharged the combustion with fresh oxygen. In the cabins and corridors above #610, smoke was suffocating sleepers such as George and Catherine Keen in #715 and John and Alice Karns in #721. Drawn up and aft through the ventilation system, the smoke was killing people in their boat deck cabins, such as Henry and Mary Hughes in #805 and William and Helen Hier in #823.

Captain Voutsinas felt his forehead sweating as he pulled on his pants, socks, and shoes as fast as he could possibly move. According to his testimony at the Coast Guard accident investigation, he grabbed a white short-sleeve shirt and rushed out of his cabin and up the steps to the bridge. He didn't take time to button the shirt.

"Where is the fire?" he asked when he arrived topside. Outside the dining room somewhere, they said.

"This all right. Stay on duty and stay in charge," he told Second Officer Ramos de Leon. "I run personally down to locate the fire and see what is the extent of the fire."

On his way down to the main deck, he met Charles Agero, who told him the fire was in #610. When he got to the corridor outside #610, he saw a small group of crew members, some passengers, and the chief engineer.

"There was several fire extinguishers lying on the floor," he would testify. "I get one in my hand and saw it was empty. The chief engineer opened the door[,] and flames and smoke, heavy smoke and big flames[,] come out. He close the door again and pull one hose. Right there is fire station. I don't see any water [coming from the hose]. Then I run up to the bridge. I see going up on the stairway there was a lot of smoke and flame. I am going through the flames there."

When Voutsinas got back up to the bridge, he told the second mate to stop the ship, close the watertight doors on the engine room, and turn to port, away from the east wind and the hazards of shallow water on the Bahamas Bank to the south.

Still, neither Voutsinas, the second mate, nor Chief Engineer Vazeos had called the staff captain to muster the ship's designated emergency squad to fight the fire.

Today, accident analysts would label the unfolding disaster on the *Yarmouth Castle* as a failure or breakdown in BRM, bridge resource management. But in 1965, BRM was an alien concept to seafarers. The concept of bridge resource management migrated in the early 1990s directly to the merchant marine industry from discoveries and changes in commercial aviation. In reviewing a spate of horrific aviation accidents from the 1970s and 1980s (such as United 173, which ran out of fuel and crashed in suburban Portland, Oregon, due to poor communication among the pilots), airlines discovered that fully 100 percent of fatal accidents and 50 percent of all aviation accidents could be traced to poor use of the human resources in the cockpit. The industry response was to codify and practice good crew resource management (CRM). Since then, the safety record of commercial aviation has improved to what it is today. According to the International Air Transport Association, there were only five fatal accidents among 32.2 million airline flights in 2022.

As with CRM in aviation, the basic concept of BRM is to have a ship's bridge team safely and effectively manage the ship's operation, in any and all circumstances that may arise. The key word here is "effectively." Under normal circumstances with benign weather conditions, things usually go as planned. It's when the unexpected occurs that things can become challenging for the bridge team. The concept of BRM is designed so each individual member of the bridge team has an assigned task, and the team works together as a whole to accomplish the end goal of operating the ship safely. When unexpected things start to occur, the officer of the watch, or the captain, can easily become "task loaded" and, from that, hyperfocused (as Captain Voutsinas and Chief Vazeos were with the fire in #610). In doing so, the same officer or officers become more and more separated from the overall situation as it continues to develop.

The problem with this on a ship, just as it is in aviation, is that both ships and aircraft are in a dynamic environment. That environment is constantly evolving. There is no pause button. So regardless of what might be occurring, the officer in charge, be it in an aircraft or on a ship, can never lose sight of the big picture. In order to keep focused on the big picture effectively, the officer of the watch must be able to manage the bridge team in a competent manner. Doing so requires delegation of responsibilities and following set procedures. No one person can effectively manage everything at once. Working as a team is key to being effective. But in the early-morning hours of November 13, 1965, there was little professional teamwork in play aboard the SS *Yarmouth Castle*.

At about the same time that the ship's second officer had alerted the captain of the fire, Margaret Masters asked cruise director José Martinez again to help her find her way back to cabin #B1. Her companions from the North Broward County Senior Citizens Club, such as Lloyd Lamn, had already headed off to their cabins. So, Masters and Martinez started for #B1 on the main deck. When they were almost at the corridor leading to her cabin, they ran into Lamn. He looked anxious and in a hurry. He said he smelled smoke, acrid, toxic smoke.

Almost immediately, the three of them arrived at the corridor outside #610 and saw two other men in white uniforms with fire extinguishers in their hands standing in front of the open door to the cabin. Reddish-orange flames seemed to be drawn up to the ceiling but not out of the door.

Other passengers started coming out of their cabins into the corridor. Cruise director Martinez told them to get on deck and go to the top of the ship.

Meanwhile, veteran firefighter Lamn worried that the fire was spreading beyond control, and that the captain and others were too focused on #610 and not on the rest of the *Castle*. As he started up the stairs from the forward lobby to the promenade deck, Lamn's worst fears were confirmed. He told accident investigators he heard "crackling in the center of the boat around the ventilator system" in the area of #614. On the promenade deck he saw smoke coming out of the cabins. He began banging on doors, along with Martinez and a purser, shouting "Wake up! Wake up! Fire!" This was bad. Lamn was old enough to vividly remember the catastrophe that occurred when the liner SS *Morro Castle* caught fire off Asbury Park, New Jersey, in 1934.

The *Morro Castle* had been a 480-foot liner built in 1930 to carry passengers between New York City and Havana, Cuba. On September 8, 1934, the ship was returning to New York in stormy weather with 318 passengers and 230 crew members when she caught fire.

A little before three o'clock in the morning, the ship was just 8 miles off the coast of New Jersey when a fire broke out in a storage locker. In the next thirty minutes, flames spread through much of the wooden superstructure of the *Morro Castle*. Shortly after the radio officer sent his first and only SOS distress signal, the fire burned through the ship's hydraulic lines and electrical circuits. The *Morro Castle* was now totally without lights, radio communication with rescue vessels, and the ability to steer the ship. Meanwhile, rough seas and windy conditions made it difficult to launch the lifeboats. With the fire whipped by the winds, it spread quickly. Passengers and crew fled to the ends of the ship.

In the absence of lifeboats and rescue vessels, and facing imminent incineration, the passengers and crew began jumping into the roiling seas. Many died when hitting the water because their bulky life vests broke their necks or knocked them unconscious.

Rescue ships were slow to arrive. When they reached the burning ship, the darkness and rough seas made it extremely difficult to maneuver rescue lifeboats and to spot people in the water. Two Coast Guard ships remained too far away to spot survivors. It was not until after first light, when commercial radio stations began reporting bodies washing ashore, that the Coast Guard sent search aircraft.

Meanwhile small, private boats set out from New Jersey coastal inlets to rescue survivors from the water. Citizens gathered on the beaches of Asbury Park to help the injured, reunite families, and collect corpses. By late afternoon the smoldering hulk of the *Morro Castle* grounded in shallow water near shore. Although official estimates differ, at least eighty-four passengers and thirty crew were lost.

With the wreck's nearness to the Asbury Park boardwalk and the Convention Hall pier, the *Morro Castle* became a macabre tourist attraction featured on postcards and souvenirs until the ship was finally refloated and towed away for scrap. The accident investigation found that negligent maintenance and crew incompetence, as well as the flammable superstructure and paint on the ship, were primary causes for the disaster and loss of life.

Now, in Lloyd Lamn's mind, the *Morro Castle* nightmare was happening all over again.

Two decks above the fruitless firefighting at #610, the drinkers and the card players were still laughing and carrying on. No one in the bar had heard an alarm or ship's horn warning of trouble. But as Charlie the bartender was restocking his shelves and coolers between serving shots, highballs, and Heineken, a female passenger named Erna Groeger (cabin #832) dashed into the Neptune Bar, shouting, "Fire! Fire!" Then a man she would describe to investigators as an "elderly gentleman" stumbled through the door. He "was very, very scorched black and kept saying, over and over again, 'Help me, help me,'" Groeger would testify.

One of the men in the lounge opened the door out to the deck saloon. Thick, dense, yellow smoke came through the door. He slammed it shut.

Charlie, the bartender, shouted for everyone to follow him. But he really did not have a plan.

CHAPTER 8

Who's in Charge?

0120 hours, Saturday, November 13

Moments after Captain Voutsinas made his way back up to the bridge from the fire in #610, smoke suddenly billowed into the radio room aft of the bridge and chart room on the *Yarmouth Castle*. Voutsinas told his radio officer to go out onto the starboard bridge wing and send an SOS light signal from the Aldis lamp. With the radio room going up in flames, this was his most immediate way to beckon other ships for help. He knew that the *Bahama Star* must not be far behind him. The two ships were competitors in the Miami–Nassau cruise ship business, and the *Star* had left the cruise ship dock in Miami less than an hour after the *Castle*. There was another ship out ahead, too, that might see his signal and come to the rescue.

As the radio officer started flashing out his SOS, a wave of superheated air blasted Voutsinas, Second Officer Ramos de Leon, helmsman/watchman Arcadio, and another lookout. Visibility dropped to nearly zero on the bridge as the men's skin felt the sting of 1,000-degree heat.

Through the swirling smoke, Ramos de Leon saw Voutsinas seem to freeze. He would describe the chaos to Coast Guard investigators. He said he saw the captain fall back against a bulkhead with his head in his hands and begin repeating, "We are lost. We are lost."

Someone swore in Spanish, "*Carajo. De puta madre* [Damn. Son of a bitch]."

"*¡Fuera!* [Get out!]," called Ramos de Leon. "*¡Ahora, hombres!* [Now, men!]."

Feeling his way through the smoke and out onto a bridge wing, the second officer grabbed a fire axe. When he and the two seamen came to a patch of clear, breathable air on the walkway in front of the bridge, he smashed open a bridge window and reached in through the flames to activate the horn switch and blast the abandon-ship signal: six short blasts followed by a long blast. Later, at the accident investigation, many passengers and crew would claim they heard no horn blasts. Others heard one long groan from the ship's horn. All that some of those aboard heard was the roar of the flames and the choking and screaming of burning, terrified passengers and crew.

Now the captain and any pretense of bridge resource management (BRM) had vanished amid the smoke.

The five major principles on which BRM is based include the following:

1. Obtaining and maintaining situational awareness
2. Allocation, assignment, and prioritization of resources (i.e., "teamwork")
3. Effective communication
4. Assertiveness and leadership
5. Consideration of team experience

Obtaining and maintaining situational awareness is accomplished by utilizing all means available to the bridge team. First and foremost, even in today's high-tech world, is to look out the window. This may seem obvious, but it needs to be reinforced, particularly in light of an ever-increasing dependence on technology. International Regulations for Preventing Collisions at Sea, or "COLREGS," rule five states: "Every vessel shall at all times maintain a proper lookout by sight and hearing as well as by all available means appropriate in the prevailing circumstances and conditions so as to make a full appraisal of the situation and of the risk of collision."

Situational awareness in today's world goes far beyond maintaining a physical lookout. Visual means of maintaining a lookout come first. Then comes maintaining a radar watch on appropriate range scales, using radar to track targets (other ships), and using radar for navigation. Additionally, the use of ECDIS (electronic chart and information systems) is another means of maintaining situational awareness, as is the use of AIS (Automatic Identification Systems). Today, AIS data are often overlaid onto radar and ECDIS displays. In busy harbors or congested coastal areas, maintaining a radio-listening watch on the proper frequencies is also a big part of situational awareness. An equal part of all of this is being aware of what is happening on one's own vessel.

Proper delegation of responsibilities plays an important part in BRM. The officer of the watch or the master must specify in the standing orders what each bridge team member's specific responsibilities are. These responsibilities must be made known and understood by all crew who have roles as part of the bridge team. Bridge teams must also train to work cohesively as a whole.

Conveying information effectively is essential within the team, within the ship's crew as needed, and with other vessels. Listening well is as important as conveying messages. Officers in charge of a navigation watch must exhibit good leadership qualities and be assertive in making decisions. As a challenging situation is evolving, it's important to be able to make correct decisions quickly. The ability to digest all the information, assess the situation, and come to the correct decision without delay is crucial. This is the mark of an effective leader.

Equally important is the bridge watch officer's ability to assess the team, their experience, and their limitations. This must be taken into account as part of the voyage planning. Training seafarers in the principles of BRM has become a complex process.

Initially, in the early 1990s, when BRM first came into development, each individual professional maritime training center offered three-day or four-day courses based on individual instructors' ideas. Usually, these courses were a blend of both classroom discussions and simulator training. This format has changed significantly in recent years. The 2010 Manila Amendments of the STCW code have detailed course content, simulator training, and required credentials for instructors.

At the same time, the STCW code has mandated that navigation and engineering watches shall be maintained according to the principles of BRM. However, it remains to the ship's master to make sure that his or her crew performs to the letter of these mandates. In the event of an unforeseen emergency arising, part of practicing good BRM is adherence to the ship's station bill. This document describes in detail the duties of each crew member in the event of specific emergencies, such as fire, man overboard, or abandon ship.

But on the night the *Yarmouth Castle* burned, the ship's master could make sure of nothing. He was lost to his officers, crew, and passengers in a cloud of smoke. Even the minimum safety protocols and mandates aboard the ship, such as they were in 1965 (along with adequate training for a night watchman), were little more than expressions of intentions and far from common practice.

Up on the boat deck, Murray Bell and his wife were on a late-night stroll, still avoiding their cabin. The air was refreshingly cool, and the waning gibbous moon cast a silver trail across the sea. Bell was thinking that it was for just this kind of serenity that he and his wife had booked this cruise, when suddenly the Bells heard glass breaking and shouting. Then "a naked man came through the window on the port side of the ship near cabin #810," Bell would testify. The man appeared badly burned. Bell and his wife ran back to the man and saw the man's wife still in the cabin, surrounded by thick, black smoke and screaming for help. Bell pulled her out through the broken window. He heard someone in the crew telling passengers to go to the fo'c'sle deck at the front of the ship.

Meanwhile, Chief Engineer Vazeos had left the firefighting outside #610. He would testify that a few of the crew remained to fight the fire while he raced down to the engine room. No one had to tell him that unless he immediately got better water pressure in the fire hoses and started shutting off oxygen to the fire, this ship would become a fiery and deadly monument to the Greek god of the sea, Poseidon. The ship he had come to think of in a paternalistic way as "his ship" after a decade with the "old girl" deserved better. More than five hundred souls on board deserved better.

He heard the ship's horn give off one long, weak moan as he raced belowdecks. Things were not peaceful in the engine room. Smoke was continuing to drift in through the ventilation system until the chief shut down all the power ventilation blowers. Then as the sprinkler alarm in the #2 fireroom (for the boilers) began rattling away, the chief began opening valves to increase the pressure both in the sprinkler system and the network of firefighting hydrants and hoses located strategically around the *Yarmouth Castle*.

None of these increases should have been necessary, he told himself. The normal 95–100 pounds of pressure in those systems should have been more than adequate to energize them. Something was wrong. All he could do was open his values to the maximum extent and hope for the best. While he was wrestling with the valves, he heard the bridge telegraph sound, and saw it was ordering all stop on both engines. This was bad. Liners, by their very nature of sailing to a strict schedule, almost never stop their engines in the middle of a voyage.

Like Vazeos, cruise director José Martinez was on a mission. He would tell investigators that after racing through the corridors of the promenade deck (along with Lloyd Lamn, Ralph Whyley, and others), banging on doors and waking passengers, Martinez had sprinted two decks down to the crew's quarters to rouse the purser and others to help him wake more passengers. Now as he got back up to the main deck, he found that the scene had changed drastically from what it had been just a couple of minutes before. Passengers were pushing into the main lobby from all directions, in all manner of dress and undress. Heavy smoke was pouring in from the port side of the ship.

Martinez shouted for the passengers to go aft as he wheeled both his arms toward the stern of the ship. Then he went back down to A deck and started knocking on doors to wake more passengers. He led them up the stairway near the doctor's office to the promenade deck, and finally to the open deck around the swimming pool at the stern.

CHAPTER 9

Rousеd

0130 hours, Saturday, November 13

On the main deck, Charles Agero had seen enough of the fire at #610 to know that he had to start waking passengers, just as Whyley and Martinez were doing. He testified to Coast Guard investigators that he was running toward the forward lobby shouting and knocking on doors, when he came face to face with an image out a horror film that nearly stopped his heart. A burned, nude woman appeared out of the smoke, crying, "Please save my fourteen-year-old baby."

Like Agero, Chief Mate Francisco Argilagos had turned his attention to the passengers too. When he had heard the second mate call down to the captain through the voice tube about the fire at about 0110, he had hustled from his cabin up to the bridge, then gone in search of the fire. After observing the heat and flames at #610, not seeing the captain anywhere to be found for guidance, and finally finding his return to the bridge blocked by a massive cloud of smoke on the promenade deck, Argilagos surmised that the *Yarmouth Castle* was a lost cause. The best he could do was try to save as many lives as possible in the only ways he knew how. He was not waiting around for orders from a missing captain or from the officer on watch, who seemed to be quickly getting overloaded. But like a growing number of the crew, he was not following any set procedures. He was freelancing.

A former Cuban naval officer, Argilagos was in his early thirties and a refugee of the Cuban Revolution, trying to rebuild his life in Miami's cruise ship industry. He had started as the third mate aboard the *Castle* a little more than a year and a half ago and had worked his way up through the ranks. This was his first trip as the chief mate, and he took his new position of responsibility seriously. His first move was to home in on the sound of screaming coming from cabin #M-1 on the promenade deck.

"I broke the window with a broomstick," he would testify. "Then I ordered quartermaster Pedro Luis to break all the windows on the starboard side. I put hose #15 in operation. There was pressure in the hose. Quartermaster Cheril manned the hose. But first I helped a heavy-set woman and a thin woman out of the cabin. I opened the door to the lobby facing #G-1. There was a solid wall of flame. There was another [fire] station aft on the starboard side of the promenade deck, and I opened that hose and gave it to a crew member. There was pressure in the hose. I had it directed on the crew's stairway. There was smoke in the stairway but no fire."

Argilagos went aft, where he saw many passengers and crew gathering. He was carrying his master key, and as he moved toward the stern of the ship he unlocked and opened the doors to interior cabins. Then he found a locker with life vests and gave them to a room steward to start passing out to the assembled passengers and crew.

Now he had to find a way to get past the smoke and flames to the boat deck. He had to start launching lifeboats before the fire spread to them.

Like many other "good Samaritans" in the crew, Chief Mate Argilagos was operating on good intuition and noble intentions as he did his best to save lives, but by today's standards, he was woefully unprepared and unsupported to face off with the tragedy unfolding aboard the *Yarmouth Castle*.

Today all ships' officers are required to have formal training in basic and advanced marine firefighting. This is a requirement under the STCW code. Unlicensed crew members, such as able seaman and oilers/QMEDs, are required to have basic marine firefighting training. This has to be refreshed every five years. Initial classes are five days in length; refresher training is two days. Training is a comprehensive blend of classroom lectures and actual firefighting in a steel mockup of a real ship or in a concrete multistory building. Additionally, under the ISM code, ships are required to hold monthly fire and abandon-ship drills as well as safety training on specific subjects.

Typically, today, deck officers will attend a bridge resource management class every three to five years, with a focus on ship handling and navigation under adverse conditions. Shipping companies, maritime pilot organizations, and their customers have recognized the value in continued training. Most courses today are three days in length and are combined with classroom discussions and simulator exercises. Usually, seafarers from the same company will attend classes together. Some may serve on the same ship together, and some may not. Simulator exercises are designed to increase the stress level on the watch officer incrementally, stressing teamwork and problem-solving.

Today's full-mission bridge simulators are very realistic in the way the simulated ship reacts to maneuvering inputs, engineering casualties, and the simulated environmental conditions. Wind, current, reduced visibility, and interactions with other vessels and harbors are accurately portrayed. Trainees take turns playing different roles in the bridge team during the exercises. After each exercise, a debriefing session is held to go over what went well, what didn't, and what could be improved upon. Equally as important as the simulator exercises, the classroom discussions are usually based on analysis of past accidents as well as firsthand experiences of the students in attendance. Seafarers who have been doing this since the 1990s, for the most part, agree that the training has improved as time goes along.

None of this existed back in 1965. Deck officers such as the *Castle*'s first officer Francisco Argilagos reported aboard with their license and stepped into the watch rotation, and that was it. The scenario was pretty much the same for able seaman and unlicensed crew members such as watchman José Arcadio. Some of those crewmen came with a high degree of skills and initiative, such as Argilagos, and some others, such as Arcadio, needed training before being given responsibilities with life and death consequences.

Ship's hostess Ruth Wright would testify that she was just about asleep when she heard the sound of the steel fire doors on the deck below her closing. She knew how they sounded from practicing fire drills more than fifty times on the *Castle*'s sister ship *Yarmouth*, where the captain was a stickler for safety.

Sensing a serious situation, she tried to turn on the light, but there was no electricity. Then she heard one of the Jamaican crewmen screaming in the corridor, "Fire! My god, fire!" followed by the sound of crockery or glass breaking.

She grabbed her flashlight, rolled out of bed, and opened the door. A wave of heat and smoke almost knocked her off her feet before she shut the door. She went to her open porthole and pulled herself halfway out on her back. Looking up, she could see the bridge of the ship on fire. Almost directly above her, the canvas cover on a lifeboat was burning, and sheets of the burning canvas were falling past her face. When she glanced down, she saw the portside pilot door open and three seamen launch the paint dinghy, hop in, and drift astern. The ship was moving forward, but much more slowly than usual.

Then she heard the maître d' calling her name from the deck above.

"Throw me a rope. Pull me up," she called.

He shook his head as if to say he had no rope. "Jump," he shouted.

She realized that if she was going to have to go in the water, she needed her life vest, so she held her breath and slid back into her cabin to fetch the vest and put it on. By the time she started sliding out the porthole again, she could feel the heat from the fire starting to sear her legs.

The smoke and the fire in the cabin were too intense, and "I had to jump," she would tell accident investigators later. "I dove into the water."

While Wright was taking her plunge, passenger Joan Reynolds was climbing the stairs to the promenade deck in her slacks and robe. She was still trying to find someone on the crew to help her investigate the source of the smoke she had smelled down on the main deck. When she reached the saloon lobby on the promenade deck, she saw a lot of people milling around in nightclothes. Then "smoke seemed to come from above very suddenly," she would say at the Coast Guard hearings.

She tried to escape the smoke by heading up to the boat deck. But the smoke in the Blue Lounge was even thicker, and she lost her way. She was beginning to panic when she found an exit door to the portside passageway. The passage seemed to have less smoke up forward, so she ran in that direction. Passengers Nathan and Betty Barkin suddenly appeared in front of her, with their clothes burned to shreds and their skin scorched. Still, there was no sign of anyone on the ship's crew.

"Come with me," she told them.

Eventually, they broke out of the smoke into clear air on the bow of the ship. Other passengers were arriving; many had serious burns. Charlie the bartender climbed up from the deck below to help with the injured, and a steward found blankets to wrap burn victims such as the Barkins. Someone pulled a fire hose out, but it had no water pressure. Now what?

Carl Apuzzo, in cabin #835, wasn't waiting for direction from the crew, he would tell investigators. As soon as he woke to the scent of smoke, he shook Willie and told her they had to get out of there. The cabin door was hot, and Carl knew instinctively not to open it. There were flames and death out in the hallway. The Apuzzos dressed in what seemed like no time at all, pulled on slippers, grabbed their brand-new life preservers, and climbed out the opened window of their stateroom to the promenade deck. At the last minute, Carl took his wallet and cabin key. Then he tucked them into his dob kit. He held it with his teeth as they scrambled out of their cabin, and the ship's horn started its long, but fading, bellow.

They saw smoke on the forward port side of the ship, and flames rising above the bridge. Apuzzo sensed that sooner rather than later, they would have to abandon the ship, so he found a steel ladder leading up to the boat deck and the lifeboats. On the boat deck, the Apuzzos joined two men trying to pull the canvas cover off a lifeboat. But even with the four or them working together, they could not make the cover budge.

Apuzzo would testify that he was sure it was only a matter of a minute or two before this section of the ship became an inferno. This is when he spotted a life raft lashed to a bulkhead.

He called to Willie and one of the other men. At the hearing, Carl would remember that they "loosened the raft and pushed it over the side. The man jumped over the side into the raft."

The drop to the water had to be over 60 feet from the boat deck, and Carl feared that the man had broken his neck, the raft, or both when he landed. But he couldn't tell because the ship was still moving forward, and the raft was drifting astern.

"The smoke was getting intense, and my wife and I decided we should leave the ship," Apuzzo would testify to the Coast Guard.

But Willie didn't want to jump. It was so far down to the water, and she didn't swim.

At this point, a woman passenger appeared out of the smoke, Willie Apuzzo would later tell her daughters.

"What do we do?" she asked Willie.

"Pray."

"Oh, god; I don't know how," said the woman.

"You already are." Willie was trying to comfort her. But then flames roared up around the woman, and she was gone.

"Fire was coming up from the deck below," Carl Apuzzo would tell Coast Guard investigators. "We held hands and jumped into the water together."

CHAPTER 10

Burned and Dying

0135 hours, Saturday, November 13

Gift shop operator Charles Agero was still dealing with the burned woman and worried about finding her lost fourteen-year-old son.

"In the forward lobby was a couch," he would testify, "and I saw fire underneath the couch. I had the hand fire extinguisher, and I discharged it, then threw it away. [I] grabbed the burned lady, and I dragged her over to my store. Then I returned to the same place, looking for her fourteen-year-old child. [I] could not go beyond the men's room, too much smoke. There were some people in the passageways, and I knocked on doors and banged on doors while passing through."

On his trip through the ship, he didn't see anyone fighting the fire and didn't see any officers or crew members. He went along the port passageway one deck below, but he couldn't get beyond room #610. Suddenly, there were people flooding out of the staterooms and scrambling in both directions. He realized that this section of the ship was quickly becoming a death trap. The lady's child must already be lost, and he would be too, unless he got out of here now.

He returned for the burned lady at his shop, but when he got there, she was gone. He thought he should rescue the valuables he kept for passengers in the shop's safe-deposit box in the store. He would tell investigators, "The smoke and panic was too much, so I left the safe and went on deck. I showed people how to put life jackets on and gave them mine; my assistant Ann Fonda was with me, and she did the same. My lifeboat was #5, but it was on fire."

Down in the "Glory Hole," Roy Drysdale was out of bed and dressed. He was stuffing his prized belongings in his suitcase when the smoke became so thick that he thought it would kill him if he tried to breathe. He pulled a damp towel over his face, left his suitcase, and started feeling his way toward a stairwell leading on deck.

Drysdale would tell his interviewer on CRS Radio Network that on his way toward the outside of the ship, he saw a woman "so badly burned, she had no breasts." She seemed to Drysdale like the walking dead. "The fat was just dripping off of her. . . . She had no ass. . . . You could see the muscle contractions as she walked." And she kept asking, 'Where are they?'"

He knew she was referring to her family, who most likely had already perished.

"I told her not to worry. They were all right." Drysdale thought that when she heard that, she felt some kind of release. She just fell over and died.

He knew the moment had come for desperate measures. This fire was a killer and out of control, and George Vazeos's "old girl" was in no condition for the fight.

In hindsight, US Coast Guard investigators would say that the obsolete construction details of the SS *Yarmouth Castle* made her an accident waiting to happen. The ship's structural members—hull, deck, and superstructure plating—were riveted steel construction. But the *Castle* had wood construction in the upper parts of the ship as a weight-saving measure. This was typical of passenger ship construction for her era (1920s).

The ship had a total of six decks. The lowermost two decks were of steel construction. Above the main deck, construction methods were mixed, with wood used increasingly in the uppermost decks. The aft end of the main deck outside the deckhouse and the boat deck outside the deckhouse were sheathed with wood planks over steel. The boat deck inside the deckhouse and the promenade deck were of wood construction. All of the uppermost decks and housetops were of wood construction covered with painted canvas. The outer sides of the promenade and boat decks were made of steel. Interior partitions, passageways, staterooms, and public rooms all were of painted wood.

As built, the *Evangeline* / *Yarmouth Castle* was fitted with both natural and mechanical ventilation throughout the ship. Natural ventilation consisted of opening portholes in the outboard staterooms of the main deck, and opening windows in the outboard staterooms of the promenade deck and boat deck. Wood-framed, opening glass skylights were fitted in the public-room overheads on the boat deck. Light and air shafts were provided for public toilet spaces and inboard staterooms on the boat deck.

Mechanical ventilation was arranged with a series of ducts routed to the living quarters on D deck, the inboard passenger staterooms of the main deck, the dining room, and the ship's offices. The ship's galley and pantry were fitted with a separate mechanical ventilation system consisting of exhaust fans and dedicated ductwork. An additional set of ducts and fans served all the public and private toilet rooms. All of this resulted in a maze of ductwork hidden above the false ceiling on each deck.

Large fore and aft ducts were fitted within the overhead of the port and starboard passageways on the main, promenade, and boat decks. Smaller ducts were routed to these main ducts from various locations, creating a spiderweb of ductwork on each level of the ship. The large fore and aft ducts led to vertical risers within the boiler casing, fitted just forward of midships on the ship's centerline. These vertical risers led to electric exhaust fans aft of the smokestack on the uppermost deck. In the event of a fire, manually operated dampers would need to be closed by crew members assigned to this task. None of the ductwork was insulated, nor was it required to be at that time.

After the ship began her work as a Miami-based cruise ship in the 1950s, technicians installed air-conditioning. Eventually all staterooms, the dining room, and all remaining public rooms were air-conditioned. Due to the piecemeal installation, the ship ended up with two different types of AC systems. As the AC was installed in various spaces throughout the ship, the existing mechanical ventilation systems were left in place, with the ends of the duct runs blanked off by various means. The air shafts to the inboard staterooms were also left in place and blanked off. Many of these air shafts were of wood construction. This maze of ductwork would become a major factor in the disaster unfolding aboard on November 13, 1965.

As with SOLAS requirements, United States Coast Guard regulations are updated periodically as the science and technology of shipbuilding, safety at sea, and ship operations evolves. When the *Evangeline* returned to Bethlehem Shipyard in Quincy, Massachusetts, in 1946 after her service as a troop carrier during World War II, much had changed regarding passenger ship regulations from the time she was built, almost twenty years prior. SOLAS had been redrafted in 1929 and would again be changed two years later, in 1948. US regulations had by now come under the administration of the Coast Guard. Substantial changes had taken place in US laws as well, particularly in the area of ship construction.

When the SS *Evangeline* entered Quincy Shipyard for conversion back to commercial passenger service, the ship had to meet all the current requirements relative to fire-retardant construction. What this meant was that large portions of the ship's upper works, which had been constructed of wood, needed to be rebuilt with steel. As the engineering staff of the War Shipping Administration (WSA) delved deeper into the technical details of the project, they came to the realization that to do this would add considerable weight to the ship up high and have adverse effects on the ship's stability, carrying capacity, and draft.

The WSA (which was paying for the ship's reconversion to passenger service) took all of this into consideration and approached the Coast Guard with concerns as to the cost of the project. In view of these concerns, the Coast Guard determined that the requirements could not be "reasonably and practicably complied with." As such, they modified the requirements to permit the repair and restoration of the existing type of construction. The original wood construction and joiner work throughout the vessel were retained. The spiderweb of current and obsolete ventilation ducts throughout the vessel remained. Sprinklers were not fitted in the toilet spaces. In essence, SS *Yarmouth Castle* had all the ingredients to become a bonfire. Now she was.

Adele Simister and Mabel Stroud were trapped, and they knew it, Simister would later tell *Life* magazine. The corridor outside their cabin was thick with smoke, and flames were licking at their door. In their cabin, they found their life vests and put them on. There were whistles on their vests, and they began to blow them, relentlessly, shrilly, hoping someone would come and rescue them. While Simister stacked suitcases and climbed atop them to open the cabin porthole, Straub tried to stabilize the suitcases, but she felt something like ice shooting up her legs. It wasn't ice at all. It was fire rising from the cabin sole.

"Del, Del," she shouted, "what are we going to do?"

"I don't know. My legs are burning too."

It was at this moment that Roy Drysdale heard Adele Simister blowing her whistle. He looked over the side of the ship from the deck above and saw her leaning out her open porthole, with her whistle in her mouth.

He climbed down over the guardrail and shouted, "Lady, lady, give me your hand."

Simister saw "his encouraging smile." She dropped the purse in her hands into the flames rising from her cabin floor and reached up to Drysdale. She stretched for his hand. Once he had pulled her through the porthole, she clung to his body as other members of the crew reached over the guardrail and lifted them both to safety.

"My friend is still in the cabin," she cried, "and it is on fire."

Drysdale went down headfirst with his legs hooked to the guardrail. Then he reached into the porthole, shouting "Lady, lady."

He could see Mabel Straub. She was standing in the center of the cabin, looking like she wanted to climb the stack of suitcases her friend Adele had used to get out of the porthole.

"Help me," she begged. But her nightgown was already on fire. Possibly stoked by the fresh oxygen from the open porthole, the fire seemed to actually roar, and Stroud fell backward into a pillar of flames. It felt like a flamethrower had suddenly been turned in Drysdale's direction and blown him back up on deck. He lay there blinded by smoke, shaking with anguish.

"Something's wrong, Charlie." Charles Matias would testify that his wife, Edna, was in the lower berth in her tiny cabin, and she had begun kicking the berth above her to wake her husband.

He said he was sure the commotion out in the corridor was just drunks. Edna wasn't so sure, so she boosted herself out of bed and opened the door. Smoke roiled it.

"Get back," he told her. "Close that door."

But she stepped out into the corridor.

"Edna, come back." He was screaming as he dropped from his upper berth to the cabin sole.

Matias shouted his wife's name again and ran into the corridor, he would tell investigators. Deep-red flames were spreading up the walls and across the ceiling around him. Edna was nowhere in sight. For an instant he hoped she had somehow made it through this gauntlet of fire. He pictured her back home in Berwyn, Illinois, decorating their new apartment. But then the heat burning his cheeks brought him back to the present. Maybe Edna made it out, but he could not go into those flames. He retreated back into the cabin and punched the glass in the porthole with his bare fist. He did not know he had this kind of strength, but he hit the plate glass again and again until it shattered, and the jagged pieces fell away.

For a second or two, he turned back to the door and looked into the corridor. It was a furnace now, so he turned away and crawled out the porthole onto the exterior deck of the ship. He had the idea that maybe he could circle around the fire and find that Edna had come out on the other side. But the fire seemed to span the ship from port to starboard, and the flames were shooting up like geysers into the night. No one could survive that. As he backed away from the heat and spewing smoke, he was crying.

CHAPTER 11

Chaos

0140 hours, Saturday, November 13

Margaret Masters did not, at first, like the way that cruise director José Martinez had abruptly ordered her to get on deck and go to the top of the ship. She did not appreciate that her new, special friend on the ship's crew had lumped her in with all the other passengers who had begun coming into the corridor outside the fire in #610. She would imply at the Coast Guard hearings that she initially felt dismissed and abandoned by Martinez. There was little smoke beyond #610 and no panic as passengers began following Martinez's direction, climbing the steps in the main lobby, and heading for what they expected to be an oasis at the Neptune Lounge on the boat deck. As she climbed those stairs, she simply couldn't understand why Martinez had left her.

But now, up on the boat deck, she realized that Martinez had surmised almost from their first encounter with the fire in #610 that this was not an isolated problem in a single cabin. He had responsibilities to more than just her alone. The whole ship and all those aboard were in peril. Martinez had sent her and the others up to the boat deck because he already knew that the time had come to load and launch the lifeboats. The first people on the boat deck would have the best chance to make it into a lifeboat before the *Yarmouth Castle* became a ball of flames.

Near the Neptune Lounge, she encountered what she would recall at the hearings as "confusion, people trying to get outside the lounge area." There was a lot of shouting. Some of the ship's crew were trying to form passengers into queues and load people into lifeboats #7, #9, and #9A near the rear of the ship on the starboard side. A passenger she knew from her travel group named Dr. Stuart gallantly gave her his life vest.

She was glad to see that a number of the folks such as Dr. Stuart and his wife from the North Broward County Senior Citizens Club were already on the boat deck, too, and boarding the three lifeboats. But dozens of her charges from the club were not here. She knew that many of the Broward County seniors had cabins in the middle section of the ship forward of lifeboat #7. That entire section of the ship was now roaring with flames and billowing black smoke. God, help them all.

It was not long before she was guided into a lifeboat and told to sit "on the floor with a Spanish-speaking girl." As the crew swung her lifeboat out from its davits and lowered away, she saw the lights go out on the boat deck. For at least the second time since boarding the *Yarmouth Castle*, Masters gave a silent prayer to her lucky stars. Now everything was either in dark shadows or lit by the glow of flames. As the lifeboat lowered toward the water, the air seemed filled with the crackling sound of burning wood and choking smoke from the inferno on the ship.

Fires by their very nature create drafts. Heat rises, as does smoke and toxic gas. The more oxygen that gets fed to a fire, the more vigorously it will burn. When the fire in room #610 started, it most likely smoldered for a period of time before developing further. Heat, smoke, and toxic gases given off by burning paint and materials in the mattresses would have risen to the ceiling in the room. As the smoke and toxic gas rose, it would have entered the ventilation ducts in the overhead. By means of a natural draft, with the hot gases encountering the cooler air within the ducts, smoke and gas spread the length of the ductwork, spilling out of any openings along the way. This explains why passengers in staterooms in some parts of the ship and in passageways in others smelled smoke well ahead of the realization that there was a fire.

As the fire gained ground, it eventually fully involved #610, radiating heat outward and upward. Once the flames reached into the false ceiling and ductwork above, fire was free to travel the length of the ship fore and aft. Gaps in the fire-screen bulkheads that had been noted during the Coast Guard inspection in Jacksonville in May 1960 had never been sealed up. Nor had the wood and glass skylights been removed and sealed up with steel covers. Old air shafts framed in wood acted as chimneys conducting the heat, smoke, and toxic gas upward. With the fire burning horizontally inside the ductwork, it jumped decks upward and aft as it burned through the wooden decks and within the superstructure. Up forward, fire propagated via the vertical risers within the stack casing to the decks above.

Adding to this nightmare scenario was the galley vent system that was fitted on the opposite side of #610's forward bulkhead. The inside of the galley vent ducts had never been cleaned as directed by Coast Guard inspectors back in July 1959 and January 1962. Years of solidified grease had built up inside the galley ducts, along with dust and debris. Once fully involved, temperatures inside #610 near the ceiling would have been in the neighborhood of between 1,200 and 1,500 degrees Fahrenheit. This amount of heat would continue to radiate outward and would be directly transmitted to the adjoining galley ductwork. These temperatures are well above the range for the built-up grease within the ductwork to autoignite. Once this occurred, the galley ductwork would have turned into a virtual flamethrower. This phenomenon is, in fact, somewhat visible in photos of the ship burning in the area where the galley vent exits the superstructure on the boat deck. As the fire gained in intensity, it burned outward and upward, consuming everything in its path. The ship's wooden superstructure components and extensive interior wood joiner work provided plenty of fuel to keep the fire burning.

Eighteen-year-old Guy Leslie was covering the switchboard in the main entrance lobby when the lights went out. He was a new bellman, and this was only his second trip on the *Yarmouth Castle*. Everything about the ship still felt new and grand to him compared to the simple life he had left behind in Jamaica. But now he sorely wished he were at home. For the last fifteen minutes or so, he had been urged by a passenger (Lloyd Lamn) into helping him sniff out the source of smoke up forward in the galley area, but they had found nothing more than a few whiffs of something that might have been cigar smoke. But when the usual switchboard operator said he needed to take up the search for the smoke, Leslie was told to "mind the board" and not leave his station.

Now the lobby was dark. He could hear the ship's horn letting out a long groan. The scent of smoke had suddenly become ten times stronger.

He would tell accident investigators that he was wondering what he should do, when someone locked him in a flashlight beam. In a split second, two older ladies in nightgowns grabbed him by the arms, pulled him into stateroom #621, and slammed the door behind them. The air in the cabin was fresh.

"We've got to get out of here right now, young man," one of them told him. "The ship's on fire. We'll all die out there." She nodded toward the door.

"Will you help us?" asked her companion.

He wasn't sure what she meant until he followed her gaze to the porthole. It was wide open. Leslie could see the reflection of the moon on the water.

"I went to the porthole," he would tell Coast Guard investigators, and "got one old lady out. Got out first. Lay on the rail of the second [promenade] deck. Grabbed her by the arm. Helped her out of the porthole. She jumped into the water." At this point the *Yarmouth Castle* had come to a complete stop.

After rescuing the women in #621, Leslie joined other crew members on the promenade deck, breaking cabin windows from #701 to #711 to help more passengers escape. "There were no lights," he would testify, "but [the] fire was bright enough to see." At some point he found a rope ladder to hang over the side. He had lowered it to a porthole to help "another elderly woman" escape when he fell off the ladder and started to swim for his life.

CHAPTER 12

A Dereliction of Duty

0145 hours, Saturday, November 13

The smoke was dark and suffocating on the *Yarmouth Castle*'s bridge when Captain Byron Voutsinas finally returned topside after spending scores of minutes trying to fight the fire at #610 on the main deck. Almost as soon as he reached the bridge, he became separated from the crew on watch. He could no longer see them but could only hear them coughing, choking, imploring him for guidance. What should they do next? They were stuck here on the bow. The ship's bridge was catching fire from beam to beam.

"I saw on the sun deck [above the boat deck] was almost everywhere fire," he would say at the Coast Guard accident hearings. He was a Greek, and his English was less than perfect.

With smoke clotting in his throat, Voutsinas felt stunned.

"I lost them [the second mate and the watchmen] in the smoke," he would testify. "I presume everybody was trying to get to his lifeboat."

He began to hyperfocus on the need to send another SOS signal. His only hope of sending out a radio distress call was to get to the emergency radio in the #3 lifeboat, the motor lifeboat on the boat deck about 50 feet aft of the starboard wing of the bridge. At this point he spotted the ship's second electrician through the smoke and told him they had to launch the #3 boat and get help. None of the other men who had stood the watch on the bridge saw him go. They were scrambling toward the bow of the ship, where the smoke and flames could not yet reach them and where there was clear air to breathe.

"When I was going to launch that particular boat, there was the fire very close to us and smoke," the captain would tell Coast Guard investigators. "Smoke was choking us and we couldn't do it. . . . We got part of the lifeboat cover off, but the deck where the lifeboat was resting was on fire."

Driven back by the heat, the smoke, and the flames, the captain and the second electrician started forward on the starboard side of the boat deck, hoping to reach lifeboat #1 and launch it.

"The boat deck open like a crater," Voutsinas would testify. "One big area open up like crater and flame come out and smoke. When this fire come up, the second electrician got into the fire[,] and his clothes start to burning and his face was burning and he start to scream, and he say, 'Captain, I am dying.' And he jump from the sun deck, which is about 70 or 80 feet high to the water. So, I am left alone there."

To escape the flames, the captain went down a small steel ladder to the boat deck below.

"I was trying to go forward between the lifeboats and the staterooms where they have windows outside to the boat deck," he would tell Coast Guard investigators. "One of the windows break the glass. The smoke and flames come out and hit me on the face and stop me. The smoke choke me and I fall down. And then after a while I recover. I think for seconds I pass out. I get my breath again, so I escape, and I went forward."

At this moment, most of the flames and smoke were blowing over the port side of the ship, but still the visibility on the forward end of the boat deck was extremely limited.

Finally, a voice answered from somewhere in the smoke, "Captain, I am here." It was the *Castle*'s boatswain. He told his skipper, "The fire is going all over the ship."

"We have to do something here to try to launch one of the boats," said Voutsinas.

He heard passengers screaming, and he had to try to get them out of the fire. "The flames were coming closer and closer. . . . Lifeboats #1 and #1A on the starboard side of the ship were almost on fire."

As the captain kept shouting into the smoke to see if there were others still alive or trapped, the staff captain and another crewman appeared. The staff captain was choking so badly on the smoke that he could not speak at first, but eventually Voutsinas heard from the staff captain that the ship was afire across her entire breadth and over its whole length. He did not know that hundreds of passengers and crew were gathered in relative safety near the swimming pool back aft and were launching the lifeboats near the stern of the ship. Neither did he know that two of his officers and a clutch of crew and passengers were huddled on deck in the bows of the *Castle*. But the flames were creeping ever closer to him. Voutsinas decided he must launch a lifeboat and save the people who were here, trapped with him, on the forward end of the boat deck.

The captain, the boatswain, the staff captain, and a deckhand struggled with the help of a flashlight in thick smoke to release and to lower lifeboat #1, and they eventually freed the boat and prepared to lower away.

"I helped some passengers (three or four) to get to the boat," Voutsinas will testify. "Very heavily injured and blood all over. One of them couldn't even see, and they were screaming."

As his shipmates lowered the nearly empty lifeboat, Voutsinas remained on the deck. He was deep in thought. "I stand there for a minute to try if I can do anything. My thoughts were the whole ship was on fire. While I was up there, the only thing I could see was smoke and fire."

The captain pictured the other eleven lifeboats on his ship. Most of them were 26 feet long and 9 feet wide. They were made of riveted steel sheet and had a carrying capacity of fifty persons. If all the boats could be completely filled and launched, there would be barely be enough room in the lifeboats for the 572 passengers and crew aboard the *Yarmouth Castle*. But now, not all those boats were usable. Voutsinas had personally witnessed most of the lifeboats at the forward end of the ship on fire or surrounded by flames. He feared that possibly the boats back aft were equally unusable or inaccessible.

Maybe lifeboat #1 was the only lifeboat in play. If this were the case, lifeboat #1 was useless as a rescue vessel. It was too small a boat for too many people by a factor of nearly twenty. The only way for his crew and passengers to survive would be for them to jump into the water. He imagined hundreds of people bobbing in the water, many without life vests, flailing in the dark sea next to the burning ship.

What could he do? "How long these people swim around the boat?" he asked.

The best thing he could think of was to take this boat and go in search of additional help. He knew that the *Finnpulp* and the *Bahama Star* were nearby.

"There was a necessity to get out some signal," he would explain later at the hearings, still clinging to his obsession "to attract some vessel in the vicinity to come close."

The man was on a mission. He grabbed ahold of the falls for the lifeboat and lowered himself down into the boat. Then he took command and told his oarsmen to pull away from the *Castle*. "The glass from the Promenade Deck, heavy big glass from the windows they [passengers and crew still aboard] were breaking and coming [down] on us in the lifeboat. It was very dangerous."

Some of the ship's crew were already in the water. They swam to the lifeboat and climbed aboard while the captain took the boat's Very pistol and began firing distress flares into the night sky.

"You were actually pulling away from your ship?" One of the Coast Guard investigators at the accident inquiry would ask Captain Voutsinas, in clear astonishment that the *Castle*'s master would leave his ship, passengers, and crew.

"Yes," Voutsinas would say with no hint that he had violated a long-standing and nearly sacred code of seafaring, dictating that the captain must be the last of his crew to abandon his mortally wounded ship.

When pressed further by investigators, Voutsinas would offer multiple explanations for being among the very first to leave the stricken *Yarmouth Castle*:

1. He needed to be farther away from the ship to effectively fire his distress flares.
2. He needed to get to another ship (the *Finnpulp*) to find immediate medical attention for the burned passengers in his boat.
3. He needed to reach a rescue ship and request she send out a radio distress SOS for help.

A captain's premature abandoning of a ship in distress has been a maritime crime for centuries in Greece, Spain, and Italy. South Korean law requires captains to rescue themselves last. In Finland, a similar law exists.

In countries such as the United States, where no such law exists, maritime tradition holds that a ship's captain has ultimate responsibility both for the vessel and everyone aboard. In the event of an emergency, a captain is expected, even *obligated*, to devote his or her best efforts to save all those persons on the ship . . . or die trying. This tradition relates to the nineteenth-century Victorian ideal of chivalry, in that "women and children go first."

In practice and in modern-day mythology, the tradition holds that the captain should be the last person to leave a ship alive before it sinks. The corollary to this tradition maintains that if the master of a vessel is unable to save all the crew and passengers aboard a distressed ship, the captain will choose to "go down with the ship." According to maritime law, a master's responsibility for a vessel is of the highest importance, no matter what its condition.

In some cases, abandoning a ship in distress may be considered a felony. After Captain Francesco Schettino prematurely left his sinking cruise ship *Costa*

Concordia in 2012, an Italian court sentenced him to sixteen years in prison for abandoning his ship, crew, and passengers.

Books and films have portrayed Captain Edward Smith, in command of RMS *Titanic*, as having followed tradition when his liner sunk (in April 1912) after striking an iceberg. Reportedly, Smith returned to the bridge just before the ship began its final plunge and, therefore, died doing his duty.

Allegedly, in 1956, Captain Piero Calamai of the Italian liner *Andrea Doria* was determined to go down with the ship to atone for his errors leading to the disaster, which killed forty-six people.

The tradition, the obligation, and the law also extend to pilots in command of aircraft. Following the ditching of US Airways Flight 1549 into the Hudson River in 2009, the pilot in command, Chesley "Sully" Sullenberger, was the last person to leave the flooding aircraft after making sure that all his passengers and crew were safely evacuated. For his compassion and coolheadedness, Captain Sullenberger received more than a score of awards for heroism, including the French Legion of Honor medallion and the key to the city from the mayor of New York.

In the early morning hours of November 13, 1965, Captain Byron Voutsinas's fortunes were on a much-different trajectory from Sullenberger's. There were witnesses, angry witnesses. Some were officers in Voutsinas's crew.

"I had on just undershirt and no shoes," Third Mate Virgilio Quiñones would tell accident investigators.

He had been roused from sleep by a screaming woman and smoke. Rushing to the bridge to see what was wrong, he had been driven to the bow by the fire, along with the second mate, eight passengers (two wounded), and fourteen members of the crew. Among this group was Joan Reynolds, along with the Bells, and they would have a lot to say to Coast Guard investigators. For the moment, they were in the clear at the very bows on a solid-steel part of the ship, but since the fire was rapidly engulfing the entire ship just aft of them, they feared that the slightest wind shift could overwhelm them with smoke and fire.

"We threw lines over the side and made them fast to the wooden mooring-line gratings," remembered the third mate, describing how he and the others were hastily planning to abandon the *Castle*. The chief radio officer went down into the crew's quarters and passed up smoldering mattresses to the ship's former hostess Joan Reynolds to toss overboard for makeshift flotation.

They were rigging two "Jacob's ladders" (normally used to board and disembark ship pilots) over the side when they spotted a lifeboat. It was lifeboat

#1, and it had Captain Byron Voutsinas, the staff captain, the boatswain, and a couple of others in it.

"There might have been four or five people in the boat," Third Mate Quiñones would testify. "I couldn't tell because it was dark. They were 30–40 yards off. I yelled to them, 'Come here. We have passengers here. Come to this side!' I said many other things. Perhaps I said, 'It is against the law to leave people here. We have passengers here.'"

Murray Bell heard the second mate and the third mate shouting, "Bring that lifeboat back. I order you to bring that lifeboat back. If you don't, it is your responsibility. I command you to bring that lifeboat back."

Joan Reynolds witnessed "many angry comments" called out from people on the bow to the captain and his lifeboat.

"I know you," one of the mates shouted at Voutsinas. "I have your number. You will never sail again!"

"Come back and help passengers," called Second Mate José Ramos de Leon. "Remember the penalty for this." But lifeboat #1 remained drifting at a distance.

"I asked the officer [either the second or the third mate] why the boat won't come back," testified Mrs. Thomas Kneeland, who was among the group on the bow. "He said they were afraid the ship would explode."

The second mate went down the pilot ladder and told the rest of the people on the bow to follow, and he would help them. The Kneelands put on their life vests and followed.

"They threw some small life rafts over," Mrs. Kneeland would tell investigators. "I went alongside and held on. People started to jump into the water, and when my husband would warn me, I would duck and get out of the way."

The Kneelands swam to lifeboat #1, still drifting nearby and occasionally firing flares into the sky.

"They picked us both up," Mrs. Kneeland would testify. "We settled down in the stern . . . right by the man operating the tiller. There was quite an argument going on." The boatswain who was steering the boat was shouting at Voutsinas, who stood in the bows. The boatswain wanted to pick up the people in the water, but Voutsinas said, "We have got to get help. We have got to go get help!"

"The captain's argument prevailed," Mrs. Kneeland would remember at the hearings.

Then Byron Voutsinas and lifeboat #1 began pulling away from the inferno that had been the SS *Yarmouth Castle*, leaving many people still in the water.

CHAPTER 13

To the Rescue

0150 hours, Saturday, November 13

Aboard the MV *Finnpulp*, her captain Johan Lehto took a deep breath and exhaled it very slowly until he could speak without swearing. He had to muster the composure his bridge crew expected of a man who has been going to sea for twenty years, a man who had already sailed as captain of transoceanic freighters for ten years. Nothing short of being cool, calm, and collected would do at this moment. His freighter had been on a routine cargo run to Nassau in the Bahamas. But now everything had changed, and not for the better.

The watch had called him to the bridge. A few minutes ago, the *Finnpulp*'s lookouts had spotted flames coming from a ship they were tracking on radar 7.8 miles astern. Now, Lehto had wheeled the *Finnpulp* around in a tight turn and begun heading at top speed for the flames on the water. He needed his radio operator to transmit a distress message, actually many distress messages, right now.

The *Finnpulp*, the *Bahama Star*, and the *Yarmouth Castle* all were equipped with MF (medium frequency) and HF (high frequency) radios. All three ships had dedicated radio rooms with trained radio operators, such as the *Finnpulp*'s Rauno Suominen. *Yarmouth Castle*'s radio room was situated about 30 feet abaft the bridge on the same deck. A long antenna wire stretched between the ship's two masts. The *Bahama Star* and the *Finnpulp* had similar setups.

MF- and HF-frequency radios have been a very reliable means of communications between ships and shore stations for decades. From the 1950s through the 1980s, many shipping companies had a radio room in the home office. Depending on the nature of the work that a particular company's ships were engaged in, the radio room might be manned only during business hours or 24/7.

The medium-frequency range is from 300 to 3,000 kilohertz (kHz) or 3 megahertz (mHz). High-frequency range is between 3 and 30 mHz. Depending on the time of day, HF radio transmissions can be reflected off the ionosphere and back to Earth at tremendous distances. This is caused by ionospheric refraction, often referred to as "sky wave propagation" or "skip." The ionosphere is made up of loosely packed air molecules within the upper atmosphere. During the hours of daylight, energy from the sun charges or ionizes this layer of the atmosphere. This process, called "ionization," is greatest during daylight hours and diminishes at night.

Radio waves will strike this area of charged particles and refract or bend, returning toward the earth's surface. Conditions need to be just right for this to work well. This is part of the radio operator's skill set, or "art," if you will, to find the right balance of frequencies for the time of day to cover the distance needed to make contact with another station. Lower frequencies, in the 4 to 6 mHz bands, don't carry very far during hours of daylight; the ionosphere is too charged for them to work well. Lower frequencies excel during the hours of darkness. Higher frequencies tend to perform well during daylight hours, frequencies in the 8, 12, and 16 mHz range. It's with these frequencies that radio transmissions are possible at great distances during daylight hours.

The advent of more-compact and more-efficient satellite communication systems has made the use of MF and HF radio far less common today, although it is still in use. It remains the only possible means of long-distance communication in Arctic and Antarctic regions. Today, emails are exchanged between ships and any location globally via satellite communication platforms such as Inmarsat C or Mini V Sat. Voice communication is common as well, via similar means. Of course, no such advanced forms of ship-to-ship and ship-to-shore communications could facilitate the rescue of survivors on that November night in 1965 when the *Yarmouth Castle* burned.

Until about 0145 hours on Saturday, November 13, it had been a relatively routine interlude in the Straits of Florida for the *Finnpulp*'s radio operator, Rauno Suominen, he would write in his narrative (now at the Rauma Maritime Museum in Finland). There had been nothing more than the usual, intermittent radio traffic between ships and shore stations on 500 kHz. All was quiet during the mandatory silent periods each hour, from on the hour to three minutes after and from on the half hour to three minutes after. These times were reserved for distress calls only.

Earlier in the day, Suominen had contacted Lantana Radio WOE in Florida and asked the shore station to pass on the *Finnpulp*'s arrival information to her agent in Nassau and completed his daily check-in with the home office in Helsinki. Then, after 2300 hours, Suominen had set the *Finnpulp*'s radio equipment autoalarm setting. He had signed off for the night and turned to the novel he had been reading. A few sentences in, he fell asleep, book in hand. His alarm clock was set for 0600 hours, but he would be up long before that.

"Wake up, 'Sparks'! There's a ship on fire nearby," Captain Lehto had shouted in Finnish. The radioman sprang from his bunk and sprinted to the radio room in his underwear. Reaching his desk, he tuned the radio set to 500 kHz and listened for distress traffic. But he heard only the usual ship-to-ship traffic, nothing indicating an emergency of any kind. Suominen then headed for the bridge to get details and orders from Captain Lehto. Lehto gave him the position of the burning ship and told him to contact Nassau Radio. Returning to the radio room, Suominen tried raising VPN (Nassau Radio) three times on 500 kHz. But he heard nothing but silence. He tried several more times. Nothing. Captain Lehto seemed to grit his teeth at the news. What the hell was the problem in Nassau? Was someone asleep at the switch? It was infuriating. People's lives were at stake.

Lehto told his radio operator to try the United States Coast Guard in Miami and not to stop calling until he got someone.

It was not until the *Finnpulp* had almost reached the stricken cruise ship from the east when the Coast Guard acknowledged the freighter's distress call.

Meanwhile, *Bahama Star* had been approaching from the west. Suominen heard her radio operator, HPGZ, chime in with details. He identified the burning ship as *Yarmouth Castle*, a passenger ship, and Suominen relayed the news to his captain. The rescue was on, and radioman Suominen had the feeling that things were about to get hectic. There were over five hundred people on the burning ship.

Lehto called all hands on deck to their emergency stations and told his men to prepare to lower a lifeboat and rig the starboard gangway. He steered his ship to approach the burning liner with it on his starboard bow. Then the *Finnpulp* made a slow turn to her right until the *Castle* was on her port quarter. Lehto was about a third of a mile to windward of the stricken cruise ship and lowering his lifeboat, when a sleek white liner coasted between the *Finnpulp* and the floating inferno. As Lehto scanned the new arrival with his searchlight, one of the lookouts with binoculars said he could see her name on the bow. It was the *Bahama Star*.

To Lehto, she seemed dangerously close to those flames. He could hear someone on the *Star* giving orders over a loudspeaker or megaphone. On the bow of the *Yarmouth Castle*, a dozen or more people were waving frantically at the lifeboats. People were tossing deck furniture, mattresses, life rafts, and life rings overboard. Some were going down to the water on ropes and Jacob's ladders. Others were holding their noses and jumping. Not all of them were wearing life jackets. Meanwhile, the *Finnpulp*'s radio operator, Rauno Suominen, was filling the night air with urgent radio messages. Nassau Radio wasn't listening, but the US Coast Guard, 90 miles away, had their "ears on" and was scrambling ships, planes, and helicopters.

Joan Reynolds was one of the refugees from the bow of the ship still in the water. Since the fire and smoke threatened all the people gathered at the bows, she had been unable to descend the Jacob's ladders because the ladders were overloaded with panicked people frozen in fear.

"You have to jump," the chief radio operator had told her, according to her testimony at the Coast Guard hearings.

She climbed over the rail. But then she hesitated. She was a good swimmer, but she feared she might drop onto someone already down there in the shadows. It was while she stood there in limbo that she was, in her words, "half-pushed by the radio officer."

When she bobbed to the surface, Reynolds looked up and saw arms flailing from the portholes and heard screams for help. Seeing all these desperate people, she made the immediate decision to help those trapped people rather than swimming like the Kneelands to lifeboat #1, which was drifting nearby. She called up to the radio officer on deck and directed him to the passengers trying to escape through their portholes. He and other members of the crew dropped ropes and began fishing passengers out of the portholes.

By the time she reached the stern of the ship, she could see a large congregation of people on the after deck (in the vicinity of the swimming pool), but no more passengers or crew trying to escape through portholes. At this point she needed to catch her breath from all the shouting and trying to direct rescues of people from the portholes. She clinched her fingernails into the rough edge of the ship's bumper strip (at the waterline) and clung to the side of the *Castle*. It was amazing. She didn't feel cold at all. Maybe blast after blast of adrenalin was keeping her warm, but right now the sea felt like bath water.

There were two other good things. First, she saw lifeboat #7 being lowered from the *Yarmouth Castle*. Grief-stricken Adele Simister was aboard. So was cruise director José Martinez, Reynolds's friend. He had been helping passengers into the lifeboat with one foot on the deck, one foot on the boat, when the boat lurched, and he fell into it as it started descending toward the water. Second, Reynolds glimpsed a massive white cruise ship coming out of the dark and pointed nearly right toward her. She could hear its screw churning in reverse to stop it, so she turned and swam toward the approaching liner. SS *Bahama Star* had come to the rescue. At this moment, to Joan Reynolds, the *Star* looked like a gift from heaven.

CHAPTER 14

Coming Together

0205 hours, Saturday, November 13

As he laid out a rescue plan with his officers and crew, Captain Carl Brown was guiding the *Bahama Star* right up to the *Castle*. It had been just twenty minutes ago when he had peered out the porthole of his cabin and spotted "something orange on the horizon." Two weeks later, he would tell United States Coast Guard accident investigators that "it was a little blurred . . . sort of spread out too much" to be the lights of another cruise ship steaming through the night between Miami and Nassau. "That was my first inkling . . . so I went up to the bridge to see what it was."

Brown had been awakened by a call from his second mate, who had the watch on the bridge. The captain of the *Bahama Star* had made it routine for the watch to alert him when the lookouts spotted the flashing of the lighthouse on Great Stirrup Cay at the east end of the Northwest Providence Channel. Once past Great Stirrup, the *Bahama Star* would shape her course southeast for Nassau. When Brown heard the call from the bridge, he got up from his berth and looked out his porthole to make sure the light at Great Stirrup was at its usual relative bearing to his ship at this point in her overnight passage from Miami to Nassau. Brown did not want to take any unnecessary chances. There were shoals and small, low islands to starboard that his ship must avoid.

Many of the young women who came aboard the *Bahama Star* ten hours ago at the cruise ship dock on Miami Harbor had been delighted to find this tall, blond, twenty-nine-year-old in a starched, white uniform as the captain on their weekend junket to a tropical oasis. He had a ready smile, an easy laugh, and a bon vivant way of making his passengers feel welcomed to his ship. Still, they wondered privately how one so young could have ascended through the ranks so quickly to be in command of this large ship and to shoulder the responsibility of safeguarding the lives of over seven hundred passengers and crew.

But while Brown projected the insouciance of a debonair officer and gentleman to his passengers, his crew knew another side of him. As a seafarer he was conscientious, careful, calm, and extremely serious about his responsibilities. When his ship was underway, he slept little. A hitch in the navy and more than ten years in the merchant marine had taught him that there is nothing more important than vigilance at sea. While some of his older shipmates, or folks in the front office at the Eastern Steamship Lines, might have considered him a bit of a Boy Scout for his fastidious attention to safety, he believed with all his heart in being prepared for any twist of fate.

So tonight, he had splashed some water on his face, pulled on his starched whites, ran a comb through his thick, wavy hair, and headed for the bridge. As soon as he had a pair of binoculars up to his eyes, he saw that the strange, orange light he had spotted from his porthole was coming from a ship about 4 miles ahead. It was on fire. At the time, *Bahama Star* was making a speed of 14 knots on a course of 101 degrees.

"I said to the wheelman to come left and steer for that ship. I didn't give him any course," he would tell investigators. "Within a very short time, we passed the first of her [life] boats. That is the first time I realized it was the *Yarmouth Castle*."

When he saw the lifeboat (#7), his first thought was to pick up these survivors. He stopped his engines and was about to bring the occupants of the lifeboat aboard.

"It all came to me that if it was the *Yarmouth Castle* and not a freighter, there must be a lot of people still on [the blazing ship]."

Brown grabbed a battery-powered megaphone and told the people in the lifeboat they would be safe, and "to come along and follow us." He wouldn't pick them up just yet. He was going "to get the people off, the ones that were still on the *Yarmouth Castle*."

At this point, Brown saw a second lifeboat (#1) with very few people in it. He also spotted the running lights of a freighter approaching the stricken cruise ship from the east. The freighter was moving cautiously, slowing at a distance of a mile or so. *Bahama Star* was still 2 miles from the burning liner. Now her captain called all hands to their lifeboat stations and told them to prepare to lower fourteen of the ship's sixteen boats post haste.

Ship handling like the finesse demanded of Carl Brown as he brought the *Bahama Star* to the rescue of the *Yarmouth Castle* is very much an art form, a skill developed over time. Seafarers gain experience from handling different ships in varying conditions and various places. Some people have the gift and pick it up quickly. Others don't and struggle. The saying "Anybody can do this" does not apply to ship handling at all.

There are some basic principles in handling ships that apply universally. These pertain both to ships in general and to environmental conditions in which the ship is handled, such as shallow water, strong currents, narrow channels, and strong wind conditions. Generally, the larger the ship and the higher the displacement, the longer it will take the ship to respond to engine commands and to stop. The same applies to draft. The deeper the draft, the longer the ship will take to respond. Deeper-draft and heavier ships are much less influenced by adverse wind conditions. A strong current will have more of an effect on a deeper-draft vessel than one of similar size but shallower in draft.

There are generalities that apply to different hull forms as well. Ships with long, fine entries forward, such as container ships or traditional liners like the *Bahama Star*, tend to like to go in a straight line. Ships that carry their maximum beam well forward and have a more parallel hull form with a more rounded bow, such as tankers, behave differently. These ships will generally turn without difficulty, but they may be hard to stop from turning, particularly in shallow harbors or narrow channels.

The most basic machinery configuration on most ships is a single screw with a single rudder. Engine types also play an important factor during ship handling. During the era of the *Yarmouth Castle*, the *Finnpulp*, and the *Bahama Star* in the mid-1960s, there was more or less an even split between diesel engine and steam turbine propulsion in ships. Reciprocating steam engines (with cylinders and pistons) had by that time, with few exceptions, been replaced by diesels. The *Finnpulp* was a modern diesel-powered ship and relatively easy for Johan Lehto to turn back to the aid of the *Yarmouth Castle*.

The *Castle* and the *Star* were steam turbine ships from an earlier era. *Yarmouth Castle* had twin-screw, single-rudder machinery configuration. *Bahama Star* was configured with a single screw and single rudder. Both were common to passenger ships built in the first half of the twentieth century. And unlike the *Finnpulp*, these ships were difficult to maneuver. Tugs and the use of spring lines or anchors (or both) were needed for mooring and unmooring at docks.

To navigate a ship such as the *Bahama Star*, Captain Carl Brown had to send commands from the bridge to the engine room via an engine order telegraph. The telegraph is a large brass device with a round case, a flat face, and a handle with a pointer. When the handle is moved, a bell inside the brass case rings. The face on the telegraph is marked with commands such as "full," "half," "slow," "stop," "astern full," "astern half," "astern slow," and "finished with engines." There is one telegraph handle for each propeller shaft, with a corresponding telegraph in the engine room.

In practice, the bridge officer rings up a command on the telegraph such as "slow ahead." This command displays on the engine room telegraph, with the pointer indicating which command was given, and the bell ringing at the same time. The engineer on watch responds with the same command on the engine room telegraph, acknowledging the command. He then changes the throttle setting to "slow ahead." After doing this, the engineer will make the notation of the command and time executed in the engineer's bell book. The bell book is the log of all the engine commands given and answered by the engine room. An individual on the bridge handling a ship must always be aware of the lag between a bridge command to the engine room, and changes to the speed and direction of machinery in the engine room. The ship is not like an automobile that can be put into reverse or stopped quickly. Planning and teamwork are key.

For Brown, in approaching *Yarmouth Castle*, there were risks in attempting to get the *Bahama Star* in close and alongside the burning ship. He obviously had been paying attention in the past when harbor pilots maneuvered ships he had been on. At twenty-nine years old, he was young, but he was a natural ship handler who "just got it." Later in life, he would become a Miami harbor pilot, handling all manner of ships large and small. It was a job he held right through to retirement.

Although the *Star* was a poor-handling ship, Brown had a great crew and a very experienced engineering staff. He knew that the place to be stopped was upwind of the *Yarmouth Castle*. Fortunately, weather conditions were good, and he would not have to contend with adverse wind and sea conditions or strong currents. Steam supply on the *Bahama Star* was unlimited, and Brown could ring up as many bells as he wanted. But there was a limit to what could be done as far as maneuvering was concerned.

As Brown approached the *Yarmouth Castle*, he had to slow the *Star* down gradually so as to avoid giving a "full astern" bell to stop when alongside. The key was to get the ship stopped and in position with a minimum of maneuvering and to avoid maneuvers that could cause the ship to come to a stop out of position. Backing "full" could do that. So, from "full ahead," Brown ordered "half" and then "slow ahead." Because *Bahama Star* was larger and heavier than *Finnpulp*, she took longer to stop. Timing was important. As Brown felt the "way" (forward momentum) come off his ship, still some distance from *Yarmouth Castle*, he ordered "all stop."

The *Star* continued to move though the water but was gradually slowing down. Within a couple of ship lengths of where he wanted to be, Brown ordered "slow astern" with rudder amidships. Standing on the port bridge wing, Brown watched his "wheel" (propeller) wash in relation to the hull. Seeing the wash approach the aft end of his boat deck, he ordered "all stop." In position and upwind of the *Yarmouth Castle*, he could now drift and maneuver as needed while his crew launched the *Star*'s lifeboats to start rescuing people from the *Yarmouth Castle*.

Brown saw that the *Castle*'s top two decks were ablaze from the bridge back to the stack. Flames soared into the night sky and cast a glow over the ship and surrounding water. Many of her lifeboats were still hanging in their davits. The forward boats were engulfed in fire. Through his binoculars, Brown could see a crowd gathering on the stern and desperate faces protruding from portholes. He had to get to these poor people as soon as possible, had to get his ship as close as he could. It would not be long before the flames in the middle of the *Castle* spread to both ends.

"We came up astern of her [*Yarmouth Castle*]," remembered Carl Brown at the Coast Guard hearings, "almost dead astern of her, and made a pass alongside of her and the closest point was 100 yards. . . . I still had a little too much headway, and I had to back down the *Bahama Star*."

As Brown tried to stop his ship, he was on the port bridge wing of the *Star*, adjacent to the bow of the *Castle*. Some of the people trapped there had not yet gone overboard. There was a woman on the bow, screaming for help, Brown would still remember, fifty years later, when interviewed for the Discovery Channel feature *The Floating Inferno*. Her voice pierced his heart. It suddenly made the life-or-death nature of this disaster all too real. It echoed like an imperative from the gods. He had souls to save tonight, lots of souls.

He picked up his megaphone and keyed the mike. "We are here to save you. My boats are coming for you now. Get in the water."

"The 100 yards was too close for me," he would tell investigators. "We were feeling the heat. And we were on the windward side. Smoke and fire were being blown away from us." Even so, the heat from the fire on the *Yarmouth Castle* had started bubbling up the paint on the side of the *Star*. When she came to a complete stop, she was 200–250 yards from the *Castle*.

"Our boats were being prepared," Brown would tell investigators. "By the time we got there, most of them were ready to go down. . . . The bridge was burning so badly [that] we hadn't been there for ten minutes before it collapsed. . . . Our boats seemed to be afraid she would explode. I had to tell them to get alongside the *Yarmouth Castle*. They were expecting the people to jump, and the people didn't want to jump. The boats were hanging off about 60 feet. . . . I told them on the bullhorn to go down by any means that they had, ladders or ropes, which I saw a lot hanging over the side. . . . I was afraid they would jump into the boats and be injured."

CHAPTER 15

The Rise of Heroes

0225 hours, Saturday, November 13

Like the Apuzzos, the Bells, and Joan Reynolds, ship's hostess Ruth Wright was in the water when the *Bahama Star* made her approach. Wright was near the stern on the port side of the *Yarmouth Castle* when she heard people calling to her from above on the deck.

"They threw a ladder down in the vicinity of [cabin] #750 or #754, and I climbed back aboard," she would explain at the hearings.

Once on deck, she tried to get across the main lobby to her assigned abandon-ship station, to help load and launch the lifeboat. But the smoke was too intense. She could not make it, so she found a new way to help.

"There were a number of Jamaicans [crewmen] around, and they carried out my orders," she would tell investigators. "I sent them into the staterooms to find [life] jackets because I knew there are jackets, one for every bunk on the ship."

Chief Mate Francisco Argilagos saw the running lights and sweeping searchlights from the *Finnpulp* and the *Bahama Star* coming closer. But he had more-immediate concerns. Within the last half hour, he had come to the conclusion that Captain Voutsinas was probably dead or trapped at the bows of the ship and unable to take command of the evacuation of the *Castle*. He told Coast Guard investigators that, according to the chain of command, the responsibility for the lives of all these frantic, scared, and injured people fell squarely on him. He needed to get as many of them as possible to the stern of the ship on the boat deck, pronto, where there was no fire yet, little smoke, and at least four remaining lifeboats, Now, covering his nose with a handkerchief in order to breathe, he made his way to the Neptune Ballroom. Calmly and decisively, he began to shepherd wandering passengers toward the remaining lifeboats.

With the help of the quartermaster, the second boatswain, and another crewman, Argilagos began loading lifeboat #9. As soon as it was loaded, the crew began lowering it, and the chief mate turned his attention to at least two hundred people crowded around the swimming pool. For a split second he noticed how strange it seemed at this moment that water was gushing into the pool from a large pipe, while the fire hoses themselves, strewn over the deck, looked flaccid and limp, with little or no pressure.

"The fire is coming!" Someone shouted and pointed to huge flames that had erupted in the vicinity of lifeboat #5.

"We must be orderly. We need to load the other boats." The chief mate's voice boomed above the crowd. "Women and children first."

Argilagos sensed that the survivors were on the verge of stampeding toward the remaining three lifeboats. He needed help, now. And he got it. Ruth Wright, gift shop operator Charles Agero, his assistant Ann Fonda, Roy Drysdale, and Lloyd Lamn began pitching in with other members of the crew to form the passengers into three separate queues to fill lifeboats #9A, #10, and 10A.

"I told the passengers not to panic; the *Bahama Star* ***is*** coming," Ruth Wright would remember at the accident hearing. She was still dripping wet from her swim down the side of the ship. As she shepherded people toward the lifeboats, it struck her that the twinkly party lights were still on back here near the stern of the ship. They seemed so forlorn and out of place now.

After leaving the fire at #610, Chief Engineer George Vazeos had been in the engine room, he would testify, closing down the ventilation systems, stopping the ship, taking a boiler offline, and cross-connecting the fire pump and bilge pump to try to get more pressure to the sprinkler system and the fire hoses. In short, he was now fully focused on his essential responsibilities to "the old girl," no longer wandering around the ship trying to detect the source of the smoke or devoting his limited time and energy to fighting the fire at #610.

When he had heard the ship's whistle begin its prolonged bellow, he knew that the time was coming to abandon ship. He sent a runner to the crew's quarters to rouse all the engine room staff who were off duty and have them report to the engine room immediately. He also had them open the pilot door, amidships on the starboard side. This door was less than 10 feet above the water and would allow the engine room crew a quick and easy escape when the time came. In the absence of a direct order from the captain or the bridge, it was his call as to when his men could leave their stations. Before he made this call, he wanted to see how things were going topside.

"I went upstairs to see what happened," he would say at the hearings. "I went to the promenade deck. I saw some people. They fight the fire. Well, I can't help in there, and then I went to the sun deck. The boat deck, the port side. They have the #10 lifeboat and #8. They [the chief mate, Agero, Wright, Lamn, Drysdale, and others] try to let down the boats. I help them. . . . The passengers get off with the three boats. . . . By that time, everybody was in the lifeboats except fifty; no more than fifty passengers was in the aft. I mean there was no place for them, no lifeboat for them."

Meanwhile, the lifeboats from the *Bahama Star* began picking up survivors, who, following Brown's urging, were climbing down Jacob's ladders, sliding down ropes, or jumping to the water.

"They [the boats] came alongside with their people," remembered Brown at the hearings, "and I shouted down to them . . . 'Go back as soon as you get the passengers out and get another load!'"

In the aftermath of the *Yarmouth Castle* disaster, the media and many observers would label Captain Carl Brown a hero. When such praise came his way, Brown would, for the rest of his life, dodge the label of "hero" with an embarrassed smile and a shake of his head. He would always say he was no hero the night when he and his crew made it their mission to rescue the passengers and crew of the *Castle*. He would say he was just doing his job. By custom, every seafarer has the obligation to respond as quickly and completely as possible to another vessel in distress. In the early-morning hours of November 13, 1965, Captain Carl Brown was that seafarer.

His modesty was genuine, which made him all the more likable and admirable. No question that he was an angel of mercy of the first magnitude to the passengers and crew of the *Yarmouth Castle*. But by most modern definitions of a hero, he was right to say the label did not fit him. Contemporary psychologists at places such as Stanford University have undertaken deep studies of heroism. They almost uniformly agree that true heroism roots in compassion, empathy, and the willingness to make a significant personal sacrifice for the benefit of others. By this definition, the *Yarmouth Castle*'s singing waiter Roy Drysdale was heroic when he risked his life as he dangled over the side of the burning ship to pull Adele Simister through a porthole to escape death by immolation. Joan

Reynolds was heroic when she chose not to swim to lifeboat #1 after jumping off the bow of the *Castle*. Instead of putting her own welfare first, she paddled the length of the ship, shouting up to people on deck and guiding them to rescue passengers trapped in their cabins on the main deck through portholes in the side of the burning liner.

Carl Brown clearly felt empathy and compassion for the people trapped by the fire aboard the *Yarmouth Castle*, but he was not risking his own physical, emotional, moral, professional, or financial well-being to rescue those people. In the strictest sense of the definition, he was not heroic. His rescue of hundreds from the *Yarmouth Castle* was, however, a noble act, performed with exceedingly competent leadership and seamanship under challenging circumstances. No doubt, the writer Ernest Hemingway would have said that Brown exhibited a remarkably high degree of courage and "grace under pressure."

"The flames were eating fore and aft, blazing into the sky," wrote David Nevin in *Life* magazine. "Metal turned red and softened and fell. The *Yarmouth Castle* was listing [now], taking on water. As Captain Brown watched from the *Bahama Star*, he identified the strange sound he had been hearing. The *Yarmouth Castle* was moaning. . . . Her list increased [to port], and a note of urgency crept into the calm voice bull-horned through the night."

CHAPTER 16

Man Up

0245 hours, Saturday, November 13

Captain Johan Lehto on the *Finnpulp* ordered the helmsman to turn hard to port as he neared the *Yarmouth Castle*. The Anschutz gyrocompass repeater next to the helm on the bridge had started clicking off the degrees faster and faster as the ship came around. Two-thirds of the way through the turn, Lehto spoke again. He told his helmsman to ease to 20 degrees left, then steer for the *Yarmouth Castle*.

The *Finnpulp* responded to her helm without delay. Unlike Carl Brown's challenges maneuvering the cumbersome and antiquated *Bahama Star*, Lehto's turning the *Finnpulp* around to the aid the *Yarmouth Castle* had been a simple maneuver for her captain. Northern European motor ships such as the *Finnpulp* have always been held in very high regard by seafarers. The Scandinavians and their European neighbors had begun building motor ships long before the rest of the world caught on. Lehto's ship was a modern motor cargo ship, launched with the latest in machinery and cargo-handling gear when she was built. Harbor pilots often refer to these ships as "handy," meaning they are very responsive and handle well.

Having been with the ship since she was delivered from the yard in 1953, Captain Lehto knew the *Finnpulp* well. With her 5,600-horsepower diesel engine and single screw propelling the 379-foot hull, the *Finnpulp* could squeeze into almost any berth in even the tightest harbors. At sea she responded to her single rudder with ease and had a turning radius of less than half a mile at full speed (15 knots) in deep water. From a stop at an anchorage with the rudder hard over and a strong ahead bell, the ship could turn even tighter. Chief Engineer Valter Mattias Toikka and his engine room crew knew their ship and her machinery, as well as their captain. They were all old hands at the job, worked well together, and had pride in their ship and company. It showed tonight.

Now, after steaming at 15 knots, the *Finnpulp* had covered the distance back to *Yarmouth Castle* in less than thirty minutes. The wind was light from the east as Captain Lehto slowed his ship a mile from the *Castle* and rounded up to put the burning liner on his port quarter. When the *Finnpulp* came to a full stop, her crew lowered the starboard gangway and the port motor lifeboat. Now, the *Finnpulp* was a bit more than a third of a mile to windward of the *Castle*. The night was calm. Lehto could drift, send out his lifeboats to rescue survivors, and maneuver as needed while mindful of his position in relation to the *Yarmouth Castle*.

Scanning the scene with a searchlight, Lehto spotted three lifeboats. One (#1) was nearly empty and only 200 yards to leeward, pulling for the *Finnpulp*. The other two were about 500 yards away, full, and drifting.

Captain Byron Voutsinas would testify about approaching the *Finnpulp* in the #1 lifeboat: "I thought we have not sent out an SOS signal. Nobody knows what is going on in that ship. They don't know the lifeboats are burning. Most people won't show up in the water, and I have the injured in the lifeboat. . . . I am going to give word to the freighter to send the SOS and to launch his lifeboats down. Because he probably didn't know our lifeboats were on fire, so he was going to wait to take off the passengers, and we would lose time and lose lives. So, we went close to the freighter."

"We have injured," called Voutsinas, who was standing in the bow of the #1 lifeboat, trying to look very much in charge. The crewmen he had plucked out of the water back alongside the *Castle* were rowing.

The chief mate of the *Finnpulp* shouted to Voutsinas, "Come along the starboard side" to where the gangway was deployed.

When the lifeboat was next to the gangway, some of the crew from the *Finnpulp* and some of the crew from the lifeboat lifted out the burned passengers such as Nathan and Betty Barkin and then folks such as the Kneelands.

Voutsinas, his boatswain, the staff captain, and several able seamen remained in the lifeboat.

"We have not sent an SOS signal, and we are trying to survive as many passengers as possible," Voutsinas called up to Lehto, according to his official testimony.

The freighter captain was on the starboard bridge wing, watching as his crew helped the burned victims and the Kneelands aboard the freighter. Later, he would tell investigators that he never heard anyone on the #1 lifeboat ask him or his crew to send out an SOS. Of course, by now the point of sending out an SOS was moot. The *Finnpulp*'s radio operator, Suominen, had summoned the United States Coast Guard in Miami more than thirty minutes earlier. Now Suominen was in constant dialogue with the Coast Guard, and he was talking to the radioman on the *Bahama Star* to coordinate rescue efforts.

There would be conflicting testimony about what happened next. Voutsinas would claim that following dropping off the Barkins and the Kneelands, his boat rowed "back fast to the stern of the ship, of the *Yarmouth Castle*."

But when investigators finally interviewed Captain Lehto after his ship reached Montreal weeks later, Lehto would tell a different story, corroborated by the Kneelands. According to testimony given by these witnesses, the lifeboat lingered alongside the freighter.

Seeing this, Lehto began growing even more impatient than he had been forty-five minutes ago, when he learned that Nassau Radio had not responded to his radio operator's multiple calls. Deep breaths could not subdue his building rage. This underutilized lifeboat was staffed by at least three men in white officers' uniforms who appeared to have abandoned their ship. Furthermore, the lifeboat hanging off the starboard gangway was preventing Lehto from launching his second motor lifeboat, which was urgently needed to rescue the passengers and crew of the *Yarmouth Castle* as flames were overwhelming the ship.

Suddenly the freighter captain whipped his megaphone to his mouth, keyed the mic, and growled down to Voutsinas and company. "Go back and pick up some more survivors!" He might well have added "goddamn it" to punctuate his order.

After a few seconds to cool down, Lehto grabbed his megaphone again. This time he told the men in the lifeboat that they were not coming aboard his ship until they did their duty. At the time, he did not know that Voutsinas was the captain of the *Yarmouth Castle*. That was a good thing for Byron Voutsinas, say people who knew Johan Lehto. The *Finnpulp*'s skipper revered the noble traditions of the sea and had no tolerance for slipshod seamanship in any form.

It would not take long after the *Yarmouth Castle* disaster for the story to get out about Byron Voutsinas's hasty departure from his ship in its hour of need. The media and many observers at the time branded Byron Voutsinas as a coward. But like applying the hero label to Captain Brown, calling Captain Voutsinas a coward was a misrepresentation. A coward is someone who protects himself first (and at all costs) in the face of a perceived threat. Voutsinas's actions and testimony, as well as the testimony of those who witnessed his departure from the *Yarmouth Castle* in the ship's hour of need, do not describe a man fleeing danger for personal safety. They show a man stressed to the point that he could not muster leadership under pressure.

After the *Castle* caught fire, stress caused Voutsinas to obsess over controlling small pieces of the problem at hand. He squandered many precious minutes of response time by hyperfocusing on quelling the flames in #610 when the fire was already spreading throughout the ship's wooden superstructure. Later, he was blindly driven by a compulsion to reach the *Finnpulp* and send a radio distress message rather than to pick up people in the water around his lifeboat or to stay with his ship and direct the loading and launching of the *Castle*'s remaining lifeboats.

Twenty-first-century psychological theorists might well speculate that Byron Voutsinas had trauma in his past that left him prone to unproductive obsessive-compulsive responses in the presence of extreme stress. Professional seafarers who know the story shake their heads in dismay at Voutsinas's behavior and say he was simply the wrong man to command an ocean liner. Unlike Carl Brown on the *Bahama Star* and Johan Lehto aboard the *Finnpulp*, Voutsinas probably had something in his past, and possibly in his training, that did not afford him the presence of mind, the aplomb, and the leadership skills required to save lives effectively when his ship caught fire.

Reportedly, the management of Yarmouth Cruise Lines had been warned. The *Yarmouth Castle*'s previous master had known Byron Voutsinas in his capacity as the liner's staff captain and had told company managers that he did not recommend Voutsinas to become master of the old girl. Yarmouth Cruise Lines had promoted Voutsinas anyway.

CHAPTER 17

Boat Brigade

0250 hours, Saturday, November 13

"Our boats started a ferrying process," Captain Carl Brown of the *Bahama Star* would recall at the hearings. "They were going back and forth as far, as fast, as they could. Most of our boats are propelled by oars, and it took a little time to get back and forth. Two motorboats [from the *Finnpulp*] were operating. The *Finnpulp* was there, and they helped us a lot by towing [with their motor lifeboats] our oar-propelled boats. They did a big job on that."

But the rescue was going far too slowly for Brown. He felt his stomach twist into a knot as he stood on the port bridge wing of his ship, watching the rescue efforts through his binoculars. He had been overseeing this evacuation of the *Yarmouth Castle* for more than a half hour, watching the fourteen lifeboats from the *Star*, the five boats from the *Castle*, and the two motor lifeboats from the *Finnpulp* plucking hundreds of passengers from the sea and ferrying them to the open pilot doors on the *Star*. But the fire was getting ahead of the rescue boats.

"It looked like whatever resistance there had been to the fire containing it in the original section was destroyed, and she started to burn out," he would testify. "She burned until we could see the flames running up her mast. The paint was burning on her mainmast, and the flames started to come out of her after deckhouse, which was a little square house on their upper deck. Her lounge started to burn, and half her lifeboats were involved in fire."

The sailors in the rescue lifeboats (and the crewmen such as Roy Drysdale, José Argilagos, and George Vaseos) who were helping passengers aboard the

Castle to abandon the ship heard Brown's voice boom loud and clear across the water from his megaphone. "You haven't got much time!"

Meanwhile, Willie and Carl Apuzzo were still floating in their bulky orange life vests on the wine-dark sea, blowing their whistles and hoping someone in the lifeboats would see them. They had drifted into the shadows, away from the *Castle* and the area near the stern where the lifeboats were concentrating their efforts. The water had felt warm when they went overboard an hour ago, but little by little they had begun to feel chilled, and now they were starting to shiver. Willie had shooting pains coming from her back and chest. She had hit the water awkwardly when she jumped from the ship, and the slap of the water against her life vest had broken three or four of her ribs. Carl's hands and feet were starting to feel numb.

The Apuzzos were learning firsthand how even warm water can disable and kill. People often imagine that hypothermia occurs only in cold water, but there is a corollary known as "warm-water" or "silent" hypothermia. Unless the water temperature is greater than 90 degrees Fahrenheit, a person in the water will lose heat. But unlike in cold water, heat loss in warm water is gradual. Nevertheless, the prolonged cooling of the body will lower core temperature.

During such prolonged immersion like the Apuzzos were experiencing, the skin temperature can remain within the comfort range for a long time, while the core temperature slowly drops. By the time a person in warm water starts to shiver, their core temperature may have already fallen dangerously low.

Water cools a human body twenty-five times faster than air. As the core temperature drops below 95 degrees Fahrenheit in a human body, a series of debilitating things occur. The muscles of a body's limbs will grow dysfunctional. Bodily fluids will start to congeal in the tissue. This is what Carl Apuzzo was beginning to feel. First, he had begun losing sensation in his fingers, hands, toes, and feet. Now his legs and arms were beginning to go numb.

Trying to swim during the early stages of hypothermia had only hastened his body's loss of heat and accelerated the growing paralysis of his limbs. If he did not get out of the water soon and find some blankets to wrap around himself to increase his core temperature, he could be in serious physical trouble. At first, he would feel fatigue and lethargy, then disorientation. He might begin to hallucinate. Eventually, he would feel very sleepy. Finally, he would become unconscious and die. Fortunately for the Apuzzos, in the 83-degree water of the Northwest Providence Channel, they still had some time before the worst happened.

Carl told Willie that they needed to rally if they wanted to see their family back in Miami again. The couple began blowing on their whistles for all they were worth.

It was when one of the Finnish motor lifeboats shut off its engine to listen for the calls and whistles of survivors they couldn't see in the dark that the boat's coxswain heard the Apuzzos whistling, homed in on the sound, and eventually spotted the couple with a strong flashlight.

"They picked us up," Carl Apuzzo would tell investigators later at the accident investigation hearing. He had to pause as the memory of their rescue came flooding over him again, and he felt surging emotions of both fear and joy. "Then [it] went to the *Yarmouth Castle* to pick up more people."

While some of the survivors such as the Apuzzos were being whisked by a motor lifeboat to the *Star*, where a doctor and nurse awaited, along with a staff and "good Samaritans," providing blankets, hot coffee, and soup, things felt more desperate in the *Castle*'s lifeboats.

At the Coast Guard hearings, passenger Bernice Shestack remembered someone on the crew breaking out the window from her stateroom #K-1 and helping her and her "girlfriend" out of the smoky cabin.

"We went up on the boat deck. There was a boat swung out and parallel with the side of the rail, with some crew members and passengers. A man said, 'Hurry up, ladies. Right here,' and we got in the boat. I estimate that when it was fully loaded there were about ten crew members and thirty passengers. They had a difficult time lowering. The cables were sticking. There was a lot of debris, including paint cans in the boat. When the boat was being lowered, it was zigzagging. The cables weren't going down evenly."

This was the #7 lifeboat. It was only the second lifeboat to leave the *Castle*, and, like the #1 lifeboat with Captain Voutsinas, this boat labored (along with a third boat from the *Yarmouth Castle*) toward the *Finnpulp*.

Like the Apuzzos, the Bells had been waiting a long time for rescue, they said at the hearings. They had followed the Kneelands down a rope (about 15 feet aft on the starboard side of the ship) during the evacuation of the bow. But about 10 feet down the rope, Mrs. Bell had lost her grip and fell into the water. Her husband dropped off the line and found his wife. One of the mates who was already in the water helped Mrs. Bell climb aboard a floating pallet while Murray Bell clung to the side of the pallet with the mate.

At this point, a second crewman lowered himself from the deck and sat in a loop of line about 4 feet above the water and kept the other three company, waiting for rescue. While they waited, they could hear a woman screaming hysterically for help up on deck. It was a shrieking that Murray Bell would hear in his dreams for the rest of his life. But he came to realize that the screaming was not just the sound of terror and desperation. It was a beacon to rescuers. The sound of that screaming eventually attracted one of the *Bahama Star*'s lifeboats to the bow of the ship to rescue all the remaining survivors there.

As it drifted aft along the side of the burning liner, the lifeboat rescued six or eight more people. One of those was Joan Reynolds. After her efforts guiding rescuers to people trapped at portholes, then clinging to the *Castle*'s bumper strip to rest, she had begun swimming to the *Bahama Star*. She was going strong when the lifeboat came for her. Part of her wanted to complete her swim, but common sense kicked in. She accepted the ride. It wasn't long before she was aboard the *Bahama Star* with a blanket around her shoulders and a cup of chicken soup in her hand.

Aboard the *Yarmouth Castle*, a group of crewmen directed by Chief Mate Argilagos stood in a line and spread their arms like a human barrier. They were holding Ruth Wright and perhaps a hundred other passengers back around the swimming pool and telling them they had to wait their turns. Meanwhile, two queues of passengers were being loaded aboard lifeboats #9 and #9A on the starboard quarter of the ship.

Always the volunteer fireman, Lloyd Lamn found a new way to help save lives as the boats lowered. He found three short pieces of rope and tied them together with square knots. Then he tied the line to a railing on deck and slithered down to where the three lifeboats were bobbing. Some were overloaded and in danger of swamping, so he redistributed the passengers until the lifeboats looked more seaworthy. It was not long before the lifeboats were met by the one of the *Finnpulp*'s motor lifeboats and were towed off like a train to the *Star*. But Lamn did not go with them. He had crewmen pull him back aboard the *Castle*. At this point they probably thought he was one of them. One thing for sure: he was not leaving the *Yarmouth Castle* until the last passengers were off.

But not all was lost for Wright and the remaining survivors around the pool. Once again under the direction of the chief mate, the men in the human barrier began shepherding passengers toward the smoky port side of the ship. Here they were loaded into the *Castle*'s last usable lifeboat, #10.

Lamn would testify that he saw no officers among all the people packed aboard. The chief steward seemed in charge, and the people in the boat were having a hard time getting organized. First, some of the elderly and heavier people we having difficulty getting into the boat. One woman was yammering compulsively, worried that no one had put the drain plug in the bottom of the lifeboat. Once the boat hit the water and the crew released it from the falls, the boat could not pull away from the burning ship. An oar snapped as a passenger tried to row. Then someone shouted that the boat was leaking, and called for a flashlight to find and plug the leak. But amid the chaos and panic, a calming voice prevailed.

"There was a cruise director or a hostess in our boat," one passenger would tell investigators. It was Ruth Wright. She was "short, blond, with a bandana on her head [to cover her singed hair]. She was doing a good job of pulling spirits [up] and keeping harmony."

Eventually, Wright began to sing. The tune was a work song like "Row, Row, Row Your Boat," and the cadence she set got the men at the oars in sync. Eventually, they pulled their boat in a wide arc, out from the dark, smoky side of the *Yarmouth Castle* and around into the searchlights beaming from the *Bahama Star*. From here, Wright knew that the rest of their trip to safety would be a piece of cake.

At this point in the night, with the boats rushing to rescue all the remaining people from the *Castle*, Carl Brown, like Ruth Wright, was struck by the glow of lights on the dying ship. "The lights were still on, as each deck would burn out," he would testify. "She wouldn't have any more lights, and there would be lights below that. And the lights kept burning. "It was eerie, he thought, as if Neptune or Poseidon were, little by little, claiming this ship as his own. The ship's list to port had worsened to more than 10 degrees, and now she was down a bit by the head too. The end of the *Yarmouth Castle* was near, and there were still people aboard her, maybe a lot of people.

Brown had seen the 1958 movie *A Night to Remember*, about the sinking of the RMS *Titanic*. Nobody had to tell him what was coming for those people still on the *Castle* if they didn't get off the ship soon. His radio operator had told him that the Coast Guard had begun launching four search-and-rescue aircraft a half hour ago from their new base at the Opa Locka Airport near Miami. They were also deploying three rescue helicopters. Brown sure hoped that all those birds would get here soon.

CHAPTER 18

So Long, Old Girl

0330 hours, Saturday, November 13

Carl Brown heard the approaching rumble of twin, radial aircraft engines and knew that help had finally arrived. Like a lot of boys growing up during World War II, in the golden age of aviation, he had been charmed by airplanes. He could tell that the muttering he heard approaching overhead was the sound of Wright 1820 Cyclone engines. The nine-cylinder power plants had been used on dozens of famous aircraft, from B-17 bombers to Douglas DC-3s airliners. And the distinctive raspy note to these particular engines came from a Coast Guard search-and-rescue flying boat, a Grumman Albatross, flown by Lt. Hugh Huleatt. Arriving on scene at 0345, Huleatt was the Coast Guard's on-scene commander and had launched first from AirSta Opa Locka. The first helo would arrive an hour later, at 0445.

For the first time since he came on the bridge of the *Bahama Star* hours ago to bring his ship to the rescue of the *Yarmouth Castle*, Brown left the bridge wing and ducked into the ship's radio room, aft of the bridge. He told his radio operator he heard a Coast Guard plane.

The radioman said the Coast Guard pilot wanted to know Brown's immediate needs. "Light," said Brown. He wanted more light for his rescue operation. The moon was declining in the western sky. It was getting harder for the rescuers in the lifeboats to see people floating on the shadowy water.

By the time the captain got back out on the port bridge wing, the circling plane had its searchlight on, and it was dropping parachute flares from 2,500 feet over the scene. Suddenly the sky and sea took on a bright, metallic glow, and there were no shadows anywhere. Brown could see what looked like the last three or four dozen people clustered on the stern of the *Castle*, awaiting rescue.

Let'*s get this done,* he thought, *and done right*.

As ordered by Johan Lehto back at the *Finnpulp*, Captain Byron Voutsinas had returned to his ship with lifeboat #1. But here he dithered again. He rescued only one passenger. It was a man barely bobbing above the water, shouting that he could not swim.

"The lower part of the stern was free of flames and full of people," Voutsinas would tell investigators. "I went there on the stern. I didn't went up. Just I was close there. All the lifeboats, they were coming close. . . . I left [the staff captain] in command with the boatswain and took another empty lifeboat and went to the starboard side. . . . I climbed up on deck and went forward."

At this point in Voutsinas's interview with Coast Guard investigators, a Coast Guard officer would ask him skeptically, "You came across an *empty* lifeboat from your vessel?"

Voutsinas would respond that he meant "empty of passengers," but then he would veer away from his previous narrative. He would claim he directed the congregating lifeboats (there were as many as twenty at this point) to hang back and form a column so that passengers would come down from the ship, board the nearest boat in the queue, then clamber from boat to boat to boat until they reached the last lifeboat in the line. He claimed that he shaped the flotilla of boats into "some kind of bridge" to the *Bahama Star*.

It never happened. The plan sounded so bizarre and convoluted that one of the senior Coast Guard officers interviewing Voutsinas in Miami threw up his hands and said, "That isn't quite clear to me."

Abruptly, Voutsinas gave up talking about directing the lifeboats and doubled back to explaining that he climbed a chain ladder to the promenade deck. Once on deck, he claimed he directed passengers to the stern. In truth, he seemed to have wandered around without displaying any effective leadership. He said he saw no other officers at this time. He also admitted that he gave no orders to his crew.

"When I stay up there," he told investigators, "I meet the chief engineer, and we stay and we look that all of the passengers are out of the ship, and the crew [too]."

Maybe this actually happened, but the chief engineer would describe no such collaboration. Voutsinas's story simply did not jive at many other points with the testimony of his officers who were there as the flames began to fully engulf the *Yarmouth Castle*. She was starting to seriously down flood through her open pilot door on the port side near the waterline.

Gift shop operator Charles Agero was aboard nearly until the end, and at the accident hearings he remembered vividly those final minutes aboard as time was running out on the burning ship.

Like Agero, most of those remaining on the ship were crew members, along with Lloyd Lamn, who had helped Chief Mate Argilagos board passengers and launch all the usable lifeboats on the stern of the ship. During the loading of the final boat, Agero and his assistant Ann Fonda had been directed to board lifeboat #10, which was nested in #10A.

"The upper boat (#10) was stuck," Agero would testify. "It wouldn't go back or forth. I saw the chief mate and the chief engineer working on the machine that cranks the boats. We were sitting in the boat, looking down at what they were doing. The boat started to swing, so Ann and I got out of the boat and went back to the swimming pool area. Ann said she couldn't swim, so we didn't jump."

They stayed here for about a half hour, watching as many of the other people trapped on the stern, cinching their life vests tight, climbed over the rail and jumped to lifeboats waiting nearby to fish them out of the sea. All the while, Agero and Fonda watched the swimming pool continue to fill with water like it was still preparing to give the passengers another day in paradise.

"Then the chief mate yelled down to us to come up because this was the last boat," Agero would tell investigators. "There was a ladder, and with the help of a couple of crew members, we climbed up to the sun deck and got in the boat. The boat was #10A, and there was Ann and I, a young married couple, an old man [Charles Matias] who lost his wife, about five crew members, [and Lloyd Lamn]. The chief mate did not get in the boat. He was directing everybody about what to do. . . . We did not know how to row. I did not know how to row. We tried to get away from the ship, but instead we got back to the ship. Then there was a lot of hollering and arguing. We drifted back past the stern of the *Yarmouth Castle*. Then everybody argued whether to go to the freighter or the *Bahama Star*."

Eventually, a motor lifeboat from the *Finnpulp* came along and towed #10A to the *Star* and safety. During all this drama, Agero never saw Captain Voutsinas, who would claim that he and the chief engineer had been directing the final evacuation of the ship. All the leadership came from Chief Mate Argilagos. Meanwhile, the fire raged ever closer toward the stern. The ship listed farther to port. Her bow seemed to be losing buoyancy fast and sinking toward the sea. For those left aboard, it was getting harder to walk upright on the slanting deck.

When it seemed there were no passengers left aboard, Francisco Argilagos ordered the remaining crew to jump in the water.

"I went to the boat deck, to the promenade deck," he would tell investigators, "and at cabin #751 found a few passengers. *Bahama Star* lifeboats were then picking up people."

Argilagos made a final walk along the promenade deck. The flames were raging, relentlessly consuming what was left of the ship and searing his skin whichever way he turned. At this point, seeing that there were no passengers or crew, Argilagos assumed he was the last living soul aboard. He heard someone calling his name in Spanish and asking him to come off the ship. When he looked over the rail, he saw a motor lifeboat from the *Finnpulp* approaching the starboard quarter of the *Yarmouth Castle*. The *Castle*'s second mate, José Ramos de Leon, was aboard the lifeboat and beckoning to Argilagos.

"When I came down the line [to the lifeboat]," remembered the chief mate, "I saw the shape of what appeared to be the captain, dressed in white with a life jacket on. He was running to the stern [of the ship]." This was the first time that Argilagos had seen the captain for hours.

After picking up a few other passengers who jumped from the stern and ferrying them to the *Star*, the first, second, and third mates of the *Castle* returned to their ship one final time in the Finnish motor lifeboat. When they circled the ship, they saw neither bodies nor survivors. The ship was listing more.

In the engine room, even with no view of the outside world, Chief Engineer George Vazeos could feel that the old girl was getting more and more out of trim. He wanted to keep the lights on as long as possible, but as he walked around and checked on his generators, pumps, boilers, and condensers, he could feel in his bones that the ship was taking on water at a distressing rate, and the list in his ship was getting worse by the minute. He could feel her bow pitching down. So, he scrambled topside to the promenade deck one last time to see if the lifeboats from the *Bahama Star* had evacuated the last of the people huddled around the swimming pool.

"I don't see nobody," he would testify. "I no see crew."

But Vazeos saw something else. He saw what Agero, Fonda, and others had seen. He saw water gushing from a big pipe into the swimming pool. Now, he finally understood why even with his increasing the water pressure to the sprinkler system and the fire-control system, there had been little or no water coming from so many of the ship's firefighting hoses and sprinklers. The pipe filling the swimming pool had been sucking the water pressure out of the rest of the system.

"*Skatá*," he may well have said in his native Greek. "Shit."

Then he went back down to the engine room and told the engineer on duty to close the suction-injection valve to stop the condensers.

"All right. It's time to go," he said, according to his testimony.

One of the motor lifeboats picked up the engineers, the donkeyman, the plumber, and a couple of more people at the open pilot door. As they were backing away from the ship, they saw that the captain was all the way in the back of the *Castle*.

"We went with the boat, and we picked him up," Vazeos would tell investigators. "The captain say, 'Let's try to make a couple turns around the ship to see if maybe we find somebody in the water.' We don't see none. Only we see the flames."

Following the disaster, Voutsinas would assert to everyone willing to listen that he was the last man to leave his dying ship, that he had followed the noble tradition of seafaring, that he had done the honorable thing in the end. There is a chance that the captain was telling the truth. But two men would beg to differ.

By the time the last of the survivors were leaving the *Yarmouth Castle*, two Coast Guard helicopters were circling overhead, training their searchlights on the *Castle* and dropping more parachute flares.

"They tell me to jump," Roy Drysdale would remember during his interview on CRS Radio, "but I don't want to . . . I don't want to swim because the sharks were out there."

So while the remaining passengers were leaping into the sea to be picked up by lifeboats, Drysdale and a friend decided that they would try to remain on the ship until the fire burned itself out. They thought there might be opportunities to salvage some of the valuables left behind on the *Castle*, such as the fancy watches for sale in Charles Agero's duty-free gift shop.

Being seasoned crewmen, Drysdale and his friend knew all the passages deep in the ship on D deck that might lead them beneath the smoke and the fire to the gift shop. So, they held wet towels over their noses and started forward through the belly of the ship, hoping to pop up at burned-out sections of the main deck and start scavenging for valuables. But while the flames were gone in some areas, the heat and the smoke eventually drove them back. They found themselves gasping for air at the same open pilot door on the starboard side that the chief engineer and his men had left from. And they felt the list in the ship increasing. Water was pouring in through an open door on the side of the hull used for loading automobiles. The *Castle* was in her death throes.

Drysdale and his shipmate knew they had to get off the *Castle*. They went out the door, stood on the bumper strip at the waterline, and hoped a lifeboat would appear. The ship's list to port made it easy for them to lean back against the metal plating of the hull and keep from falling in the water. But 30 feet over their heads, the fire raged and showered them with sparks. Finally, the crew of a motor lifeboat came to the rescue. They spotted the two young men standing on the bumper strip, with white towels still pressed to their faces.

"That's how I came to be the last man off the *Yarmouth Castle*," Drysdale would tell the CRS radio interviewer more than fifty years later. And he would admit that, oh yes, he had a pocket full of salvaged watches from the gift shop that he had wanted to keep dry at all costs on the night of the fire. In the weeks to come, money from the sale of those watches would be all that stood between Roy Drysdale and abject poverty. He would never receive a dime, not even for his lost belongings, from the Yarmouth Cruise Lines.

"About forty-five minutes before she sunk, I got in a lifeboat and went over there [to the *Yarmouth Castle*] to take another look," the chief engineer of the *Bahama Star*, William Dagner, would tell investigators.

His lifeboat circled the flaming wreck at a distance of "about 8 feet." The lights were still on in the engine room and on D deck. He looked in every porthole he could. From the lifeboat, he surveyed the decks too.

"We checked the ship, both sides," Dagner testified. "We returned to [the *Bahama Star*] and I told the captain there wasn't any more passengers that we could see at that time. . . . On the last pass, the only place you could have gotten aboard was the bow section. . . . The heat was too great to board her back aft. . . . The blisters were sometimes about 5 feet in diameter, and then it would catch fire on the hull, on the outside. . . . There was an eerie sound in the fire . . . a sort of howling noise."

As the motor lifeboat turned away from the burning ship, someone said, "Goodbye, old girl."

"Amen," said several others. Some of the seafarers bowed their heads.

Back on the *Star*, Carl Brown radioed Johan Lehto, the three HU-16As circling overhead, and Coast Guard Miami. Brown said he was satisfied that every living person aboard the *Castle* or floating in the sea had been rescued. The *Bahama Star* was now ceasing rescue operations. The lifeboats were returning to their respective ships. Fifty-one passengers and forty-one crew from the *Castle* were on the *Finnpulp*, along with two lifeboats from the burning ship. The *Bahama Star* had rescued 240 passengers and 133 crew. More than eighty passengers and two crew were missing.

At this point, Coast Guard Miami released the Finnish freighter to proceed on her way to her destination (Nassau), but before she got underway, she transferred the worst of her burn victims, such as the Barkins, to the *Star*. The Coast Guard requested that the *Bahama Star* remain on station.

For the passengers, survivors, and crew aboard the *Bahama Star*, there was nothing to do but sip coffee or soup and wait. The *Castle*'s crew members gathered in one corner of the *Star*'s dining room. Many, such as the mates, were exhausted. They pulled blankets over their heads, curled up on the floor, and tried to sleep. Carl Brown offered his cabin to Byron Voutsinas. Except for about a dozen severely injured persons being treated on the stern of the *Star*, many of the former passengers from the *Yarmouth Castle* filled the ship's lounge.

The Apuzzos, the Bells, and the Kneelands hugged, prayed, and wondered how they could get messages to their families back in the United States. Willie Apuzzo was having a hard time breathing. Her chest had a crushing pain from smoke inhalation and her broken ribs. But she was not worried about herself. She was worried about her daughters and how they would react when they heard the news about the fire on the *Castle*. Her twins, Mary and Helen, were just thirteen. They were at home in the care of their eighteen-year-old sister, Denise, a college student. Willie hoped that Denise would get them all in the family car and drive them to the church to pray. Willie had raised her daughters as devout Roman Catholics. She hoped that they could find some comfort in their faith now.

Adele Simister and Charles Matias were in shock over their losses. They stared blankly off into space. Sometimes they wept quietly. So did Joan Reynolds, who found herself wondering how it happened that she had survived so much. Why was it that she was one of the lucky ones?

Margaret Masters thought about luck too. She had started this cruise wishing on her lucky stars that this trip would be something grand to remember for her and all her charges from the North Broward Senior Citizens Club. Now, more than half the people in her group were missing, presumed dead. Would her lucky stars give her the strength to face off with the families and friends of all those who were lost? She didn't think so. She didn't believe in lucky stars now. Neither did Lloyd Lamn. He never had. And he was angry. In his mind, this catastrophe was no act of fate. None of this had to happen. None of these people had to die. Yarmouth Cruise Lines had really screwed this up. They needed to pay for their negligence.

Meanwhile, from the burned-out hulk across the sea, an incessant howling rose from the ship that for most of her life had been called *Evangeline*. She had been named after the heroine in Henry Wadsworth Longfellow's nineteenth-century poem of the same name. It is an epic about star-crossed lovers. For Carl Brown and many others who had to listen to that howling coming from the burning ship, the sound was all too human. It sounded like a woman mourning the death of a lost love and the bitter end of her days.

CHAPTER 19

Stunned

0603 hours, Saturday, November 13

The radio operator on the *Bahama Star* had not felt more urgency than at this very moment as he broadcasted on frequency 2182.

The *Star* had about twelve critically injured people who should be taken off immediately, he told Coast Guard Miami and the USCG rescue helicopter #1407. The injured were on the afterdeck.

As the light of predawn began to spread over the disaster scene from the east, the helo arrived on scene and was circling at an altitude of 200 feet above the *Star*, hundreds of feet below the fixed-wing HU-16As still dropping flares from a higher altitude.

USCG #1407 was a Sikorsky HH-52 Seaguard helicopter. Coast Guard personnel called it the "Flying Lifeboat." It was an amphibious rotorcraft that had been introduced into the Coast Guard's aviation search-and-rescue service in 1958. Eventually, the Coast Guard would operate ninety-nine HH-52s, as the mainstay of USCG helicopter operations for twenty-six years. Typically, a 52 carried a pilot, copilot, aviation petty officer (hoist operator), and corpsman (medic).

Most of the passengers on the *Bahama Star* had been awake all night watching the rescue and trying to help tend to the needs of the hundreds of survivors coming aboard. Now, Brown used the ship's public-address system to ask the curious passengers and survivors to remain well clear of the stern of his ship while the helicopter maneuvered into hoist position. Brown knew that helicopter rescue operations were always a careful dance between the aircraft and the vessel below. But he took some comfort in watching the dawn coming on calm and clear. The wind and sea conditions were benign, the visibility was good, and the stern of the *Star* made a reasonable pickup zone. Still, like his radio operator, Brown felt the urgency of the moment. His ship's doctor had told him that some of the injured, such as Nathan Barkin, had third-degree burns over most of their bodies. They would die if they remained aboard.

Like Brown, hundreds of the passengers, crew, and survivors aboard the *Bahama Star* held their breath and hoped for good fortune as they watched the big Sikorsky flying lifeboat wheel into its final approach to the ship. Using his radio, the hoist operator (who had an unobstructed view of the *Star* below) kept a sharp eye out for obstructions and loose debris as he guided the pilot into position. Fortunately, Brown and his crew had cleared away all the deck chairs and other furniture that might be sent flying by the rotor wash from the hovering helicopter.

As USCG #1407 made its approach to the ship, the winch operator lowered the corpsman down to the deck, using a "horse collar." As soon as the corpsman landed, the helo dropped downwind of the ship and hovered. Immediately, the corpsman began assessing the medical condition of the injured and deciding who was most in need of urgent transport and whether to use the "Stokes litter" or rescue basket. The corpsman then started prepping the injured for medevac and briefed the ship's crew on how it would take place. He shouted over the whine of the jet engine and the beating of the rotor blades. No question, the badly burned Barkin couple would be first. They would need to be hoisted in the Stokes litter, and the corpsman signaled the helo to hover close and to lower the litter.

One of the dangers in a helicopter hoist is the static electricity that builds up in the hoist cable and can be transmitted to the litter or basket via the cable. The cable and basket or litter must be grounded before it can be safely handled. Brown and hundreds of others watched from a distance while, amid the chopper's rotor wash, the corpsman grabbed the lowered litter with a "deadman stick." It was about the size of a police officer's nightstick, with an insulated handle, a brass rod sticking out of one end, and a length of wire with a large spring clip to ground the litter to a metal part of the ship.

Then with everyone on deck briefed, and Nathan Barkin bundled and strapped into the litter, the corpsman radioed the helicopter to begin the hoist. Once the litter was clear of the deck, USCG #1407 dropped downwind of the *Star* and continued to hoist Barkin.

When the litter was level with the floor in the helo, the hoist operator grabbed the litter with one hand and pulled it inboard. In short order, #1407 moved back into position and lowered the litter for Betty Barkin. When she was aboard, the helo made room for one last burn victim. Then it vanished on a beeline for the Princess Margaret Hospital in Nassau, about 65 miles away.

Almost before Captain Carl Brown had a chance to heave a sigh of relief or refill his coffee mug after USCG #1407 rushed off toward Nassau, another Coast Guard rescue Sikorsky appeared from the west.

It was after this helicopter had hoisted its third "medico" (injured person) and started for Nassau that Brown heard one of his mates on the bridge blurt out, "Look there!"

For an instant or two, he didn't understand, but then he saw the mate pointing to the *Yarmouth Castle*. Since ending the rescue, Brown had let his ship drift back to a safer distance of a half mile or so from the *Castle*. At this point, as the morning dawned, the flames on the ship had all but subsided. A plume of smoke trailed away overhead. The sun was just cresting the horizon, and it gave the smoke a strange, rosy hue. The *Castle* had been losing buoyancy rapidly during the last hour. While she had been down by the head earlier, she had started to settle by the stern since rescue efforts had ceased. Her list to port had increased to more than 20 degrees.

As hundreds looked on, the gutted hulk of the SS *Yarmouth Castle* seemed to teeter for a few seconds. Then she lay down on her port side, rolled bottom up, and slipped away stern first with one final sigh. There were a few tremendous bubbles, and then the water became still as glass. Nothing remained on the pale, blue sea but a single, abandoned lifeboat. It was as if a grand dame from the Roaring Twenties named *Evangeline* had never existed. But, of course, she had. More importantly, so had eighty-seven human beings who went down with her. Eighty-five of those lost had been passengers, such as those from the North Broward Senior Citizens Club who had come with Margaret Masters to let the salt air, calypso rhythms of the islands, Gombay punch, gambling tables, and duty-free shopping cast all their worries to the wind.

Carl Brown noted the time. It was three minutes past six o'clock in the morning. He knew that he would remember this moment, its loss, and its heartache for the rest of his life. When the memories came flooding back later, he would feel himself choking up. Then he would brush back the tears.

By midmorning, twelve of the injured were being treated at Princess Margaret Hospital in Nassau. Three of them, including Nathan Barkin, would perish from their burns, bringing the death toll for the disaster to ninety persons.

Meanwhile, two Coast Guard cutters, the *Cape Shoalwater* and the *Cape Knox*, had arrived at the accident scene. *Cape Shoalwater* arrived at 0940 and relieved Lt. Huleatt in Grumman Albatross #7229 as on-scene commander at 1048. *Cape Knox* arrived a short time later, at 1105. Released by the Coast Guard in Miami, *Bahama Star* departed the area at 0830 and followed the *Finnpulp* to Nassau. *Cape Shoalwater* and *Cape Knox*, along with helicopters, spent the rest of the day searching an ever-expanding area for additional survivors or bodies. None were found, only a long trail of debris stretched out in the currents of the Northwest Providence Channel.

Back in the Unites States, newspapers such as the *Miami Herald*, the *Palm Beach Post*, and the *New York Times* were in a frenzy to report every angle of the *Yarmouth Castle* fire.

The media circus began, complete with photos of the burning ship in a ball of flames, victims on stretchers, and a weeping Adele Simister. The front page of the *Miami Herald* on Sunday, November 14, was entirely devoted to the disaster. A banner headline proclaimed, "90 Missing After Inferno Sinks Cruise Ship with 550 on Board." Secondary headlines stirred up controversy, saying, "No SOS Sent; Fire Cause Still Mystery" and "Survivors Say No Boat Drill." Then came a human-interest story titled "I Watched Ship Sink in Flames."

The *Palm Beach Post-Times* of November 14 played up the disaster's connection to local South Florida communities, with headlines such as "Many from Area on Cruise Ship" and "Panic on Ship Reported." There was also a front-page list of "Known Area Injured." In smaller type, below the fold, there was a glimmer of hope amid the horror. The headline read, "One Local Couple Reported Safe."

On November 15, the *Miami Herald* sounded a funereal tone with "Ship Fire Probe Opens; 84 Lost," "22 Senior Citizens of Broward Lost," "Abandon All Hope for Missing Persons," and a list of the "Missing at Sea." One journalist called the *Yarmouth Castle* "the death ship." Another writer interviewed passengers who complained that "everything on the ship rattled." Several stories included testimony from survivors about the slack fire hoses, lack of warning alarms, dysfunctional lifeboats, and a lack of organized leadership from the crew.

The next day, the *Miami Herald* printed an editorial calling for a congressional investigation. The author wrote, "It ought to be a national responsibility that cruise ships in the future comply with higher standards of safety in return for the right to sail from American ports."

By Tuesday, November 17, the *Yarmouth Castle* disaster was no longer front-page news, but investigative reporters started searching for something or someone to blame. One headline read, "Crew Charges Captain Left Them, Passengers Stranded." Another announced, "$3.2 Million in Suits Filed."

An article in the *Miami Herald* on November 20 titled "*Castle* Owner Proves to Be Mystery Man" seemed to be insinuating an organized-crime connection. It identified Jules Sokoloff as the owner of Yarmouth Cruise Lines' parent corporation and linked him to "a Miami Beach Bank, which has changed hands a half-dozen times," a 120-unit apartment building "under incessant threat of foreclosure," and a failed Jamaican hotel.

A week after the disaster, the *Miami Herald* still had reporters digging deep for the causes of the catastrophe, which the paper was now calling "a voyage of death." One reporter got wind of an FBI investigation into possible arson on the ship and ran with a speculative story titled "Problem Child, 36, Added to Ship Probe."

As the rumors began to get out of hand, the United States Coast Guard recognized it had a duty, sooner rather than later, to set the record straight for the families of the lost, the survivors, cruise ship passengers sailing from American ports, and the public in general. The question was how, when, where, and under what authority could such an investigation be undertaken.

CHAPTER 20

The Investigation and Beyond

Late November 1965

Even though the *Yarmouth Castle* was a Panamanian-flagged vessel, sailing in international waters, the United States Coast Guard launched into a full-scale investigation of the accident because the ship's home port of convenience was Miami, and almost all her passengers were Americans. Furthermore, the government of Panama did not have the resources for an investigation. The Panamanian authorities requested that the USCG investigate on their behalf.

Known officially as a Commandant's Action by the Marine Board of Investigation, the hearings, held at the Coast Guard headquarters in Miami, began on November 22, 1965. Over the course of nineteen days, Coast Guard officials interviewed more than seventy witnesses. In the end, the investigation amassed over three thousand pages of direct testimony and thousands more pages of supporting evidence. The results were damning to the Yarmouth Cruise lines and Captain Voutsinas.

The Coast Guard Commandant's Action Report concluded that the "proximate cause" of the disaster was the failure to detect the fire early on. Contributing to this failure were the inadequate and untrained security patrol and the lack of a sprinkler head in room #610. The construction of the ship, which contained excessive flammable material, allowed the fire to quickly spread out of control. The high death toll was due to the fact that the general alarm and PA system were not immediately used to alert passengers and crew. Many windows were found to have been improperly maintained, further preventing escape.

The action report drew twenty-two conclusions about the fire and disaster, but "the source of ignition could not be determined." The hearing board speculated that the fire may have started by a "malfunction of the lighting system in room #610, which had been jury[-]rigged." On the other hand, the fire might have started "when sparks entered room #610 through the natural ventilation ducts during the blowing of the boiler tubes." The fire might also have resulted from "unintentional or careless acts of persons entering #610 during the evening . . . such as failure to extinguish a cigarette [or] placing of mattresses so that they came in contact with the jury-rigged lighting circuit."

There was another possibility that rapidly spread as a wild rumor among the crew and survivors. The rumor claimed that the fire had been intentionally set. That it was murder. One variation of the rumor, published less than a week after the fire in the *Miami Herald*, speculated that a fire had been set deliberately by a passenger who was twice suspected of arson by his own family.

Another version of the rumor claimed that the fire in #610 had been set to disable or destroy the ship and thereby collect insurance money to pay off the *Yarmouth*'s and *Yarmouth Castle*'s hefty shipyard bills for the post–Hurricane Betsy damages. This rumor has persisted and has been given new life over subsequent decades by survivors sensationalizing their stories in print, radio, and film interviews. But in the wake of the catastrophe, the US Federal Bureau of Investigation (FBI) chased down the rumors and found no evidence of any intentional foul play.

The Coast Guard's Commandant's Action Report said, "The master and ship's officers [principally Chief Engineer Vazeos] who arrived at the scene [of the fire in #610] failed to take firm and positive action to organize the crew to isolate and combat the fire or to awaken and evacuate passengers in the area."

The hearing board had particularly harsh words for Captain Byron Voutsinas. The board concluded that "the decision of the master to leave his ship to allegedly go to the rescue vessel to assure the sending of the distress signal demonstrates negligence, abandonment of command responsibility, and a overall failure to approach and cope with the difficulties attending the accomplishment of a task of this order of magnitude."

The board of inquiry further noted that while the ship's firefighting procedures were adequate, they were not properly implemented by the crew. In addition to the failures of the *Yarmouth Castle*'s captain, officers, and crew, the Coast Guard report highlighted the way the ship's port engineer delayed and skirted fully addressing the safety recommendation of Coast Guard inspectors over the years. It also describes a culture of deferred maintenance, profit-driven quick fixes (as opposed to timely and proper repairs and upgrades), low pay, and inadequate training.

As for the high death toll, the Coast Guard investigators observed, "Over half of the people missing and presumed dead were assigned state rooms on the boat deck[,] and their loss is attributed to the rapid rise of smoke, heat, and fire in the forward staircase on the boat deck and rapidly spreading horizontally and preventing passengers exiting through the passageways."

In light of these findings, the United States embassy in Panama (where the *Yarmouth Castle* was registered) "endeavored to obtain, without success, an informal statement from the responsible official in Panama's Ministry of Justice concerning actions taken or contemplated by the government of Panama in the *Yarmouth Castle*." Getting no response from Panamanian officials (by April 1967), the embassy assumed that "no disciplinary action has yet been taken by the government of Panama in the matter."

In contrast to citing the shortcomings of the ship's captain, officers, and crew aboard the SS *Yarmouth Castle*, the Commandant's Action Report praised the rescue efforts of the crews aboard the MV *Finnpulp* and the SS *Bahama Star* for performing their duties "in an exemplary manner and in keeping with the highest traditions of the sea."

In September 1967, the commandant of the United States Coast Guard issued an official letter of commendation to captains Johan Lehto and Carl Brown for their timely and efficient rescue of the passengers and crew from the *Yarmouth Castle*. The mayor of Miami presented Carl Brown with a "Key to the City" in recognition of the lives he saved. As for Captain Byron Voutsinas? He never went to sea again as a professional mariner. Rumors around the docks in Miami said he had moved to New York and started a Greek restaurant, but nobody was really sure.

Buried among the many thousand pages of testimony and evidence collected for the Commandant's Action Report is a report from the FBI of a highly critical nature. It offered a seasoned seafarer's impression of the South Florida cruise ship industry at the time. The report states that on December 14, 1965, the FBI in Miami interviewed Captain Andre Armatruda. He had been employed by the Eastern Steamship Company from 1954 until 1964. During this time, he had severed mostly aboard the *Yarmouth*, the *Evangeline* / *Yarmouth Castle*, and the *Bahama Star* in the capacity of staff captain, assistant port captain, second officer, chief officer, and master.

According to the FBI, "Captain Armatruda advised that he had no specific information as to the cause of the fire [on the *Yarmouth Castle*]. He stated, however, that in general the management of the companies that operated ships of this type, under a foreign registry, was not good."

Armatruda further "stated that there was no control [over the maintenance and operation of the Miami-based cruise ships] by any government agency, and the only control rests with the company itself."

He added, "The company is interested in making money and, therefore, operates the ships as cheaply as possible."

Armatruda pointed out that "the crew very often has little or no experience, and they are low paid. . . . The company operates the ships with as small a crew as possible. . . . The crew members have no social security and no health insurance. . . . Very often when the ship comes into port, the crew is dismissed rather than pay their wages while in port. This necessitates the hiring of a new crew before the ship sails again."

Armed with the Commandant's Action Report, and incriminating testimony such as that of Captain Armatruda, a cadre of personal-injury lawyers went to work trying to sue Yarmouth Cruise Lines, its parent company Chadade Steamship Corporation, and its owner, Jules Sokoloff, for negligence both in the maintenance and operation of the *Yarmouth Castle*. Within a week after the catastrophe, lawyers had filed suit for $3.2 millions in damages, and that was just the beginning. The lawyers and their clients sought financial compensation for the families of the victims of the disaster and for the other survivors. Since both corporations were registered in Panama, and Sokoloff was a Canadian citizen, the lawsuits were a protracted and uphill fight. According to international maritime law at the time, the owners of the *Yarmouth Castle* could be sued only for the insured value of the ship, which was a mere $240,000. As a result, the families of those who died on the *Castle* received approximately $2,700 for the loss of a loved one. Getting that money came slowly.

The late 1960s marked a series of coming-of-age changes for the Miami cruise ship industry. With mounting expenses and legal exposure due to the *Yarmouth Castle* disaster, owner Jules Sokoloff dissolved the Yarmouth Cruise Lines in 1967. He sold his remaining ship, the SS *Yarmouth*, to Greek interests the same year. It was scrapped in 1969 in Greece. That was the same year that Eastern Steamship Lines sold the SS *Bahama Star* to another Panamanian company, which renamed her *La Janelle*. She was wrecked on the breakwater at Port Hueneme Harbor, California, in April 1970.

In 1969, Carl Brown left the cruise ship industry to become a harbor pilot in the Port of Miami and married his wife, Janet Thurman, of Beckley, West Virginia. He changed his last name to Netherland-Brown to honor his mother and worked in this capacity until 1991, when, as seafarers say, "He swallowed the anchor."

The captain retired with Janet to begin a new life with their son, Louis Netherland, in Rogersville, Tennessee, near where Captain Netherland-Brown had spent most of his youth. While living there, he and Janet became leaders in several preservation projects. Their work began after the purchase of the Hale Springs Inn, which Brown ran as Tennessee's oldest continually operating inn until 1999. Following the preservation of his inn, Brown restored Rosemont Mansion and several other historic buildings in Rogersville before his death in 2007.

Seven years after the *Yarmouth Castle* disaster, her owner, Jules Sokoloff, passed away in Ventura, California, at the age of fifty-nine. Ed Stephan, the former general manager of the Yarmouth Cruise Lines, went on to form the multibillion-dollar Royal Caribbean Cruise Lines, with Knut Kloster and Ted Arison.

No criminal charges were ever brought against the captain, crew, or owner of the SS *Yarmouth Castle* for the deaths of the ninety people who perished during the disaster of November 13, 1965.

But the families and communities never fully recovered from their grieving. The city of Pompano Beach, Florida, lost almost two dozen citizens on the *Yarmouth Castle*. Their loved ones and friends placed a memorial to those lost at sea in a local cemetery. Fifty years later, the living still gather at that memorial to remember, honor, and grieve for those who had "crossed the bar" in the *Castle*. Even people who knew none of the dead have mourned. The Canadian folksinger Gordon Lightfoot honored the lost with his haunting song "Ballad of the *Yarmouth Castle*."

In June 2019, a curious posting appeared in the log of requests for materials under the FOIA (Freedom of Information Act) from MARAD, the United States Maritime Administration. The request was submitted by a man named Dade Sokoloff.

When requesting materials from MARAD, a person must give a reason, and that reason is accessible to the public at large via MARAD's log of FOIA requests. In his request, Dade Sokoloff had written the following:

"Jules Sokoloff was my father. He was the owner of Yarmouth Cruise Lines at the time of the *Yarmouth Castle* fire. While I was very young at the time of his death, it has recently come to my attention that he may have been the subject of FBI investigations for activities involving organized crime. I would like whatever information may exist for the sole reason of piecing together a more complete picture of my father, his life, and his real professional activities."

It seems the ghosts of the *Yarmouth Castle* will not rest.

EPILOGUE

Observations in Hindsight

Yarmouth Castle and the SOLAS Conventions

After the *Titanic* catastrophe in April 1912, the Inter-Governmental Maritime Consultive Organization (IMCO; changed to the International Maritime Organization, or IMO, in 1958) drafted the first of the Safety of Lives at Sea, or SOLAS, conventions. Most maritime nations are members of the IMO and are signatory to the SOLAS conventions, which is international law. The idea of SOLAS was to describe and codify standardized regulations for ship safety.

In its early form, SOLAS left a lot of room for interpretation. And, to a degree, the general nature of the language in the early SOLAS conventions allowed for the possibility of the *Yarmouth Castle* disaster. Fire protection and extinguishment stipulations occupied only a half page in the original SOLAS convention document. Requirements called for a "continuous patrol system" to be organized, so that any outbreak of fire would be promptly detected. Ships of less than 4,000 gross tons should be equipped with two fire pumps. Larger ships were required to carry three powerful pumps operated by steam or other means.

Under the early SOLAS conventions, no requirements were specified for fire main pressure or volume in gallons or cubic meters per minute. The only requirement was for the pumps to be capable of delivering "a sufficient quantity of water in two powerful jets simultaneously in any given part of the vessel and shall be available for immediate use before the vessel leaves port." Fire service pipes and hoses were required to be of "ample size and suitable material." The "branches of each pipe shall be so placed on each deck that the fire hose can be easily coupled to them." Regarding firefighters' equipment, the requirements of the day stipulated, "Two equipments, consisting of a smoke helmet and a safety lamp[,] shall be carried on board and kept in two different places." All the fire-extinguishing equipment was required to be inspected annually, by a government-appointed surveyor. Drills were to be held "once a fortnight" and recorded in the ship's log. Although well intentioned, this type of language is largely subjective and open to individual interpretation. Clearly, not much thought was given at the time either to fire protection or equipping ships' crews to fight fires effectively.

Over the years, the SOLAS conventions have been modified and updated to remain relevant to improvements in maritime safety and technology. The convention was redrafted in 1929, 1948, 1960, and 1974. A new protocol was drafted in 1988 and amended again in 2014. During intervening years, annual amendments are regularly made as applicable. These updates are done by members of the IMO's Maritime Safety Committee. The original SOLAS convention contained eight chapters with a total of seventy-four articles. Each article described in detail the requirements of the chapters. Chapters included subjects such as ship construction for both new and existing ships, lifesaving appliances, fire protection, and safety of navigation, among others. Over time, the number of chapters have expanded, and the current SOLAS regulations today include a total of twelve chapters.

The United States Steamboat Inspection Service, which operated as part of the Department of Commerce, stipulated and provided oversight for passenger ship regulations under US law. The Steamboat Inspection Service became part of the US Coast Guard in 1939. This occurred at the same time that the Lighthouse Service became part of the Coast Guard. Henceforth, the Coast Guard assumed the role of inspecting US flag commercial ships of all kinds, including passenger ships. Laws pertaining to construction and outfitting of US flagships fall under Title 46 of the Code of Federal Regulations, generally called the "CFRs." Title 33 of the CFRs covers manning and operation of ships. As with SOLAS, USCG regulations both under Titles 46 and 33 of the CFRs are updated periodically as the science and technology of shipbuilding, safety at sea, and ship operations evolves.

The *Yarmouth Castle* disaster prompted significant updates to SOLAS regulations, since her wooden superstructure was a major cause of the fire's rapid spread. The updated law brought new maritime safety rules, requiring fire drills, safety inspections, and structural changes to new ships. Under the law, any vessel carrying more than fifty overnight passengers is required to be built entirely of noncombustible materials such as steel.

Early in 1966, the Coast Guard in conjunction with the Maritime Commission made a study of existing US-flag passenger ships. None of the US ships then operating in oceangoing service were found to have wooden superstructures.

Two ships operating on the Great Lakes and one on Western Rivers did have wooden superstructures. The ships on the Great Lakes were the sister ships SS *North American* and SS *South American*, built at Great Lakes Engineering Works in Ecorse, Michigan, in 1911 and 1913, respectively. Operating on the western rivers was the *Delta Queen*, a stern-wheeled steamboat reminiscent of a late 1800s-era river vessel. The *Delta Queen* had been built at Dumbarton, Scotland, and shipped to Stockton, California, in pieces. Assembled on-site, she was launched in 1925.

All these ships with wooden superstructures were required to cease operations and were laid up. The *Delta Queen*, through much political wrangling, was able to obtain a congressional waiver to continue operating. Through extensions of the waiver, she continued to sail until 2008, when the last extension ran out. In 2018, the US House of Representatives voted to reinstate an exemption to permit the *Delta Queen* to sail again. But the vessel has required extensive restorations and safety upgrades before carrying passengers. She is currently moored in a shipyard in Houma, Louisiana. Both the *North* and *South American* never returned to service.

Evangeline / Yarmouth Castle Reconversion

Following World War II, the US War Shipping Administration was still in possession of the *Evangeline / Yarmouth Castle* when she entered the drydock in Quincy, Massachusetts. It was the responsibility of WSA to return the ship to Eastern Steamship Lines in serviceable condition. The ship had been run hard during the war years and had seen minimal maintenance. Returning a passenger ship to her owners after use as a troopship was not so straightforward. Aside from cosmetic work such as cleaning and painting, considerable interior and systems refurbishment was required. Interior decorative joiner work was often removed from passenger ships to make room for additional troop berths. Any remaining joinery or woodwork was usually in tough shape. American GIs had the habit of carving their initials into anything close at hand. All this damage had to be either repaired or replaced. Where problems arose with the *Evangeline / Yarmouth Castle* was in compliance with ship construction regulations.

When the ship was delivered from her builders in 1927, the original SOLAS convention of 1914 was in effect, along with US Steamboat Inspection regulations. By 1946, many of these regulations had changed. Notably, the use of combustible materials such as wood for superstructure construction had been largely restricted.

By contrast, at the same time the *Evangeline / Yarmouth Castle* was being refurbished in Quincy, naval architect William Francis Gibbs was in the process of designing the SS *United States*. To say the SS *United States* was a remarkable ship in every way is an understatement. *United States* was also the most powerful passenger ship ever built. She set the transatlantic speed record from Ambrose Light to Bishop Rock on her maiden voyage, a record among large passenger ships that stands to this day. Among her many attributes, the ship was designed to be built entirely with fireproof materials. When she was delivered from her builders, Newport News Shipbuilding and Drydock, in June 1952, the only wood on board the 990-foot ship was the grand piano and two butcher blocks in the ship's galley.

Meanwhile, the SS *Evangeline / Yarmouth Castle*, a virtual antique from the Roaring Twenties, entered Quincy Shipyard for conversion back to commercial passenger service. The War Shipping Administration had the daunting responsibility to ensure that the vessel was in compliance with all applicable standards and regulations current at that time. The US Coast Guard was responsible for ensuring compliance both with SOLAS and US regulations. Considering the extensive scope of work that would be required, the Coast Guard determined the conversion work to be "a material alteration" of the vessel and pursuant to the provisions set forth in 46 USC 369. This meant that the *Evangeline / Yarmouth Castle*, just like the new SS *United* States, would have to meet all the current requirements relative to fire-retardant construction. Detailed plans of the alterations would have to be submitted to the Coast Guard for approval, prior to the work being started.

To counter the stability issues that would arise with the additional steelwork required, additional ballast would be needed. Once the stability calculations were completed, engineers determined that the weight of the steelwork would add an additional 100 tons to the superstructure. This weight, along with the accompanying required ballast, would reduce the ship's deadweight capacity by approximately 450 tons. Deadweight capacity equates to a ship's cargo-carrying capacity represented in tons. The net result would be an increase in draft along with the loss of carrying capacity. Draft, the depth of a ship's hull below the water's surface, becomes a navigation consideration when entering or leaving smaller ports, which tend to have shallower water.

Conversion costs aside, the impact of draft restrictions on the *Evangeline / Yarmouth Castle* were considerable. Particularly so in view of ports the ship would most likely be called upon to serve. Harbors such as Nassau, Bahamas; Port-au-Prince, Haiti; and Kingston and Port Antonio, Jamaica all were popular cruising destinations at the time. These ports had relatively shallow entrance channels and depths alongside the berths.

Facing these challenges for the reconversion of the *Evangeline*, the Coast Guard acquiesced to the War Shipping Administration's requests for exemptions from current SOLAS and USCG regulations. The Coast Guard did so subject to certain requirements. This decision would later prove to have fatal consequences. These requirements set forth by the Coast Guard included the following:

1. The main stairwells to be trunked in with incombustible material behind the paneling
2. The installation of hinged metal fire doors enclosing the stairways
3. Staterooms, passageways, stairways, and public spaces to be covered with a seven-zone automatic sprinkler system

All these requirements were completed in the course of the conversion work at Quincy Shipyard.

Yarmouth Castle's Safety Equipment

When the *Castle* left the shipyard after her reconversion, she was well equipped (by 1950–1960s standards) to address the possibilities of various emergencies, including fire. In hindsight, she really did not lack for equipment.

The sprinkler system was a dry-pipe type, with water retained in a 260-gallon tank; fusible links were fitted on each sprinkler head. Air pressure was maintained within the piping. Upon actuation of a sprinkler head, the air pressure would drop and water would start flowing from the pressure tank. As pressure dropped, a sprinkler system pump rated at 300 gallons per minute would start and maintain pressure on the sprinkler system. The system was designed so that once a sprinkler head was activated, an alarm would sound both on the bridge and in the engine room, indicating the sprinkler system was operating. On the bridge a lighted panel indicated which of the seven sprinkler zones was activated. Piping was arranged so as to be able to feed the sprinkler system with the fire pump in addition to the sprinkler system pump, if needed.

A manual fire alarm system was installed on the ship, with fire alarm stations placed strategically throughout the ship, including passenger areas. Activation of a pull box at an alarm station would alert the bridge and engine room. A lighted panel on the aft bridge bulkhead, similar to the sprinkler panel, would indicate which alarm box had been activated. Furthermore, a general alarm system was fitted with twenty-nine bells and accompanying switches throughout the ship. Additional general-alarm switches were installed on the bridge and in the engine room. The ship was also fitted with a public-address system, which was operated from the bridge. This system served the entire ship. The ship was not equipped with a dedicated alarm system for the crew's quarters.

Kidde Rich smoke detectors were placed throughout the ship, also with an indicator panel on the bridge. Unlike common practice today, these twelve detectors were located only in the cargo holds, chilled freight holds, and the paint locker. No smoke detectors were fitted in any passenger or crew cabins or any of the public spaces. This system was serviced by an outside contractor, Miami Fire Equipment, in June 1965.

The ship's fire main consisted of a network of pipes routed throughout the ship, with forty-six hose stations mounted on interior and exterior bulkheads. Each hose station was equipped with a hydrant valve, a 50-foot-long fire hose, and a bronze hose nozzle. Three dedicated 400-gallon-per-minute steam-powered fire pumps provided water pressure to the system. Two additional smaller electric pumps were available as well. As was common practice then and today, cross-connection piping was fitted so the bilge and ballast pumps could be connected to provide additional pressure if needed. Both the bilge and ballast pumps were somewhat smaller than the fire pumps, rated at 250 gallons per minute. Noteworthy was the fact that the ship's swimming pool was filled by using the fire pump system. A branch pipe from the fire main on the promenade deck was fitted with a valve to direct fire-main water into the swimming pool, located on the boat deck at the very stern of the ship.

In addition to the ship's fire main, portable CO_2 and foam-hose-reel-type extinguishers were located in the ship's engineering spaces, including the two boiler rooms, the engine room, and generator rooms. A fixed CO_2-extinguishing system supplied by eighteen 50-pound CO_2 cylinders served the boiler rooms through a system of ¾-inch steel pipes. Soda-acid-type fire extinguishers were located in the public spaces, crew's quarters, and passageways. In total, the ship was equipped with seventy-two portable fire extinguishers. Steam smothering was also possible in the ship's holds and paint locker. Fixed CO_2 systems are still in use today and, if used properly, are very effective.

The fire team equipment consisted of two self-contained compressed-air-breathing devices, one self-contained rebreather, six general-purpose gas masks, and two ammonia gas masks.

Lifesaving equipment consisted of thirteen lifeboats and eight rafts. One lifeboat was propelled by a diesel engine and equipped with a marine radio transmitter; this was boat #3. The remaining boats were equipped with oars. Lifeboat construction was riveted steel, which included buoyancy tanks in each end of the boat. Individual boat capacity varied among boats. Oar-propelled boats had a capacity of fifty persons, and the motor lifeboat carried thirty passengers. The motor lifeboat and the nested boats were smaller than the rest. Rafts were of foam construction, covered with a vinyl paint. Each raft was certified to accommodate twenty people, for a total raft capacity of 160 and a combined boat and raft capacity of 790 persons.

Three boats aft were nested, two on the port side and one on the starboard. All the boats rested in wooden chocks on the boat deck and were fitted with canvas covers. Boats were launched with the use of Welin Crescent davits that had to be cranked out by hand. The boats were lowered to the water by wire falls rove from the head of each davit, down to a block and bail in the lifeboat, and then back up to a block at the head of the davit, and thence to electric winches mounted on deck. The steel bails attaching the falls to each end of the boat were released simultaneously with a device called the Rottmer releasing gear. Rafts were launched by untying the lashings and physically pushing them over the side.

A total of 715 kapok or cork life jackets, sixty-nine for children, were stowed in various locations. Life jackets were provided in each passenger stateroom and in the crew's quarters, with one allocated for each bunk. Additional life jackets were stowed in boxes on deck. Fourteen ring buoys stenciled with the ship's name and home port, strategically mounted in brackets on the weather decks, were provided in the event of a man overboard.

Yarmouth Castle Regulatory Certifications

By 1965, *Evangeline* / *Yarmouth Castle* had been sold several times and reflagged twice, first as Liberian and then as Panamanian. At the time of the disaster, *Yarmouth Castle* was certified to carry 426 passengers and 172 crew members. At full capacity, this would allow a maximum of 598 persons on board. The ship was classed by the American Bureau of Shipping (ABS) as an oceangoing passenger ship. She was issued a Passenger Ship Safety Certificate by ABS, serving as an agent of the Panamanian government. This certificate was issued under the provisions of the International Convention for Safety of Life at Sea (SOLAS) in 1960. ABS surveyors made annual inspections of the ship's structural and machinery condition, as well as to ensure compliance with SOLAS.

Since the ship was operating from a US port, with American passengers, the US Coast Guard issued a Certificate of Examination for Foreign Passenger Vessels. Coast Guard inspectors conducted comprehensive annual inspections and quarterly reinspections. This was done to ensure compliance with SOLAS and applicable US regulations. For the most part, Coast Guard inspections would include examination of the ship's documents and firefighting and lifesaving equipment, as well as observation of the efficiency of fire and abandon-ship drills. The purpose of the quarterly inspections was to ensure continued compliance. SOLAS regulations were, and still are, the same for all ships of each classification, regardless of flag state.

Individual flag state regulations vary widely in scope and detail. US and European regulations are among the most stringent. Foreign passenger ships sailing from US ports were required to comply only with SOLAS, their own flag state regulations, and provisions of the US Foreign Passenger Ship Examination requirements. They were not required to comply with the much more stringent US regulations. In addition to construction and equipment standards, US regulations also stipulated crew requirements. These crew requirements, specified on US Coast Guard Certificates of Inspection, stipulated how many crew members of each license, grade, and ratings were required on each ship. Each license and rating require a demonstrated degree of competency as determined by testing, practical evaluations, and accumulated sea time. Under the US system, the more senior the license and the more advanced the rating, the more extensive the requirements are to advance.

Yarmouth Castle Inspection History and Trends

Both the US Coast Guard and the American Bureau of Shipping maintain inspection records of ships that come under their purview. In examining records related to the *Evangeline / Yarmouth Castle*, trends begin to emerge. What becomes apparent is that as the span of time increases from when the ship was reflagged Liberian and, subsequently, Panamanian, deficiencies increase in number and scope, particularly in respect to the ship's overall material condition, the condition of the safety equipment, and the crew's proficiency at emergency drills. Some of the same deficiencies were noted repeatedly by inspectors.

Another trend that emerges is repeated patterns in the emergency drills and inspections required and observed by US Coast Guard inspectors. During lifeboat drills in Miami and Jacksonville, boats on both sides of the ship were swung out. However, in all but one exception between 1954 and 1965, only the starboard boats were lowered to the water. The reason for this was that each time the Coast Guard was aboard for an inspection, the ship was moored with her port side to the pier. This also helps explain and corroborate the testimony of the seaman in charge of caring for the lifeboats, regarding the condition of the falls winches. He claimed that the brake bands were in rough shape and in some cases frozen and in need of repair, along with some other lifeboat equipment. The Coast Guard made a point of refuting this claim as part of the hearings, but the evidence speaks for itself.

After each annual and quarterly inspection, when deficiencies were noted, Coast Guard inspectors would issue notices of violation on Form 835, which is still in use today. This form would describe the deficiency and specify a time by which it had to be corrected. Additionally, inspectors would make further recommendations that would need to be complied with, usually in a longer time frame such as the next shipyard period or drydocking.

Of the repeated deficiencies noted on 835s between 1955 and 1965, several deficiencies had a direct bearing on the outcome of the disaster. Crew proficiency at fire and lifeboat drills was mixed. Unsatisfactory fire and boat drill performance was noted eight times between 1960 and 1965. High crew turnover rate no doubt was a contributing factor in this situation. Defective watertight and fire-screen doors were noted and required to be repaired in ten instances between 1958 and 1965. Note was made of the ship's watch key system on three occasions between 1959 and 1964. In September 1964, a notation made by the attending Coast Guard inspector specified, "Install watchman key system so a readable record is always available."

Careless stowage of flammable materials was noted every year from 1959 through September 1964. Lifeboats and associated launching equipment were found to be seriously deteriorated on numerous occasions between 1958 and 1964. Lifeboats were found to be holed on seven separate inspections. Lifeboat falls and launching equipment were found to be deteriorated as well. On January 26, 1962, the attending inspector noted in Item 4, "Start a program of turning down lifeboat winch brake drums. All drums are very rough and irregular and are tearing up brake linings."

As if these deficiencies were not bad enough, two additional areas of concern posed serious hazards. Jury-rigged, makeshift wiring had been noted repeatedly between 1959 and 1965. This situation was so pervasive that the ship's second electrician, Theodoros Sakellaros, testified during the hearings that when he was awakened and notified of a fire, he was thinking, "It was the usual trouble, some short circuit or something." Coast Guard inspectors made repeated note of the poor wiring on almost every inspection. During the January 1962 quarterly reinspection, the inspector noted in Item 9, "Keep constant check against jury-rig wiring throughout crew's quarters."

The serpentine labyrinth of ducts that wove its way above the false ceilings on each deck did not go unnoticed either. Inherent problems with the ship's HVAC (heating, ventilation, air-conditioning) systems were legion. All the ducting was uninsulated and thus had the ability to conduct heat rapidly though the duct material itself. Dampers within the ductwork, designed to restrict or stop the passage of heat, smoke, flame, and toxic gas, were minimal and manually operated. The only dampers installed were at the end of each fore and aft trunk on each deck, where they penetrated the fire-screen bulkheads. Since these were manually operated by a steel lever, they relied upon a crew member being able to get to the location of the damper and close it before a fire were to spread that far, an unlikely scenario in the best of situations.

Compounding the problems with the archaic and extensive ductwork were all the modifications that had taken place over the years, and in particular the addition of air-conditioning. The original, mechanical ventilation ducts left in place after the AC was installed provided additional uncontrolled paths for fire to spread through the overhead on each deck level. One inspector wrote, "Removed panel in B Deck port side of aft stairway, found openings above fire screen bulkhead. Required same to be closed up on a progressive basis and completed next dry-docking." Following inspections, either the Coast Guard or ABS always noted if previous deficiencies were rectified. But no mention was made in the October 1960 inspection reports of the observations made in May regarding the fire-screen bulkheads. Nor was any mention made in future inspection reports.

Twice Coast Guard inspectors issued discrepancies with regard to the condition of the inside of vent ducts. In July 1959, an 835 was issued with instructions to clean the inside of the pantry duct system. Again, in January 1962, another 835 was issued, instructing the crew, "At next shipyard[,] clean all ducts throughout vessel." The shipyard period that followed this inspection took place in October 1962, in Jacksonville. Again, no mention was made in the inspection record of the ductwork being examined during the October inspection, nor was any mention made of the ducts having been cleaned in compliance with the 835 issued in January.

The last ABS inspection was conducted by ABS surveyor H. E. Hopkins when the ship was drydocked in Tampa, Florida, from mid-September to mid-October 1965. ABS attended the vessel on several occasions during this period, examining the hull and machinery as well as the safety equipment. Previously, ABS had conducted a SOLAS 1960 inspection aboard the ship while she was docked in Miami on June 9 and 23. Deficiencies were noted at that time. Panama had not yet ratified the 1960 SOLAS convention but was intending to do so. Because of this, SOLAS 1948 still applied to the *Yarmouth Castle*. However, Panama requested ABS to inspect the ship for compliance with SOLAS 1960, as applicable to existing vessels. Notably, the 1960 standards, as in the case of previous standards, exempted existing vessels from current construction standards, except as determined by the administration (flag state) concerned. Therefore, application of the 1960 ruling in respect to the *Yarmouth Castle* applied primarily to equipment, not construction.

The deficiencies noted during this fall 1965 inspection were as follows:

1. Three (3) 20-person life rafts together with complete equipment, including provisions to be installed
2. Smoke signals for two (2) lifebuoys on bridge and smoke signals for each lifeboat to be installed
3. Renew defective automatic self-igniting lights on lifebuoys.
4. Direction Finder: Calibration to be checked at sea and results entered in logbook
5. Spare charges for soda acid and foam portable fire extinguishers to be stowed aboard
6. Hose test side port doors and check all watertight doors. Overhaul watertight doors Nos. 2, 3, 4, 5, and 6 manual operate.
7. Food and water for lifeboats to be furnished and examined
8. Whistles to be attached to all life jackets
9. Orange shelter covers for lifeboats and rigid life rafts
10. Change boat No. 2 from port to starboard.
11. Size and position of markings on lifeboats, life rafts, and buoyancy apparatus to be changed and corrected
12. Copy of illustrated table of Lifesaving Signals to be placed in watertight compartment in each lifeboat and on the bridge
13. Smoke detector diagram and instructions to be posted alongside of cabinet on bridge bulkhead
14. International shore connection to be installed (This is for attaching civil fire hoses to the ship while in port.)

Three inflatable life rafts required by SOLAS 1960 had been ordered from Dunlop but had not yet arrived and were not on board the ship at the time of the inspection. These missing rafts were noted as deficiencies. ABS did note that all other deficiencies from the June SOLAS inspection, numbered 2 through 14, had been rectified. On October 15, 1965, ABS surveyor Charles Garvey issued an extension for a provisional Passenger Vessel Safety Certificate. This extension, issued before the ship left Tampa, was valid for three months, expiring in January 1966. Garvey issued the extension "on the basis of a document from the supplier stating a delivery date for the inflatable rafts."

The last Coast Guard examinations took place on October 15, 1965, also in Tampa. Attending was Cmdr. Mark Welliver and Lt. Schaeffer from Marine

Safety Office Miami. At this time, the Coast Guard issued a Certificate of Examination for a Foreign Passenger Vessel. Cmdr. Welliver visited the ship for the final time on October 25 in Miami. This visit was to check for compliance with deficiencies found earlier in the month, and to observe a fire and boat drill.

The deficiencies noted on the fifteenth were inoperative gear assembly on the #3 watertight door and trouble starting the emergency generator. Commander Welliver noted during his inspection on the twenty-fifth that repairs to the #3 watertight door and the emergency generator were satisfactory. Fire and boat drills were held. The time for water to arrive in hoses on deck from the fire main was noted at forty seconds. The starboard boats were launched along with the motor lifeboat. The first boat was in the water in two minutes, and the last nested boat in eight minutes. Approximately sixty of the ship's crew participated in rowing the lifeboats in the vicinity of the moored ship. The motor lifeboat, #3, was tested in operation. A test of the ship's sprinkler system was performed on zones 6 and 7 and found to be operating properly.

No mention was ever made of the previously noted deficiencies, regarding cleaning of vent ducts or closing up openings above fire-screen bulkheads.

Yarmouth Castle Drydocking

Yarmouth Castle entered Tampa Ship Repair & Dry Dock at Hookers Point in Hillsborough Bay on September 15, 1965, leaving roughly five weeks later, on October 18. Extensive work was planned for the ship during this period. In addition to the usual ABS and Coast Guard inspections, the ship was drydocked for bottom painting and hull repairs. Inspections and repairs of steelwork in the engine and boiler rooms took place as well. The ship's turbines, boilers, pumps, and turbogenerators were opened for inspection and overhaul as needed.

During the previous summer, the ship had grounded briefly, on July 21, when departing Nassau. This grounding dented a hull plate on the port side, bending a frame. This plate, B7, 20 feet long by 5 feet wide and 9/16 inch thick, was replaced and the frame was repaired. Additional work included renewal of piping, valves, and other equipment, as well as general cleaning and painting. Safety equipment, including the firefighting and lifesaving equipment, was attended to as well. The shipyard invoice annotating each specified task listed 167 items, for a total estimated cost of $223,279. Of all the work that was done, no mention was made in the itemized shipyard bill of gaps being closed in fire-screen bulkheads.

Overseeing all this work was port engineer Steve Arapmatiz. Captain Voutsinas and Chief Engineer George Vazeos were on board the ship during the yard period. Yarmouth Cruise Line representative Peter Whelpton checked in on progress from time to time. Outside contractors were brought in to perform specialized work. A representative from RCA checked and calibrated the radio equipment and radio direction finder. Representatives from the Miami Fire Equipment serviced all of the ship's portable fire extinguishers and fixed extinguishing systems as well as semiportable hose-reel-type extinguishers. Miami Fire also checked and serviced the alarm systems, smoke detectors, and gas masks / breathing apparatus. In addition, Miami Fire Equipment serviced the smoke alarm system, which they found to be inoperative when they arrived on board the vessel in Tampa. Miami Fire fixed the nonfunctioning smoke detectors and alert panel on the bridge. By the time Miami Fire left the ship, all the fire-related safety equipment was in proper working order.

Lessons from Modern Disasters

In today's world, mariner training and operational procedures are very different from the way that things were done in the past. A history of horrific accidents over time has changed the way the industry does business. Legislation mandating formalized training and procedures has been enacted both internationally and regionally in response to various incidents.

Incidents such as the *Exxon Valdez* spill at Prince William Sound, Alaska, in 1989 precipitated the Oil Pollution Act of 1990. This 1,500-page document specifies details of tank vessel operations in US waters. It also mandated the end of single-hull tankers and tank barges carrying petroleum products. The international response to this was the MARPOL convention, promulgated by the IMO.

When the towboat *Mauvilla*, pushing six barges ahead, became lost in the fog outside Mobile, Alabama, on September 23, 1993, she mistakenly turned into Big Bayou Canot and a short time later crashed into the Amtrak railroad bridge spanning the waterway. Eight minutes later, the eastbound passenger train Sunset Limited, traveling at 72 mph with 220 passengers on board, plunged off the destroyed span and into the water at 0253 hours. Forty-seven people were killed and 103 injured in the disaster. Thirty minutes later, the towboat pilot still did not know where he was, or that he had hit the bridge.

The result of this disaster was the enactment of subchapter M of 46 and 33 CFR. "Sub M," as it is now called, comprehensively regulates the towing industry in the United States. This covers everything from shoreside management requirements to vessel equipment, crew qualifications and training standards, minimum crew levels, and much more. Legislation was a long time in coming. The industry pushed back hard, with lobbying groups attempting to forestall the Coast Guard and Congress because Sub M would be expensive. Finally rolled out in 2018 and fully implemented in 2022, Sub M has made the industry far safer. Serious accidents are way down.

Two other major changes involving worldwide shipping have been the IMO conventions for STCW and ISM (the International Safety Management convention), which entail STCW-codified training and certification of watchkeepers. Because of STCW, mariners everywhere are held to the same set of standards. Delegates at the IMO recognized that change was needed, not just in the way ships were operated but also in how they were managed.

ISM came as a result of the *Herald of Free Enterprise* disaster in 1987. The concepts of implementing bridge resource management were part of the evolution of ISM.

Herald of Free Enterprise was a cross-Channel ferry that ran between Zeebrugge, Belgium, and Dover on the south coast of England. The ship was designed to carry both passengers and vehicles. Vehicles were carried on the main deck. Referred to as the car deck, this deck ran unobstructed from one end of the ship to the other. Large watertight doors fitted at each end of the car deck permitted vehicles to drive straight on at the loading port and straight off at the discharge port. The ship was designed to accelerate quickly and would make several trips across the English Channel each day. The crossing distance was relatively short, 70 miles.

On the morning of March 6, 1987, *Herald of Free Enterprise* departed Zeebrugge, bound for Dover. The assistant boatswain, whose duty it was to close and secure the forward car deck doors, failed to do so after departure. The ship had been ballasted down by the bow for loading. Officers on the bridge, unaware the doors were open, accelerated quickly when departing the port. This resulted in the bow taking a dive and the car deck rapidly flooding. The rapid flooding of the car deck, a lethal situation on any vehicle carrier, resulted in an equally rapid loss of stability. *Herald* capsized and came to rest on her port side four minutes after clearing the jetties. Due to the extremely rapid nature of the capsizing, few inside the ship had the chance to escape. In the end, 188 people perished in a disaster not only within sight of land, but within the confines of a harbor.

One of the most important takeaways in examining the *Herald of Free Enterprise* disaster was the lack of standardized procedures by Townsend Car Ferries Ltd. for how they conducted shipboard operations. As a result, IMO drafted what would become the International Safety Management (ISM) convention. The IMO had no intention of telling shipping companies how they should operate their ships.

What was needed was for shipping companies to standardize operating procedures and then ensure that their ships' crews and shoreside support staff followed those procedures. Along with this, shipping companies would be required to draft these policies and procedures in the form of documents, subject to third-party review. These drafted, formalized procedures came to be known as safety management systems (SMS). Once a company drafted an initial SMS, it would need to be certified by an IMO-authorized third party. This same third party would also conduct annual audits going forward to ensure continued compliance.

Third-party review ensured impartiality and avoided a situation where a company official would certify their own program. This crucial point is what gave ISM legitimacy.

By developing standardized methods and procedures for just about everything, from navigation to maintenance to human resources, everyone in a ship's crew ends up on the same page. Things run more smoothly, more efficiently, and, because of this, safely. In the simplest of terms, ISM means that you describe how you are going to do something, and then you do it how you have described every time. The track record speaks for itself: ISM works, brilliantly.

Developing a Culture of Safety Aboard

Regardless of a ship's flag state, on any vessel there is either a culture of safety on board or not. Safety culture develops through the leadership of the master and fellow officers. This gets passed down to the rest of the crew, and with good leadership the entire crew works as a whole, driving toward the goal of operating the ship safely and professionally. Equally important to this equation is shoreside support. Management must do its part as well as provide ships' crews with the tools they need to successfully complete the job.

Management's part starts with developing company-wide polices and operating procedures. Shoreside management is also responsible for providing support as needed to the ship's master, fellow officers, and crew. This support includes many things, not the least of which is providing the parts and supplies needed to keep the ship operating safely and properly. Management is also required to stay abreast of current regulatory requirements.

Most shipping companies employ individuals referred to as a "port captain" and a "port engineer." These two people serve as the direct liaison between the master and chief engineer and the shoreside management team. Both the port captain and port engineer will make arrangements with outside contractors to perform various maintenance tasks, schedule inspections, arrange drydock or shipyard periods, and approve budgets.

The master holds ultimate responsibility for ensuring that the ship is operated safely. He or she must instill in their crew the culture of safety, and the ability to work together cohesively as a team. This is accomplished by instituting a program of regular emergency drills and safety meetings. By involving the entire crew in this process and delegating responsibility, everyone can and will play a part. Effective drills and training scenarios are the ones that are realistic. Dragging a single fire hose out and pumping water overboard while everyone stands around watching does not provide for an effective training evolution.

Much more effective are drills with realistic scenarios carried out in different parts of a ship, as if they were the real thing. For example, a galley fire drill might go like this. The general alarm sounds, and the crew musters at their assigned emergency stations. The chief mate becomes the on-scene leader, and the chief engineer reports to the engine room. The engineering team secures the HVAC system, shuts off electrical power to the galley, and starts the fire pumps. The bridge team activates the automatic watertight doors from the bridge, and the radio officer sends a simulated distress message. The chief officer assembles the fire team at the scene and prepares them to enter the space, simultaneously keeping the bridge advised as to the progress. Assigned crew members close all fire-screen doors, fire dampers, and external vent closures. The fire team, with a minimum of two people, is suited up in "turnout gear" and breathing apparatus.

Once ready, and knowing that electrical power is secured, the fire team enters the space with a charged hose line and extinguishes the simulated fire. In the case of galley fires, carbon dioxide extinguishers are brought to the scene as well. The lights are extinguished inside the galley to make the drill as realistic as possible. While this drill is taking place, the cabin staff, led by the ship's purser, rouses all the passengers and assembles them at abandon-ship stations.

Drills like this take time and effort. But the end result is a well-trained crew that is ready to respond to any eventuality. No two fire or emergency situations are ever the same. As such, an exact script cannot always be followed. However, by holding drills in different locations on the ship, in different conditions, the foundation is laid for a basic plan of action for any eventuality.

Every good shipboard drill or safety meeting regarding firefighting starts with a discussion about fire prevention. Fire prevention is always the first line of defense in combating shipboard fires. Three things are needed to produce a fire: heat, fuel, and oxygen. This is often referred to as the Fire Triangle. Remove any one of the three sides of the triangle, and fire will be extinguished or not start at all. In the very simplest of terms, fire prevention equates to keeping the heat sources separated from the fuel sources.

Yarmouth Castle: A Crew Unprepared for Trouble

What becomes apparent in the case of the *Yarmouth Castle* is that a culture of safety was lacking or nonexistent on board the ship. A fractured response to the fire combined with a general lack of leadership laid bare the true level of crew training and competency. Contrasting this was the exemplary performance of the *Finnpulp*'s and *Bahama Star*'s crews in executing the rescue operation. Although both the *Bahama Star* and the *Yarmouth Castle* had been operated by Eastern Steamship Lines, whose safety culture was questionable at best, crew performance was drastically different between the two ships. Captain Carl Brown, his officers, and his crew had clearly developed a cohesive and effective culture of safety aboard their ship. Because of this, all three departments on the *Star*—deck, engineering, and the hospitality staff—worked together as a team during the rescue.

In the Wake of the *Yarmouth Castle*

Life-threatening accidents aboard passenger-carrying vessels have not come to an end, despite the cautionary tale represented by the *Yarmouth Castle*. The three examples that follow, spanning the decades from the 1970s to the present day, stand out among dozens of astonishing and horrific incidents. The first is a miracle, the second a disaster, and the third an excellent example of when things go right after trouble occurs. Each is a unique story and, like the *Yarmouth Castle* disaster, a cautionary tale worthy of scrutiny.

Much has changed and improved in the field of ship safety over the past sixty years. At the same time, new risks have arisen—risks that could never have been foreseen in 1965, risks yet to be effectively dealt with. Many lessons have been learned from accident analysis. Others have not. Vigilance is not universal, and complacency still exists. Bureaucracy is slow to react, and the shipping industry remains resistant to change.

A Miracle

MV *Angelina Lauro*

March 30, 1979, Charlotte Amalie Harbor, St. Thomas, USVI

Most of the 669 passengers were ashore that afternoon, enjoying the last stop on their cruise, which began on March 24. Of the 380 crew aboard the Italian-flagged cruise ship *Angelina Lauro,* most were busy with typical port call duties; some (approximately half) were ashore.

Galley man Mateo Iacomino had just finished cleaning up in the crew's galley and left the compartment around 1500 hours. Shortly thereafter, a person whose identity was never determined entered the crew galley and turned on the electric brazier to its highest setting, #3. The brazier was filled with cooking oil and had been used as a fryer aboard the *Angelina Lauro* for some time, a purpose for which it was never intended. Sometime prior to 1520 hours, the brazier heated the oil beyond its flash point, and the oil in the brazier ignited.

Not long after this, four members of the galley crew detected smoke. They were on B deck in the passenger galley, and in the vicinity of the continental dining room and nearby ventilation ducts. The dining room was separated from the crew's galley by an A60 (one-hour) fire-resistant bulkhead. The tailor on D deck and a barman on C deck also smelled smoke.

Like the crew on the *Yarmouth Castle*, these crew members started firefighting efforts on their own, using hose lines and extinguishers. Believing that the fire was not serious, they failed to notify the bridge or engine room at the time. Meanwhile, flames were propagating through the galley exhaust trunk as well as above the false ceilings. Both the bridge and engine room were manned with officers on watch in each location. The master and staff captain were ashore conducting ship's business.

Second Mate Assanti, on the bridge, was notified of a fire by the master-at-arms at 1545 hours, via the ship's phone. The master-at-arms was in his cabin on A deck and had traced the smell of smoke to the crew's galley. Assanti sounded the crew alarm and notified the engineer on watch in the engine room, First Engineer Scala, as well as the duty fireman, safety officer, and first officer. The first officer notified the chief fireman.

Several crewmen, including the duty fireman, first officer, master-at-arms, and carpenter, gathered outside the crew's galley. They joined the galley staff in attempting to fight the fire. The duty fireman, entering the galley wearing turnout gear and breathing apparatus, found the electric fryer ablaze. The fryer was located against the aft bulkhead, which adjoined the forward bulkhead in the continental dining room. He discharged two CO_2 extinguishers, one onto the fryer and the other onto an adjoining electrical panel. Meanwhile, the fire was continuing to spread via ventilation ducts and the galley vent duct, which was full of grease.

The crew was making efforts to fight the fire, but it was rapidly getting out of control. Safety officer Mattera ordered one of the crew to go ashore and call the local fire department. A hose and nozzle were run into one of the vent ducts in the dining room, and additional hoses were run down from the upper decks inside vent trunks that appeared to be on fire.

A sprinkler system warning light was illuminated on the bridge and noticed by the second mate. He did not recall hearing any warning alarm for it. The automatic fire-screen doors were not closed for fear of injuring passengers and crew during their rapid closure. At this time, no announcement had yet been made to the passengers on board. Crew and passengers were still coming and going from the ship via two gangways that were rigged on the starboard side, one on A deck and the other on B deck. Numerous side ports and portholes were open on both sides of the ship.

When the staff captain returned to the ship at 1615 hours, he ordered the general alarm to be sounded, which was done. No one specific crew member was in charge of ensuring that the passengers were informed or evacuated at this time. The Virgin Islands Fire Department arrived shortly after 1600 hours, with Sergeant Brown in charge. Fire Chief Jennings arrived shortly afterward. Coordination between the VIFD and the ship's crew was poor at best. Language barriers between the Italian officers and English-speaking fire department personnel were a problem. No attempt was made to connect one of the fire department pumpers to the ship's fire main via the international shore connection on the ship. Firefighting water was being supplied from shore-based pumpers and also the ship's fire main, which consisted of several pumps located on the lower level of the engine room. However, the ship's fire main pressure was observed to be low.

Crews from the fire department extinguished the fire in the galley but did not know of the further extent of the fire or of the crew's ongoing firefighting efforts over the previous hour. People coming and going from the ship were hampering firefighting efforts. Finally, all boarding was stopped. At this point, Chief Jennings realized the need to evacuate the ship and started an effort, with the ship's crew, to do so. A room-by-room search was made by VIFD personnel, the ship's crew, and civil defense volunteers to ensure that everyone on board was made aware of the situation and evacuated. The ship was fully evacuated by 1745.

Down in the engine room, the engineer on watch was notified of the fire and in turn notified the electrician, who secured power to the galley and dining room. The chief engineer relieved the duty engineer on watch and assumed engineering command. The duty engineer was dispatched to the fire scene. Shortly after assuming engineering command, the chief engineer shut down all the ship's ventilation. Engine room personnel were making brief forays topside for fresh air, since the engine room was starting to fill with smoke. By 1745 hours, smoke in the engine room had reached the point where it could no longer be occupied. The chief engineer ordered the space evacuated and tripped the master switch to close all fire-screen doors on his way out. He was the last to leave.

By now, all remaining passengers and crew had safely disembarked from the ship and onto the pier. Additional help was on the way from the US Coast Guard, the US Navy, and a civilian firefighting tug owned by Hess Oil Company. The CGC *Point Whithorn* arrived and commenced firefighting efforts on the ship's seaward/port side. Lt. Eric Olsson from Coast Guard Marine Safety Detachment St. Thomas arrived and boarded the ship from the port side to assess the situation. He quickly left and joined Chief Jennings on the pier to help coordinate efforts. Costa Line representatives were on the pier by now, getting a head count to ensure that everyone was accounted for. Two navy destroyers, USS *McCandless* and USS *Core*, and a navy tug were in port for a port call and supplied crews to help. The USCG high-endurance cutter *Gallatin*, deployed in the Caribbean Sea, was diverted to the scene and ordered to assume the role of on-scene commander after arrival.

By 1930 hours the ship was burning from stem to stern. An hour later, the Amerada Hess oil terminal tug *Turquoise Bay* arrived from the Hess refinery in St. Croix. *Turquoise Bay* was equipped with an elevated tower and large monitor-type nozzles for fighting tanker and refinery fires. She also carried a large quantity of AFFF foam. She joined *Point Whithorn* in fighting the fire from the port side and took station near the stern.

By early the next morning, *Gallatin* arrived and sent teams of firefighting and damage-control parties to the ship. *Gallatin*'s crews worked around the clock for the next three days getting the fire fully extinguished. Navy, civil defense, and local volunteers pitched in as well. *Gallatin*'s executive officer, Cmdr. Moritz, led a coordinated attack. Fire teams were eventually able to reboard the ship and isolate fires to specific compartments and extinguish them effectively. The fire was finally completely extinguished on April 4, six days after it had begun.

With the fire out and the ship still safely moored, the opportunity was present to make a full examination of the ship, in an effort to determine what had happened and why. This investigation would prove telling in several areas.

The ship was built in 1939 in Amsterdam, the Netherlands, for Rotterdam Lloyd as the transatlantic liner *Oranje*. She was purchased by Lauro line in 1964 and underwent an extensive refit and modernization. This included compliance with the current SOLAS conventions at the time—SOLAS 1960, with the 1966 fire safety amendments and SOLAS Method II fire protection. Attention was paid to dividing the ship vertically into fire zones of A60 construction (able to withstand the passage of flame and smoke for one hour). These zones were spaced not more than 40 meters (131 feet) apart. In areas where ducting would pass through fire bulkheads, insulation and steel fire dampers were required and installed. Openings in the main fire-screen bulkheads were fitted with automatically closing fire-screen doors. These could be activated either from the bridge or the control room in the engine room. The doors could also be manually operated locally. Watertight doors were fitted below the bulkhead deck.

Sprinklers were installed in all passenger cabins, public areas, and crew's quarters. This was a "wet" system, with water pressure maintained in it at all times. Fusible links were attached to each sprinkler head. Fusible links would actuate at 79ºC (174ºF), starting the flow of water. With the drop in pressure from a fusible link actuating, a pressure switch would activate the sprinkler pump for that zone. The ship was divided into twenty-eight zones. Construction using noncombustible materials was not a requirement for this vessel. However, SOLAS resolution A.108 required the reduction of combustible materials as much as possible. To this end, bulkheads, furnishings, carpets, etc. were treated with a fire-retardant process. Galley vent ducts were wrapped in fiberglass insulation to provide fire-retardant insulation on the ducts. Inspections were made regularly by regulatory and classification society personnel as well as by the ship's crew. The ship received her first USCG Control Verification Examination in Miami in June 1971.

A postfire physical examination of the ship revealed some troubling points. The crew's galley was located forward and to port of the continental dining room. The ship's side shell comprised the port bulkhead in the galley. The other three bulkheads were steel, fire-rated, A60 bulkheads sprayed with asbestos insulation. The aft bulkhead abutted the forward dining-room bulkhead, and the starboard bulkhead abutted a passageway adjacent to a stair tower. An inward-swinging entrance door was fitted in the starboard bulkhead at the aft (dining room) end of the bulkhead. Located 1 meter forward of this door was a rollup serving window made of stainless steel. This rollup serving window was found to be partially open, compromising the fire integrity of this bulkhead. This allowed fire to spread through this opening to the passageway.

Upon examination of the range hood ducting in the crew's galley, investigators found that the damper at the range hood itself was not closed, but the fusible link had melted. The dining-room-side damper was closed but severely warped. The inside of the ducting was found to be heavily coated with burned grease. Portions of this ductwork was constructed of aluminum and found to be melted away in some areas. The chief cook testified that the duct was cleaned regularly, and the screens above the hood were changed out weekly. A steam-smothering line was also found inside the duct but was not used during the fire. No doubt, the route of the ducting hampered any cleaning attempts beyond what was immediately reachable.

From the investigation, it seems clear that the brazier fire spread via the range hood ducting throughout the length of the ducting and into various compartments in which the duct material had disintegrated. As in the *Yarmouth Castle*, heat and flames within the ductwork readily transferred to combustible materials within the false ceilings, which contributed to the rapid spreading of fire. Steel ductwork was found to be intact except in areas of hangar failure, where it had collapsed.

Upon examination of the sprinkler system, investigators found that all of the sprinkler heads were located below the false ceiling in the various compartments. No sprinkler heads were fitted between the false ceiling and the steel overhead. Had sprinkler heads been installed in these locations as well, they would have helped reduce the spread of fire.

Investigators found the majority of the fire-screen doors throughout the ship to be open, which indicated that the automatic function of the master switch tripped by the chief engineer was not functioning. Most likely the fire had compromised the wiring to this system by the time it was actuated. Some of the fire-screen doors were warped. Those doors had been damaged due to the melting of their aluminum frames.

Interior cabin subdivisions, draft stops, interior paneling, floor coverings, and furnishings all were completely consumed by the fire. Clearly, the fire-retardant coating applied to combustible materials proved to be totally ineffective. Numerous portholes and side port doors were open on both sides of the ship. These open ports provided a ready supply of oxygen to feed the fire. Had the fire-screen doors, vent closures, and hull-side shell openings been closed in a timely manner, they would have greatly reduced the spread of smoke, fire, and toxic gases.

From a procedural perspective, a number of points relative to fire aboard the MV *Angelina Lauro* are noteworthy. In this case the three main failure points were crew training, contingency planning, and communication. Supplemental to these three main points were individual failures that contributed to the disaster. Although the ship's crew responded to the fire and made efforts to contain and extinguish the blaze, lack of training was evident in many ways. The failure to immediately notify the bridge and engine room seriously delayed the overall response to the fire. Furthermore, no attempt was made to establish fire boundaries even after the fire had breached one of the zone bulkheads. Immediately closing fire-screen doors, vent dampers, and watertight doors and ports and shutting down ventilation systems are considered crucial in shipboard firefighting. Doing so limits the spread of flames, smoke, and toxic gases throughout the ship as well as restricts the flow of oxygen to the fire. These operations buy the response teams time to assemble, gear up, and get into position to fight the fire, while simultaneously robbing the fire of oxygen. Had these things been done on the *Angelina Lauro*, the rapid spread of fire would have been greatly reduced.

With passenger ships comes a special responsibility on the part of the ship's crew. That paramount responsibility is the safety and well-being of the passengers. In the event of a fire, the safety of the passengers must be provided for in an immediate, organized, and preplanned manner. Evacuation procedures must be developed to ensure efficiency and speed. Aboard the *Angelina Lauro*, there was no one person directly in charge of seeing to the passengers' welfare. Not until Fire Chief Jennings ordered the ship searched and evacuated was any attempt made to ensure that everyone was safely ashore. These procedures should have been implemented immediately upon the alarm being sounded. Most of the evacuations took place via the gangway on A deck; not until the last few moments was the second gangway on B deck used. Passengers and crew coming and going from the ship, using both gangways early on, hampered shoreside responders' access. Lack of a prearranged evacuation plan and poor communication between the ship's crew and the local first responders contributed to an uncoordinated, initial response to the fire.

The lack of a response command structure on the ship and a command and control center for the port also contributed to delays and confusion at different periods during the firefighting efforts with the different entities responding. The language barrier between the ship's officers and shoreside responders caused considerable difficulty. Language barriers hindered the initial response right at the outset. Confusion as to the potential danger of the ship's fuel tanks exploding further delayed efforts when firefighting was stopped to investigate this possibility. Coordination between the shoreside response and the CGC *Point Whitethorn* and tug *Turquoise Bay* was virtually nonexistent. Having a ship's officer designated as liaison to shoreside responders could have mitigated this delay without interrupting firefighting efforts. Additionally, having the ship's fire plan made available to shoreside responders would have greatly facilitated response efforts.

Investigators found shortcomings with the firefighting equipment on board the ship. Hose stations were fitted with hoses, straight nozzles, a spanner wrench, and a gate valve to the fire-main piping. Protective equipment consisted of self-contained breathing apparatus (SCBAs) and filter-type smoke masks. SCBAs are the universally used breathing apparatus for firefighting. The smoke masks used aboard the *Angelina Lauro* were found to be totally ineffective. Straight-type nozzles, although effective in some circumstances, are less than ideal for shipboard firefighting. High-velocity fog patterns from hose nozzles have the ability to absorb heat much more effectively than a straight stream. Had the *Angelina Lauro*'s firefighters been fully equipped with a sufficient number of

SCBAs, they would have substantially improved the crew's response capabilities. Likewise, equipping fire stations with variable-stream nozzles, as is required today, greatly improves the effectiveness of hose streams.

Had this accident happened while the *Angelina Lauro* was at sea, the outcome would undoubtedly have been devastating and deadly. It was nothing short of a miracle that nobody was killed or seriously injured. Despite the cautionary tale of the *Yarmouth Castle* and fourteen years of hindsight, including improved regulations for the construction and operation of cruise ships, haunting parallels loom large between the *Angelina Lauro* fire and the *Yarmouth Castle* disaster. In both cases, poor crew training and lack of a coordinated response hampered firefighting efforts. In both cases, ductwork coated with grease contributed to the rapid spread of fire, as did ductwork constructed of non-fire-resistant materials. Language barriers played a significant factor in both cases as well.

A Disaster

D/V *Conception*

September 2, 2019, Channel Islands National Park, California

During the early-morning hours, the 75-foot dive boat *Conception* was anchored in Platts Harbor on the north side of Santa Cruz Island, located within the Channel Islands National Marine Sanctuary. Thirty-three passengers and six crew members were on board at the time. Everyone was asleep, including the entire crew.

Conception was owned by Truth Aquatics, a recreational diving-charter company based in Santa Barbara, California. She was one of three vessels owned by the company, which offered multiday diving excursions in the nearby Channel Islands National Marine Sanctuary. Truth Aquatics had been in business since 1974 and was highly regarded in the recreational-diving and charter boat industry in Southern California.

Built in Long Beach, California, in 1981 to US Coast Guard requirements under 46 CFR, subchapter T, for small passenger vessels, *Conception* complied with all the regulations in place at the time she was built. She and her two fleet mates were inspected annually by the Coast Guard. She was certified to carry ninety-nine passengers on day trips and forty-six on overnight voyages.

The other vessels owned by Truth Aquatics, *Vision* and *Truth*, were of similar fiberglass-over-wood construction for hulls, decks, and superstructures. *Vision* was quite similar in design to *Conception*. Each vessel was powered by twin diesel engines and equipped with a diesel generator and high-pressure air compressors for filling scuba tanks.

The vessels were configured with three decks. A flush main deck, extending from the bow to the stern, an upper deck (which included the pilothouse and crew-berthing area forward, with an open sun deck aft), and a lower deck. The lower deck from bow to stern comprised five compartments. Most forward was an anchor chain locker accessed from a hatch on deck. Next aft was a passenger shower room. Spiral staircases led below the main deck to the shower room and passenger-berthing area. The berthing area had a capacity of forty-six persons in a combination of single and double berths. Aft of the berthing area was the vessel's engine room. This was accessed via a hatch on the forward end of the dive deck. Aft of the engine room was the lazarette compartment, which contained additional food storage and the vessel's steering gear. This compartment was also used to dry wetsuits, via a fan that drew warm air from the engine room into the lazarette.

The superstructure occupied the forward portion of the main deck, with walkways on both sides and a small foredeck. One large room comprised the superstructure on the main deck; this room was referred to both as the "galley" and "salon." Most forward to port within this space was a food preparation area with an electric oven and range, refrigerator, sink, and counter space. A serving area ran down the centerline of the compartment, with dining tables outboard to port and starboard. Seating comprised wood-framed benches covered with foam-cushioned vinyl upholstery and plastic outdoor-style chairs. Windows ran across the forward end and down both sides of the cabin. Large doors at the aft end of the compartment opened onto the dive deck aft. The only other access to the berthing area aside from the spiral staircase was an escape hatch fitted above a bunk at the aft end of the bunk room. This hatch led up to the aft end of the salon.

Conception had been chartered by Worldwide Diving Adventures, a diving-tour group, for a three-day trip in the Channel Islands National Marine Sanctuary over the Labor Day weekend. Thirty-three passengers had signed on for the weekend. *Conception* had departed Santa Barbara on the morning of Saturday, August 31. The trip began as usual, with passengers arriving early the evening before, stowing their gear, and settling into their bunks for the ride out to Santa Cruz. Information on where to stow their gear as well as bunk assignments was left on a clipboard in the salon. None of the crew members were aboard when the passengers began to arrive. Crew started to arrive between 2200 and 2300 hours, with the last crew member, the captain, arriving at 0330 hours, thirty minutes before departure. The vessel departed Santa Barbara at 0404 hours on Saturday, August 31.

After getting underway, all the crew went to bed with the exception of the captain, who piloted the vessel toward the first dive site of the trip. The following morning, a general safety briefing was held in the salon; this briefing covered both vessel and dive safety topics. Over the next two days, *Conception* stopped at various dive sites around Santa Cruz Island.

On the evening of the first, *Conception* stopped for a night dive at Quail Rock, located at the west end of Santa Cruz. Seventeen divers made a night dive between 2030 and 2130 hours. Channel Islands National Marine Sanctuary is well known for abundant marine life and excellent diving conditions. Most of the divers aboard for the trip were marine life enthusiasts and underwater photographers. With everyone back aboard from the night dive, *Conception* heaved anchor and headed east to a sheltered anchorage at Platts Harbor for the night.

During the trip from Quail Rock, the second galley hand turned off the breaker to the electric oven and range and turned on the air-conditioning for the bunk room. The range was turned off as a matter of practice, to prevent an accidental energizing of a range top burner. After rinsing off dive gear, many of the divers placed cameras, dive lights, phones, and tablets on the two aft tables in the salon. These devices or their batteries were plugged into chargers. Chargers were in turn plugged into power strips, which were plugged into two 15-amp receptacles.

Conception arrived at Platts Harbor at 2300 hours. A large private sport-fishing vessel, *Grape Escape*, was also anchored nearby. The crew made a last check around the deck, galley, berthing area, and machinery spaces before turning in to their bunks shortly before midnight. According to crew statements after the accident, there were some passengers still up in the salon when the crew went to bed.

At 0130 the second galley hand got up, as was his routine, and went to the galley to clean up after the last of the passengers. This took approximately an hour. On his way back to bed, he stopped to use the restroom at the aft end of the salon. He noted the time as 0235 hours.

Awakened by an unusual noise sometime after falling back asleep, the second galley hand was lying in his bunk when he thought he heard a passenger yelling. Getting up to investigate, he looked aft through the door to the sun deck and saw a glow emanating from the main deck below. Realizing what he saw, he turned around and started yelling fire, waking the other four crew members sleeping in the upper deck cabin.

With the other crew members alerted, the second galley hand ran aft. Reaching the stairwell to the main deck, he discovered it blocked by flames. He ran forward and alerted the crew that the stairs were blocked. He then lowered himself over the rail on the port side to the main deck. Reaching the main deck, he ran aft, hoping to access extinguishers located in the salon and to rouse the passengers below in the bunk room. When he reached the open aft doors to the salon, the entire area was engulfed in flames, including the area around the aft bunk-room escape hatch.

The mate and the first deckhand had been sleeping in the pilothouse, the captain in the starboard room, and the two galley hands in the port room. At this point the captain instructed his crew to lower themselves to the main deck from the pilothouse wing stations. The mate and first deckhand climbed over the rail and lowered themselves down. The first galley hand jumped. He misjudged the distance, striking the railing below and breaking his leg.

Reaching the deck on the port side, the mate and first deckhand discovered that the portside passageway was blocked. Smoke and flames coming out of the salon windows were extending up toward the sun deck. They then turned around and opened the bow gate, reasoning that anyone coming from below could use that for abandoning ship. By now the second galley hand, running through the smoke, had reached the bow. The mate and the first deckhand attempted to open the forward salon window, which was hinged but latched from the inside. They both tried unsuccessfully to pry the window open. Later, both would testify that the window was warm to the touch but not hot, and their view inside was completely obscured by thick smoke.

While this was going on, the captain was still in the wheelhouse. He was able to transmit two brief mayday calls before being overcome by smoke, reaching US Coast Guard Sector LA / Long Beach on VHF radio channel 16. His first call was "Mayday, Mayday, Mayday, *Conception*, Platts Harbor, north side Santa Cruz," followed by "39 P-O-B [persons on board]. I can't breathe. 39 P-O-B. Platts."

Forced out of the wheelhouse by heavy smoke, the captain proceeded out to the starboard wing station and dove overboard. The mate and first deckhand looked up at this time, seeing the captain jump and followed by a trail of smoke. Thinking that the captain was on fire when he jumped, the mate dove after him.

In a last-ditch effort to reach the passengers from the bow, the first deckhand opened the hatch to the anchor locker. Realizing that there was no doorway from the anchor locker aft, he then closed the hatch. He would later testify that there was no smoke in that compartment at that time.

With both side decks completely blocked by fire, the captain instructed the three remaining crew members on the foredeck to jump overboard from the bow. The first galley hand was in extreme pain due to his broken leg but was able to enter the water from the port bow door. Both galley hands then swam away from the vessel. The first deckhand swam toward the stern, followed by the mate once he had realized that the captain was unharmed. The captain followed the others swimming aft.

The mate reboarded the vessel via the aft swim platform and made his way forward to the aft end of the salon. Seeing the entire deckhouse completely engulfed in flames, he turned around and opened the engine room hatch. Finding only heavy smoke and no flames, he closed the hatch and returned to the swim platform. Assisted by the first deckhand, who had also climbed aboard, the mate launched *Conception*'s ridged-hull inflatable boat, RIB. This boat was stowed on the folded swim platform.

With the boat in the water, the mate jumped in and got the outboard engine started. By now the captain had reached the stern of *Conception*, and the mate pulled him into the boat. The first deckhand was still on board and made another attempt to reach the salon. Realizing that there was no way to get inside, he then attempted to reach the fire hose station and the start switch for the remote fire pump on the port side. Again finding his way blocked, he proceeded to the engine room hatch in an attempt to get directly to the fire pump in the engine room. Finding the engine room filled with heavy smoke, as did the mate, he then ran to the stern. At this time the captain yelled to the deckhand to get in the boat, which he then did.

By now, both galley hands had swum some distance from the *Conception*. The crew in the RIB proceeded to their location and got them aboard. From there, they motored over to the private fishing boat *Grape Escape*. Banging on the hull and then climbing aboard, they quickly woke the *Grape Escape*'s crew. *Grape Escape*'s captain took *Conception*'s captain and mate to the wheelhouse to make additional calls to the Coast Guard. The deckhand and second galley hand along with the *Grape Escape*'s crew assisted the injured first galley hand onto the *Grape Escape*'s aft deck.

Initially, believing that the mayday was for a medical emergency, Coast Guard Sector Long Beach notified Coast Guard Station Channel Islands at 0323 of a medical emergency at Platts Harbor. A minute later, at 0324 hours, Sector Long Beach notified Air Station Point Magu, who prepared to launch a helicopter. At 0329 hours a mayday was received from the captain of the *Grape Escape*, stating that a commercial boat was on fire at Platts Harbor with thirty-three people on board.

The first Coast Guard asset underway was a response boat medium, RBM 45643, departing Channel Islands harbor at 0342 hours, followed by RBM 45739 with a paramedic and an EMT from Ventura County Fire Department on board at 0349. Ventura County Fire boat 15 got underway at 0404 hours with members of Engine Company 54 on board.

The two response boats arrived on scene almost simultaneously along with a helo, CG6540 from Pt. Magu. By now, *Conception* was fully involved in fire from stem to stern. Both coxswains on the RBMs realized that they did not have the capacity to fight a fire of this magnitude; they immediately commenced a search of the surrounding waters for survivors. Ventura Fire boat 15 arrived on scene at 0455 hours along with Santa Barbara Harbor patrol boat 3. Both boats initiated firefighting efforts. The fire was extinguished at 0508, reflashing twice afterward.

Ventura Fire's paramedic and EMT examined the first galley hand, with the broken leg, on the *Grape Escape* and determined that he needed transport as soon as possible. *Grape Escape* departed at 0516 with the injured crew member on board, arriving in Channel Islands Harbor at 0735 hours.

Meanwhile, *Conception*, burned nearly to the waterline, sank at 0654 hours, coming to rest upside down on the seabed 20 yards from shore in 61 feet of water. *Conception*'s captain remained at the scene on board one of the RBMs until it departed at 0743 hours.

Four victims were recovered on the surface at 0804 hours. The Coast Guard cutter *Narwhal* arrived at 0841 hours, and another helo, CG6014, arrived at 0940 hours from Air Station San Diego. Searching continued until the following day, when the search was suspended on Tuesday, September 3.

After the disaster, the US attorney's office moved swiftly. A search warrant was served at Truth Aquatics office in Santa Barbara on September 8–10, as well as on the two remaining vessels in the fleet. Thousands of pages of company records, computers, and security camera servers, along with items from *Vision* and *Truth*, were seized.

Over the following nine days, divers from the FBI and local law enforcement agencies dove on the wreck and recovered all but one of the remaining victims. The last victim was found on September 11, floating close to the Santa Cruz Island shoreline.

Conception was recovered from the seabed by a commercial salvage team on September 13 and transported to Naval Station Ventura County at Port Hueneme, California. The wreckage was laid out by deck level—lower, main, and upper—in a secure area for examination. Major pieces of machinery were articulated into their respective locations. Smaller items that could not be identified by Coast Guard, FBI, or local law enforcement officers were gathered into plastic bags and placed at the examination site. Much of this material was from the main and upper decks. Four cell phones with no signs of heat damage were recovered from victims, and five from the wreckage. These phones, along with tablets and computers recovered from the site, were taken to the FBI lab in Washington, DC, to extract any relevant information.

Initially, the US attorney's office barred the National Transportation Safety Board (NTSB) from interviewing the *Conception*'s captain and crew as well as examining any of the seized documents. Later, NTSB officials were permitted to interview crew members but not the captain. Eventually, the NTSB was given scanned copies of the seized documents. Similarly, Truth Aquatics employees were barred from examining the wreckage. Truth Aquatics employees would have been able to identify the more obscure objects recovered from the wreck. Unfortunately, the Justice Department prevented some of the most qualified people available from examining the evidence and, in doing so, hampered the NTSB's ability to fully assess the circumstances surrounding the disaster.

All the victims were found to have died due to smoke inhalation. Carbon monoxide was found to be a contributory cause of death in addition to smoke inhalation in two of the victims. Passengers ranged in age from sixteen to sixty-two years old; two were minors under the age of eighteen. Of the thirty-three passengers, thirteen were male and twenty were female. The second deckhand, who was sleeping in the passenger bunk room and also perished, was a twenty-six-year-old woman.

Twenty-seven of the victims were fully or partially clothed when found. Fourteen had some form of footwear on. One person was found with a sandal on one foot and a boot on the other, indicating haste. The second deckhand was found with sandals on. It appeared as though some of the passengers were attempting to escape. Two had cell phones with them. Two were wearing jackets. One had a flashlight, and another a backpack. Silhouette areas of unburned but "sooted" wood were found near the stairs in the bunk room. This indicated that some of the victims were not in their bunks and were lying against these areas when overcome by smoke. It is likely that passengers who were awakened first alerted the others. The NTSB concluded that all the passengers were awake but unable to escape.

Conception was equipped with only two smoke detectors; both were located in the bunk-room passageways. Coast Guard regulations at the time did not require any additional smoke detectors on the vessel. Smoke detectors work on the principle that heat and smoke will naturally rise from a fire. The ceiling or overhead will be the first place that smoke and heat will begin to accumulate. Configured as the *Conception* was, with detectors only in the lower deck compartments, a deck above would have to burn long enough to fill that compartment completely with smoke before smoke reached the deck below.

Of the six crew members aboard at the time of the disaster, the captain, sixty-five years old, was the only experienced mariner. He had been working at Truth Aquatics since 1984, starting as a deckhand and then becoming a captain in 1985. The twenty-eight-year-old mate had been hired in late June 2019 and had attained his captain's license in March of that year. Prior to joining the *Conception* crew, he had worked on other local boats over the previous two years. The captain and mate were the only crew members holding merchant mariner credentials. The remaining crew members were not required to hold any credentials or undergo any formal training or certification process.

The first deckhand had been hired by Truth Aquatics less than a year prior, in November 2018. Prior to that he had worked on a day-charter sailboat. The twenty-six-year-old second deckhand had been promoted the previous week from galley hand on another Truth Aquatics vessel to deckhand on the *Conception*. This was her second voyage on *Conception*.

The thirty-four-year-old first galley hand had been employed aboard the *Conception* for three months. This was his first seagoing job. The second galley hand had worked aboard the *Conception* since October 2017. He was fifty-eight years old and had previously worked in restaurants.

In tracing the origins of the fire, crew interviews helped eliminate specific locations and equipment. None of the crew reported open flame visible on the upper deck when they first woke up. The first deckhand had described not seeing any flames or feeling heat from the anchor locker compartment when he opened the hatch.

Both the first deckhand and the mate stated that they did not see any flames or feel heat in the engine room when they opened the hatch to that compartment on two separate occasions, only smoke. It was common practice to leave a vent fan running overnight to draw warm air from the engine room into the lazarette for the purposes of drying wetsuits. With this fan running, smoke would have been pulled into the engine room via the main deck vents and then into the lazarette. Both the mate and deckhand stated they did not hear the heat-activated CO_2-fire-extinguishing system alarm sounding. This would have activated automatically if there had been fire in the engine room. Lighting was noted by the mate and deckhand to still be working in both the engine room and lazarette, which indicated that the generator was still operating when they evacuated the vessel.

All of the *Conception*'s galley equipment was electrically powered, and relatively new. The second galley hand stated that he had secured the breaker to the oven and range prior to going to bed. The only galley appliances that were energized at the time of the fire were the refrigerators. The vessel did not have a deep fryer.

Crew interviews consistently identified the aft portion of the salon area as having the most intense amount of heat and flames. The second galley hand described seeing an orange glow in the vicinity of the stairs at the aft end of the sun deck when he first woke up. He also described flames blocking the base of the stairs leading to the main deck and coming from the area of the starboard restroom. All the crew described smoke coming out of the salon on both sides aft. They also described the area around the aft doors completely blocked by flames and extending out to the restrooms on both sides. Descriptions given indicate that the fire initially was more internal to the aft end of the salon than external. NTSB determined that the fire started in the aft end of the salon.

Possible ignition sources at the aft end of the salon would include electrical-system components, passenger-owned devices being charged on the two aft tables in the salon, and improperly discarded smoking materials. Separate investigations by the Federal Bureau of Alcohol, Tobacco, and Firearms (ATF) and the NTSB differed in their conclusions about the probable cause of the fire. ATF favored a discarded cigarette that eventually ignited a large, Rubbermaid trash can under the stairs leading to the upper deck. The NTSB favored an electrical fire resulting from a "thermal runaway" in one of the many devices charging overnight in the aft end of the salon. In the end, both the ATF and the NTSB decided to declare the exact cause of the fire as "unknown."

Battery fires have become serious problems on ships and elsewhere. Lithium ion batteries have become very popular due to their high-energy capacity and ability to fully recharge after being deeply discharged. They are found almost universally in phones, tablets, and laptop computers as well as electric or hybrid automobiles. They have become very common in diving equipment, including underwater lights and strobes used with camera equipment.

These batteries have also developed a well-documented history of starting fires. A lithium ion battery being charged caught fire the previous year aboard the *Vision*. This fire was discovered by a passenger shortly after it started. The passenger pulled the charger cord out of the receptacle and tossed the charger and battery into a freshwater rinse tank, extinguishing the fire. This fire was never reported to the Coast Guard.

The really scary thing about lithium ion batteries is a condition called thermal runaway. This condition occurs when the internal battery temperature rises at a rate greater than 20ºC (68ºF) per minute. Maximum temperatures can rapidly reach 300ºC (572ºF) or greater. When this occurs, the battery is in an uncontrolled, self-heating state. This usually results in the ejection of gas, shrapnel, and particulate matter due to violent battery cell venting. Extreme heat and fire are a byproduct of this process.

Thermal runaway can occur from one of two circumstances: an internal short circuit or what's referred to as an off-nominal condition. Internal short circuits occur when the separator between anode and cathode plates within the battery breaks down, causing the short. This is common in poorly manufactured batteries. Off-nominal conditions can occur in one of four possible scenarios:

1. Overcharging a battery due to incompatibility between the battery and the charger or a poorly designed battery management system
2. Multiple deep discharges of the battery below its lowest safe discharge point, followed by recharging
3. An external short within a battery charger
4. Abnormally high or low ambient temperatures

In any case, once a thermal runaway starts, it is almost impossible to stop. A fire will start within the battery. That fire will self-generate its own heat. The fuel source and oxygen are already present. With small devices such as cell phones, the best course of action is isolation. Airlines carry insulated steel boxes for just this eventuality; should a passenger's phone catch fire, it can be placed in the box and the fire contained. Lithium ion batteries have become a real problem for ocean shipping. Hardly a month has gone by during the past few years when a fire hasn't started on a container ship or car carrier due to a malfunctioning lithium ion battery. In many cases this has resulted in the constructive total loss of the ship.

In summary, the NTSB and ATF determined that the fire started in the aft end of the salon, in the area where there was a large combustible trash can and multiple devices were plugged into chargers. Contributing to the disaster were the following factors:

1. The fire burned undetected for at least a half hour before being detected by the second galley hand.
2. Lack of a roving patrol prevented early detection of the fire, precluded firefighting and evacuation efforts, and directly led to the high number of fatalities in the incident.
3. Although meeting compliance requirements, the lack of smoke detectors in the salon prevented early detection and allowed for the growth of the fire, precluding firefighting and evacuation efforts, directly leading to the high number of fatalities.
4. Both means of escape from the bunk room, the circular staircase and escape hatch, led to the same compartment. Neither was adequate for effective escape, and neither exited to an exterior deck or a separate compartment from the primary exit.

5. The emergency escape hatch over the bunk aft was not a practical means of escape under any circumstances due to its configuration.
6. Most of the victims were awake but could not escape the bunk room at the time of the fire.
7. The vessel's hull, decks, and superstructure all were constructed of combustible materials.
8. Combustible materials were used extensively in the vessel's furnishings, including vinyl-covered foam seating, plastic chairs, paneling, and plastic waste disposal containers.
9. Crew training and experience were lacking.
10. Company oversight into operations and maintenance was lacking, jeopardizing the safety of passengers and crew.
11. The large number of devices with lithium ion batteries being charged inside the cabin and in proximity to the only exit point was an especially poor decision.
12. Had a safety management plan been in place at Truth Aquatics, unsafe practices and fire risks could have been identified and mitigated to prevent the disaster.

Considering these issues, the NTSB made ten recommendations and reiterated one previous recommendation. These recommendations included revisions to 46 CFR, subchapter T, small passenger vessels. These recommendations were as follows.

To the US Coast Guard:

1. Require that newly constructed vessels with overnight accommodations have smoke detectors in all accommodation spaces.
2. Require that all vessels with overnight accommodation spaces, currently in service, including those constructed prior to 1996, have smoke detectors in all accommodation spaces.
3. Require that all vessels with overnight accommodations, including vessels constructed prior to 1996, have interconnected smoke detectors, such that when one detector alarms, the remaining detectors also alarm.
4. Develop and implement an inspection procedure to verify that small passenger vessel owners, operators, and charterers are conducting roving patrols as required by 46 CFR, subchapter T.

5. Require newly constructed passenger vessels with overnight accommodations to provide a secondary means of escape into a different space than the primary exit, so that a single fire should not affect both escape paths.
6. Require all small passenger vessels with overnight accommodations, including those constructed prior to 1996, to provide a secondary means of escape into a different space than the primary exit, so that a single fire should not affect both escape paths.
7. Review the suitability of 46 CFR, subchapter T regulations regarding means of escape to ensure there are no obstructions to egress on small passenger vessels constructed prior to 1996, and modify regulations accordingly.

To the Passenger Vessel Association, Sport Fishing Association of California, and National Association of Charter Boat Operators:

1. Until the US Coast Guard requires all passenger vessels with overnight accommodations, including vessels constructed prior to 1996, to have smoke detectors in all accommodation spaces, share the circumstances of the *Conception* accident with your members and encourage your members to voluntarily install interconnected smoke and fire detectors in all accommodation spaces, such that when one detector alarms, all the remaining detectors also alarm.
2. Until the US Coast Guard requires small passenger vessels with overnight accommodations to provide a secondary means of escape into a different space than the primary exit, share the circumstances of the *Conception* accident with your members and encourage your members to voluntarily do so.

To Truth Aquatics: Implement a safety management system for your fleet to improve safety practices and minimize risk.

A single Coast Guard recommendation, M-12-3, was reiterated from a previous report, issued in 2005, currently classified as an "open-unacceptable response." It reads, "Require all operators of US flag passenger vessels to implement an SMS, Safety Management System, taking into account the characteristics, methods of operation, and nature of service of these vessels, and, with respect to ferries, the sizes of the ferry systems within which the vessels operate."

Obvious, parallels can be made between the loss of *Yarmouth Castle* in 1965 and the 2019 *Conception* disaster fifty-four years later:

1. The lack of a roving patrol on *Conception* mirrors watchman Jose Arcadio on *Yarmouth Castle* bypassing the port forward main deck passageway and cabin #610.
2. The extensive use of combustible materials in the *Conception*'s construction and outfitting mirrors *Yarmouth Castle*'s wooden upper superstructure.
3. Inadequate means of escape on the *Conception* mirrors windows and portholes painted shut aboard *Yarmouth Castle*.
4. Lack of crew training and experience at Truth Aquatics played a major role in the disaster, similar in many ways to training and experience levels aboard *Yarmouth Castle*.
5. Actions of the second galley hand in rousing the crew, attempting to reach the fire extinguishers at the aft end of the salon, and alerting the passengers are reminiscent of Roy Drysdale's efforts to save passengers on *Yarmouth Castle*. Neither individual was a mariner. The second galley hand was fifty-eight years old and had come from the restaurant industry.

On September 1, 2023, NTSB chair Jennifer Homenday wrote a letter to the commandant of the US Coast Guard emphasizing the need to implement a rule requiring SMS for small passenger vessels within thirty days. In 2010, Congress had explicitly granted the US Coast Guard the authority to require that operators of small passenger vessels implement safety management systems. The Elijah E. Cummings Coast Guard Authorization Act of 2020 mandates that the Coast Guard carry out all the NTSB recommendations issued or reiterated as a result of the *Conception* investigation.

A Coast Guard marine board of investigation (MBI) was established, requiring the board to convene as soon as practicable, to inquire into all aspects of the *Conception* casualty. As of June 2023, a formal MBI has yet to convene.

On November 7, 2023, a federal court in Los Angeles convicted sixty-nine-year-old Captain Jerry Boylan of the *Conception* on one count of misconduct or "neglect of a ship officer," following a ten-day trial. The charge is a pre–Civil War statute colloquially known as "seaman's manslaughter," designed to hold steamboat captains and crew responsible for maritime disasters. In May 2024 he was sentenced to four years in prison.

When Things Go Right

MV *Ocean Intervention*

December 19, 2020, off the coast of Hawaii

Trouble happens at sea. There are no two ways around it. The key to successful outcomes is staying ahead of the curve. Anticipating different possible scenarios and then training as a crew to react to those scenarios is the way to do it. With the basic groundwork and plan in place, when something does happen, a crew will be ready to deal with it. This is precisely what happened aboard the subsea support ship *Ocean Intervention*.

Ocean Intervention is a US-flagged, 243-foot, steel-hulled diving-support ship built in 1998 and operated by Oceaneering International, of Houston, Texas. Designed to perform inspection maintenance and repair work in deep-sea environments, where much of the work is with remote-operated vehicles (ROVs), *Ocean Intervention* is equipped with a diesel-electric power plant. Four diesel engines drive generators, which in turn supply power to the entire ship's electrical needs, including the electric propulsion motors and thrusters.

The ship was standing by for orders in anchorage B off Honolulu, Hawaii, in late December 2020. The day prior to the fire, the engineering team noticed the #3 generator start to "hunt" when under a load. The crew shifted to the #1 generator and replaced a sensor on the #3. The following day, generator #1 started to hunt, so the crew switched back to the #3 generator. All the generators were close to (but had not exceeded) the time for an overhaul.

Ocean Intervention is configured with an engineering control room, referred to as the engineering operating station, or EOS. The EOS is an air-conditioned room, containing all the engineering instrumentation and controls for the ship. Windows in the bulkheads provide a view of the ship's engine room. The EOS is where the ship's engineers stand watch.

On the afternoon of December 19 at approximately 1303 hours, both the chief engineer and the engineer of the watch were in the EOS. Both men heard a loud bang and saw thick black smoke beginning to fill the engine room. The engineering officer of the watch immediately notified the bridge. Neither engineer knew the cause of the noise and smoke. The chief activated the emergency stops for all the online generators, closed the fuel and lube oil supply valves, secured the engine room ventilation fans, and closed all the dampers. Both men then evacuated the EOS. With the main ship's service generators shut down, the emergency generator, in a separate compartment, started automatically, providing basic electrical power throughout the ship.

About the same time that the engineer on watch notified the bridge, the mate on watch received a fire alarm for the engine room and observed smoke coming from vents on the port stack. Arriving on the bridge shortly thereafter, the captain sounded the general alarm and directed the crew to muster at emergency stations. The captain then notified the Coast Guard in Honolulu and Oceaneering's office in Houston. Once mustered, all crew members were accounted for. Two fire teams of two persons each suited up in turnout gear and self-contained breathing apparatus (SCBAs).

At 1306 hours the fire pump was started, using hoses from on-deck fire stations. Crew members started boundary cooling on the exterior bulkheads and decks surrounding the engine room. At 1310 hours the fire teams, wearing SCBAs, entered the EOS and observed heavy smoke in the engine room but could see no sign of fire. At this point, the engine room was sealed at all ventilation and access points. After checking the other engineering spaces and finding them all clear, the fire team determined that the issue was isolated to the engine room itself. Smoke coming from the port stack was noticeably reduced by this time.

The ship's crew then began taking baseline temperature readings on deck, using an infrared thermometer. At 1328 hours, temperatures on the port and starboard side were 95 and 87 degrees Fahrenheit, respectively. The crew continued to take readings every thirty minutes as boundary cooling continued, and the space remained sealed. An hour or so later, the temperature started to drop in the engine room. The fire team then made another assessment at 1518 hours from the EOS. The smoke was now noticeably less in the engine room, with no sign of fire. At 1945 hours the chief engineer and two firefighters from a responding marine salvage company entered the engine room and determined that the fire was out, and the space was safe from any further fire risk.

The cause of the incident was a catastrophic failure of the #3 diesel generator, resulting in a connecting rod being ejected through the side of the engine block. This event was similar in many ways to what is known as a "main engine base explosion." There have been many cases in the past, particularly on tugboats where a bilge fire resulted from a base explosion and, coupled with a poor response from the crew, resulted in the total loss of the vessel.

Fortunately, in this case the crew of the *Ocean Intervention* was well prepared and well trained to respond to the situation. By removing the fuel sources and sealing up compartment ventilation, they starved the fire both of fuel and oxygen.

Ocean Intervention's crew quickly and effectively removed two of the three elements of the fire triangle. The timely and professionally coordinated response resulted in a positive outcome and minimized harm to the ship and her crew.

At the end of the day the question remains, Are cruise ships safe?

Statistically, comparing the number of cruise ships in service today along with the number of passengers carried each year, the answer would have to be yes. That said, there are big differences among cruise ship operators. Within these pages, we have attempted to bring the story of *Yarmouth Castle* to light as completely and accurately as possible, so that seafarers, passengers, and government supervisory and regulating entities such as the United States Coast Guard can use past mistakes to inform modern-day safety practices on passenger-carrying vessels. For reflection and comparison, we have included three other passenger vessel incidents. Since the *Yarmouth Castle* disaster in 1965, there have been more than forty major fires damaging cruise ships, and hundreds more people have died.

APPENDIX

The Lost

NAME	HOME	CABIN NO.
Nathan Barkin	Miami Beach, Florida	820
Norma J. Barton	Astoria, New York	811
Andrew J. Best	Boca Raton, Florida	806
Francis M. Best	Boca Raton, Florida	806
William H. Burleigh	Pompano Beach, Florida	844
Elsie Burleigh	Pompano Beach, Florida	844
Anna E. Cirlincione	Lincroft, New Jersey	620
Frank A. Cirlincione	Lincroft, New Jersey	620
George R. Crawford	Pompano Beach, Florida	808

Sarah J. Crawford	Pompano Beach, Florida	808
Carlos Davis	Lima, Peru	804
Carmen Davis	Lima, Peru	804
Dr. Lisardo Diaz-Torrens (crew)	Cuba	Doctor's cabin
Dena A. Duffy	Pompano Beach, Florida	817
Sylvia Ebner	Flushing, New York	710
Hal M. Eberle	Pompano Beach, Florida	845
Helen E. Eustice	Margate, Florida	809
Samuel Frankel	Miami Beach, Florida	G-1
Rose Frankel	Miami Beach, Florida	G-1
Estelle M. Franc	Oak Park, Michigan	810
Fred R. Franc	Oak Park, Michigan	810
Wanda B. Gang	Pompano Beach, Florida	629
Allen M. Gillan	Hamilton, Ontario, Canada	838
Lynda Ann Gillan	Hamilton, Ontario, Canada	838
Agnes Hill	Pompano Beach, Florida	815
William Hill	Pompano Beach, Florida	815
Jonathan A. Hamilton	Madeira Beach, Florida	614

Mary Hall	Miami, Florida	718
Phyllis Hall (crew)	Jamaica	Steward cabin
Helen M. Hier	Pompano Beach, Florida	823
William Hier	Pompano Beach, Florida	823
Henry A. Hughes	East Setauket, New York	805
Mary Hughes	East Setauket, New York	805
Castillo F. Hurtarte	Guatemala City, Guatemala	N-1
Ann Martin Jackson	Vero Beach, Florida	842
Louise Jackson	Vero Beach, Florida	842
Robert W. Johnson	Watertown, Massachusetts	828
John A. Karns	Winter Park, Florida	721
Alice Karns	Winter Park, Florida	721
George D. Keen	Pompano Beach, Florida	715
Catherine Keen	Pompano Beach, Florida	715
Arthur E. Lehr	Brooklyn, New York	819
Stella Lehr	Brooklyn, New York	819
Nathan Lehr	Miami Beach, Florida	634
Clarice Lobel	Bay Village, Florida	P-1
Myrtle P. Lowe	Miami, Florida	0

Morgan I. Lowe	Miami, Florida	0
Florence B. Lucchesi	Washington, DC	702
Ann J. Marple	Tulsa, Oklahoma	F-1
Edna Matias	Berwyn, Illinois	719
Jessie Mazzarisi	New York, New York	638
John Mazzarisi	New York, New York	638
Gayle M. Musson	Pompano Beach, Florida	629
Louis W. Neher	Pompano Beach, Florida	830
Margret E. Neher	Pompano Beach, Florida	830
Elsie M. O'Connell	Miami, Florida	718
Leonie Pellowski	West Palm Beach, Florida	832
Eduardo Pinedo	Lima, Peru	812
Maria Pinedo	Lima, Peru	812
Charles E. Polm	Parker, Pennsylvania	840
Mary A. Polm	Parker, Pennsylvania	840
Herman Pollock	Pompano Beach, Florida	841
Minnie Pollock	Pompano Beach, Florida	841
Della Quay	Pompano Beach, Florida	836
Omar D. Quay	Pompano Beach, Florida	836

Charlotte M. Reich	Pompano Beach, Florida	807
Helen St. Clair	Largo, Florida	T-1
Vivian St. Clair	Largo, Florida	T-1
Bertha Salke	Miami, Florida	L
Edith R. Schneider	Pompano Beach, Florida	831
Frank Silver	Chicago, Illinois	827
Elmer E. Stanley	Kenosha, Wisconsin	813
Juan P. Stanley	Kenosha, Wisconsin	813
Mabel Straub	Woodhaven, New York	615
Ralph D. Storrs	Pompano Beach, Florida	843
Ethel L. Thomas	Lake Worth, Florida	824
Winfield W. Thomas	Lake Worth, Florida	824
Flora G. Tiefenthaler	Chalfont, Pennsylvania	816
William Tiefenthaler	Chalfont, Pennsylvania	816
Pauline I. Tomasini	San Luis Obispo, California	829
Warren Tomasini	San Luis Obispo, California	829
Mercedes Vila Sole	Guatemala City, Guatemala	N-1
Charles E. Vincent	Pompano Beach, Florida	717
Salle A. Vincent	Pompano Beach, Florida	717

Betty Wand	Miami Beach, Florida	P-1
Stella M. Wiehe	Miami, Florida	L
Alice Weible	Long Beach, California	523
Florence B. Wright	Pompano Beach, Florida	847
Joseph T. Wright	Pompano Beach, Florida	847
Steven W. Wright	Redington Beach, Florida	614

ACKNOWLEDGMENTS

The core of our research for this book roots in over three thousand pages of eyewitness testimony and documents known as a Commandant's Action Report. The United States Coast Guard gathered these records during nineteen days of hearings, following the SS *Yarmouth Castle* disaster in November 1965. We found a complete record of these hearings and their associated transcripts and documents at the National Archives and Records Administration (NARA) in College Park, Maryland, and Washington, DC.

Many newspaper and magazine articles from the era rendered firsthand testimony about the events surrounding the fire and sinking of the *Yarmouth Castle*. The *Life* magazine feature "Death of a Cruise Ship" of November 26, 1965, by David Nevin added much to our stories of Ruth Wright, Adele Simister, Mabel Straub, Edna and Charles Matias, and Winston Roy Drysdale. Reportage by the *Miami Herald* and the *Palm Beach Post* not only yielded eyewitness testimony but also helped penetrate the corporate shield surrounding the actual owner of the *Castle* and Yarmouth Cruise Lines, Canadian Jules Sokoloff.

The children, grandchildren, nieces, and nephews of the crews and passengers of the *Yarmouth Castle*, *Bahama Star*, and *Finnpulp* have showed us unlimited generosity in sharing memories with us of their loved ones who, as sailors say of the dead, have "crossed the bar."

Miami tugboat captain Bill Bunting shared his memories of his friend Captain Carl Brown of the *Bahama Star*.

Thanks to the assistance of steamship historian Jeff Macklin, we were able to talk with the son of Carl Brown, captain aboard the *Bahama Star*. His son, Louis Netherland, shared his father's personal memories and photographs of his career and the *Yarmouth Castle* disaster and gave us a window into his gallant father. The captain's obituary in the *Rogersville Review* (Tennessee) added to our insights into his life. We also had the notes of an interview with Captain Brown conducted by Henry Flayhart.

Jeff Macklin arranged for us to meet the three daughters of Carl and Wilhelmina Apuzzo: Helen Apuzzo Bloodgood, Mary Apuzzo Lehman, and Denise Apuzzo Sessions. They graciously agreed to meet us one afternoon in Tequesta, Florida, to reminisce about their parents and their cruise on the *Yarmouth Castle*.

Jeff and Marilynn Macklin graciously hosted the authors in their home for three days, while examining Jeff's extensive archives.

Ms. Willamae M. Johnson, librarian at the LJM Maritime Academy in Nassau, Bahamas, and Captain Eric Wieberg gave us insight into Bahamian records of the disaster.

We found a radio interview on the CRS Radio Network with waiter/entertainer Winston Roy Drysdale, who was aboard the *Yarmouth Castle*. His vivid memories, five decades after the disaster, were haunting in their attention to detail and their ability to evoke the horror of that awful night.

A number of videos and documentaries on YouTube have informed us as well. Produced for the Discovery Channel, *Floating Inferno* by director Christopher Rowley portrays the disaster and includes the firsthand recollections of Captain Carl Brown.

Hal Burton's book *The Morro Castle: Tragedy at Sea* detailed the nightmare of the liner's burning at sea in 1934, which in its scale and details was an eerie portend of the disaster that befell the *Yarmouth Castle* thirty-one years later.

For a narrative about the origins of the Miami cruise ship industry, we consulted *Devils on the Deep Blue Sea* by Kristoffer A. Garin.

Lewis A. Fraser's unpublished biography, *Highlights of the Life of F. Leslie Fraser: A Pioneer of the Port of Miami*, gave us further details and insights into the development of the Miami cruise ship industry as it related to his father, Frank Fraser, and the Eastern Steamship Lines.

Under the Crown and Anchor: Royal Caribbean Cruise Line; The First Twenty-Five Years, 1970–1995 by B. Kolltveit and J. Maxtone-Graham provided additional insight into the end of Yarmouth Cruise Lines and the beginnings of Royal Caribbean. Ed Dunbaugh and David Crockett's excellent book *Eastern Steamship*, published by the Steamship Historical Society of America, provided insight into the early years of Eastern Steamship Lines, as well as a fleet history.

Diana Aguilera's article "The Psychology of Heroism," in the March 2019 issue of *Stanford Magazine*, and psychologist Peter Walker's analysis of stress disorders in his online monograph "The 4Fs: A Trauma Typology in Complex PTSD" helped us unravel how stress in extreme situations such as the *Yarmouth Castle* disaster elicited very different behaviors from the people involved.

Douglas Bigler's article "Warm Water Hypothermia" on the website infolific.com clued us in on this little-known topic.

In researching the MV *Finnpulp* and the history of Finnlines, the book *The Finnlines Fleet, 1947–1997: 50 Years at Your Service* by Matti Pietikainen was an invaluable resource on the company's history.

Finnpulp's radio officer Rauno Suominen provided a detailed description of *Finnpulp*'s voyage from Mobile, Alabama, to Nassau, the rescue, and his general procedures as radio operator on the ship. Ms. Outi Kivimaki of the Rauma Maritime Museum in Rauma, Finland, provided Rauno Suominen's description of events, as well as pointing us in the direction of various Finnish archives.

Mr. Timo Kuntto of the maritime museum of Finland in Helsinki provided additional insight.

The NTSB report "MAB-2126" was our source for the stories of the *Ocean Intervention* fire. NTSB report "MAR-20103" and supporting documents provided information on the dive boat *Conception* disaster.

Details of the disaster aboard the *Herald of Free Enterprise* came to us from Captain Daniel Parrott's *Bridge Resource Management for Small Ships* (International Marine).

The US Coast Guard Marine Board of Investigation report "16732/01282, MV *Angelina Lauro (Italian)*, Fire on Board While Docked in Charlotte Amalie Harbor, St. Thomas, USVI, on 30 March 1979 with No Loss of Life" provided additional insight into cruise ship fires.

Underwriters Laboratories research institute provided information on the hazards involved with lithium ion batteries, battery chemistry, and dangers of thermal runaway.

Articles in *Steamboat Bill*, now *Power Ships*, the quarterly journal of the Steamship Historical Society of America, provided details on the final days of the *Bahama Star* as *La Janelle*.

Images in this book came from many sources, including the private collections of the authors, cruise ship historian Jeff Macklin, and Louis Netherland. Additional images came from the Steamship Historical Society of America in Warwick, Rhode Island, the Associated Press, the *Miami Herald*, the *Palm Beach Post*, and the Mariners Museum in Newport News, Virginia. The three wonderful paintings, *Fire*, *On Borrowed Time*, and *A Pioneer*, came from renowned maritime artist Robert G. Lloyd.

Finally, a book like this one cannot take its final shape without the help of a legion of people. John Stone at Schiffer Publishing inspired us with his support and enthusiasm during the initial stages of this project. Senior editor Bob Biondi brought his gusto and perspicacity to this book to give it a thoughtful massage before publication.

SELECTED BIBLIOGRAPHY

Books

Burton, Hal. *The Morro Castle Tragedy at Sea*. New York: Viking, 1973.

Cudahy, Brian J. *The Cruise Ship Phenomenon in North America*. Centreville, MD: Cornell Maritime Press, 2001.

Dunbaugh, Edward, and David Crockett. *Eastern Steamship*. Warwick, RI: Steamship Historical Society of America, 1997.

Garin, Kristoffer A. *Devils on the Deep Blue Sea: The Dreams, Schemes, and Showdowns That Built America's Cruise Ship Industry*. New York: Viking, 2005.

Kolltveit Bård, and John Maxtone-Graham. *Under Crown and Anchor: Royal Caribbean Cruise Line; The First Twenty-Five Years, 1970–1995*. Miami, FL: Onboard Media / Royal Caribbean, 1995.

Parrott, Daniel. *Bridge Resource Management for Small Ships*. Camden, ME: International Marine / McGraw Hill, 2011.

Pietikainen, Matti. *The Finnlines Fleet, 1947–1997: 50 Years at Your Service*. Helsinki: Finlandia Books, 1989.

Government Reports

US Coast Guard. *Commandants Action Marine Board of Investigation Fire on Board the Panamanian SS Yarmouth Castle on 13 November 1965*. Records of the US Coast Guard, record group 26, National Archives at College Park, MD. Washington, DC: USCG, February 24, 1966.

US Coast Guard. *Foreign Passenger Vessel Examination Records Excerpts: 1957–1965*. Records of the US Coast Guard, record group 26, National Archives at College Park, MD. Miami, FL: Marine Inspection Office.

US Coast Guard. *Marine Board of Investigation Hearings Exhibits, November 1965*. Records of the US Coast Guard, record group 26, National Archives at College Park, MD. Washington, DC: USCG.

US Coast Guard. *Marine Board of Investigation Hearings Testimony, 22 November 1965–14 January 1966*. Records of the US Coast Guard, record group 26, National Archives at College Park, MD. Washington, DC: USCG.

US Coast Guard. *Marine Casualty Report*, 16732/01282, *M/V Angelina Lauro (Italian), Fire on Board While Docked in Charlotte Amalie Harbor, St. Thomas, USVI, 30 March 1979*, 16732/01282. Records of the US Coast Guard, record group 26, National Archives at College Park, MD. Washington, DC: USCG, September 1, 1981.

US Coast Guard. *Marine Casualty Report USCGC Cuyahoga, M/V Santa Cruz II (Argentine) Collision in Chesapeake Bay, 20 October 1978*. 16732/92368. Records of the US Coast Guard, record group 26, National Archives at College Park, MD. Washington, DC: USCG, July 31, 1979.

US Department of Justice, Federal Bureau of Investigation. *Yarmouth Castle Interview Transcripts, 1965–1966*. Records of the US Coast Guard, record group 26, National Archives at College Park, MD. Washington, DC: DOJ.

US Department of State. *Collection of Letters and Correspondence Regarding Cruise Ships, 1965–1966*. Records of the US Coast Guard, record group 26, National Archives at College Park, MD. Washington, DC: US Department of State.

US National Transportation Safety Board. *Safety Recommendations, USCGC Cuyahoga–Santa Cruz II collision*. M79-17-30. Washington, DC: NTSB, March 2, 1979.

US National Transportation Safety Board. *Diesel Generator Engine Failure Aboard Offshore Supply Vessel Ocean Intervention*. MAB-21/26. Washington, DC: NTSB, December 2, 2021.

US National Transportation Safety Board. *Fire Aboard Small Passenger Vessel Conception Platts Harbor, Channel Islands National Park*. MAR-20103. Washington, DC: NTSB, October 20, 2020.

US National Transportation Safety Board. *Railroad-Marine Accident Report, Derailment of Amtrak Train No. 2 on the CSX Big Bayou Canot Bridge near Mobile Alabama, September 22nd, 1993*. RAR-94/01. Washington, DC: NTSB, September 19, 1994.

Magazines

Aguilera, Diana. "The Psychology of Heroism." *Stanford Magazine*, March 2019.

Ballance, Virginia. "The *Yarmouth Castle* Disaster of 1965 and Its Legacies." *Journal of the Bahamas Historical Society*, October 2001.

Eisele, Peter. "Saga of the Surviving Coastal Twins." *Steamboat Bill* 128 (Winter 1973).

Elliott, Richard V. "High Seas Report, *Yarmouth Castle* Burned and Sank." *Steamboat Bill* 96 (Winter 1965).

Emery, John. "The Passenger Ships of Theodore Ferris." *Steamboat Bill* 275 (Fall 2010).

Johnson, Arthur. "No Fire Bell in the Night." *Steamboat Bill* 131 (Fall 1974).

Nevin, David, "Death of a Cruise Ship." *Life*, November 26, 1965.

Parkinson, Robert. "West Coast Report, *La Jenelle* Torn from Moorings." *Steamboat Bill* 115 (Fall 1970).

Parkinson, Robert. "West Coast Report, *La Jenelle* Scrapped in Place." *Steamboat Bill* 118 (Summer 1971).

Newspapers

Auerbach, Stewart. "He Abandoned Us, Crewman Charge." *Miami Herald*, November 17, 1965.

Auerbach, Stewart. "Who Owns Yarmouth Castle?" *Miami Herald*, November 15, 1965.

Auerbach, Stuart, and Steve Rogers. "Survivors Say: No Boat Drill." *Miami Herald*, November 14, 1965.

Buchanan, James. "Problem Child, 36, Added to Ship Probe." *Miami Herald*, November 21, 1965.

"Cruise Ship Owner Claims Arsonist Set Fatal Fire." *Red Deer Advocate*, December 17, 1965.

Doran, Tom. "It Was to Be a Happy Outing—but Elders Found Horror." *Miami Herald*, November 14, 1965.

Jones, Clarence. "Coast Guard OK'd Ship but Some Called Her Unfit." *Miami Herald*, November 16, 1965.

Kerr, James. "The Last Cruise of the Yarmouth Castle." *South Florida Sun-Sentinel*, November 13, 1988.

Miller, Gene. "Go Get Passengers, Boat Crewman Told—Liner Pushed In Until It Felt Heat of Blazing Ship." *Miami Herald*, November 15, 1965.

Russell, James. "Castle Owner Proves to Be Mystery Man." *Miami Herald*, November 20, 1965.

Southworth, George. "Disaster Ship Called Firetrap—Seaman's Union Rips Use." *Miami Herald*, November 16, 1965.

Werne, Jo. "22 Senior Citizens of Broward Lost." *Miami Herald*, November 15, 1965.

Whited, Charles, and James Buchanan. "90 Missing After Inferno Sinks Cruise Ship with 550 on Board." *Miami Herald*, November 14, 1965.

"Yarmouth Castle Owners Face 3.25 Million in Suits." *Palm Beach Post*, November 18, 1965.

Unpublished Sources

Fraser Lovett Narrative History. Louis Netherland collection.

Highlights of the Life of F. Leslie Fraser: A Pioneer of the Port of Miami. Jeff Macklin collection.

The Finnpulp *Voyage from Mobile, Alabama, to Nassau, Bahamas, November 1965*. Rauma Maritime Museum, Rauma, Finland.

Broadcast Interviews and Films

Drysdale, Winston. "The *Yarmouth Castle* Fire." *Caribbean Radio Show*, August 2021.

Rowley, Christopher. "Shipwreck! The Floating Inferno." Cine Nova Productions for Discovery Channel, 1997.

INDEX

"The Fun Ships" brochure for *Yarmouth* and *Yarmouth Castle* circa 1965. *Authors' collection*

Evangeline tied up in Miami, Merrill Stevens drydock to the right, swimming-pool casing visible on ship's stern. Yarmouth Cruise Lines office is to the left. *Courtesy of Jeff Macklin collection*

Evangeline moored bow out at her pier in Boston. *Courtesy of the Steamship Historical Society of America, Warwick, Rhode Island, C. Bradford Mitchell Collection*

Postcard from the winter of 1927–28, when *Evangeline* was chartered to Clyde Steamship Corp. *Authors' collection*

Evangeline returning to Boston from Nova Scotia. *Courtesy of Jeff Macklin collection*

[30] EASTERN STEAMSHIP LINES—*Land of Evangeline*

LET'S SAIL THE SEA TO ACADIA

The ROMANCE-LAND *of Evangeline*

IN his poem "EVANGELINE" Longfellow immortalized Nova Scotia. Today, the EASTERN STEAMSHIP LINES carry thousands of travellers to "the land of Evangeline" to worship at the famous shrines of history, romance and scenery which have served to make NOVA SCOTIA one of the most popular summer vacation countries in the world.

Plying between New York and Yarmouth, and Boston and Yarmouth, the luxurious steamships of Trans-Atlantic type, the S.S. "YARMOUTH," and S.S. "EVANGELINE" head the Eastern Steamship Lines fleet.

The recently adopted change in the laws of the Province of Nova Scotia will permit of the sale of liquors under a system of government control.

SCENES IN THE LAND OF EVANGELINE.

1930s Eastern Steamship Line's brochure. *Authors' collection*

Evangeline portside promenade deck at lifeboat station 6, stateroom windows to right. *Courtesy of Jeff Macklin collection*

Yarmouth Castle departing Miami for the last time? *Courtesy of Jeff Macklin collection*

Early 1960s postcards for Yarmouth Cruise Lines ships. *Authors' collection*

Capt. Carl Brown. *Courtesy of Louis Netherland*

F. Leslie Fraser greeting British dignitaries in Jamaica. *Courtesy of Jeff Macklin collection*

A Pioneer—the *Queen of Nassau* entering Nassau Harbor, 1955. *Painting by Robert G. Lloyd, courtesy of Jeff Macklin collection*

Yarmouth Castle brochure for cruises from Miami. *Courtesy of Jeff Macklin collection*

Full-page magazine ad featuring Nassau Harbor, circa 1950s. *Authors' collection*

Motor ship *Finnpulp* dressed in flags for her commissioning ceremony. *Courtesy of Rauma Maritime Museum, Rauma, Finland*

Evangeline moored at Prince George Wharf, Nassau Bahamas, July 1963.
Courtesy of Jeff Macklin collection

Yarmouth Castle moored at Prince George Wharf, with the Nassau Straw Market in the foreground.
Courtesy of Jeff Macklin collection

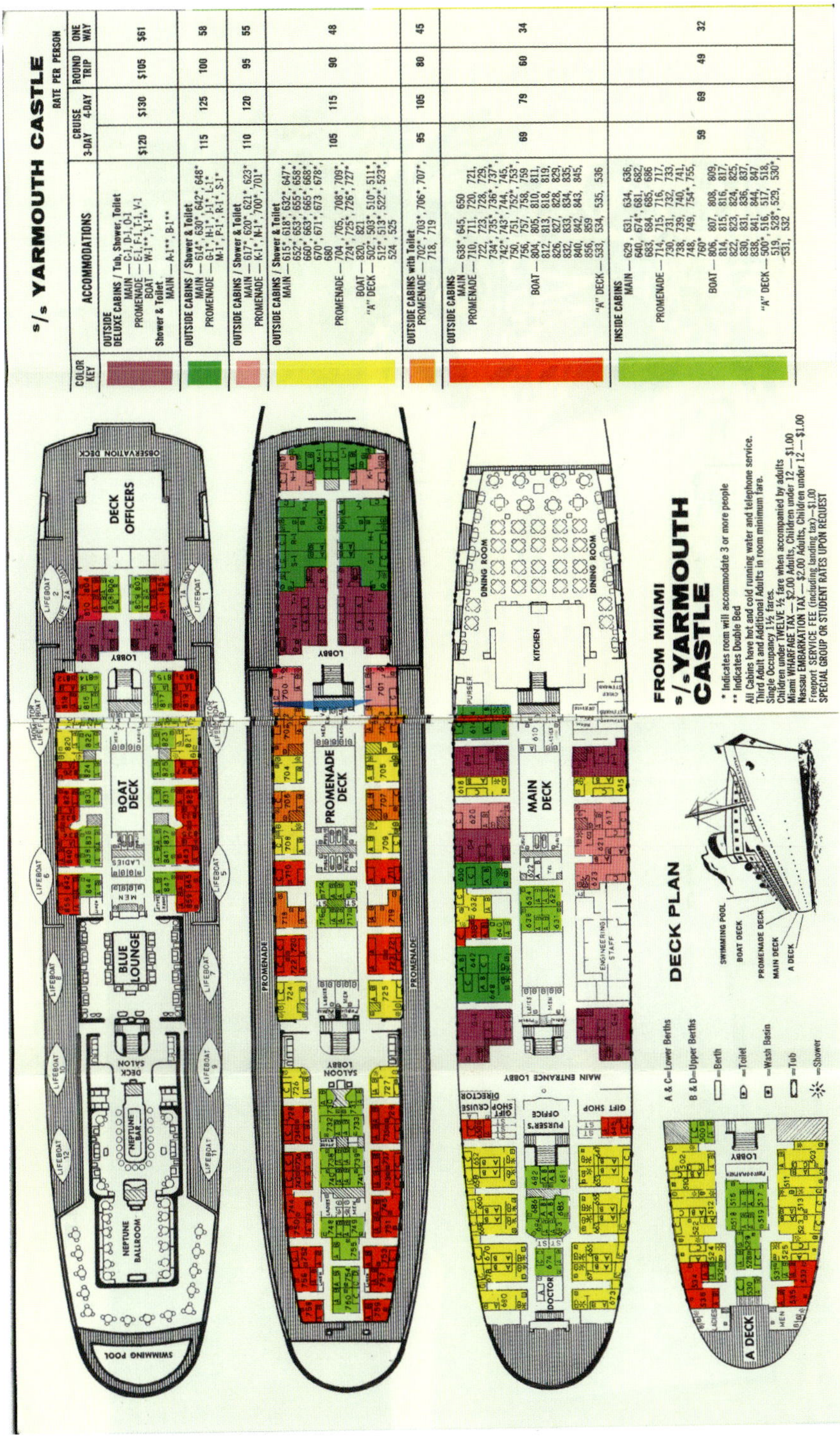

Deck plan brochure of *Yarmouth Castle*, showing decks, staterooms, and lifeboat locations. *Authors' collection*

Passengers wearing life jackets during an abandon-ship drill on board SS *Yarmouth*. *Authors' collection*

Yarmouth Castle burning; galley vent stack is in center of image, forward of the ship's smokestack. *Courtesy of National Archives and Records Administration, College Park, Maryland*

Port side of *Evangeline* boat deck, facing aft. Radio shack is to the left, with the galley vent stack visible above it. A life-jacket locker box is in the center, with boat 4 and a life raft to the right.
Courtesy of Jeff Macklin collection

Views of the bow and foredeck of *Evangeline* in Nassau and Ocho Rios, Jamaica. *Courtesy of Jeff Macklin collection*

Two photographs taken by Captain Carl Brown as he pulled alongside the *Yarmouth Castle*. In the first image, a solid jet of flame is extending upward from the galley vent stack just forward of the ship's smokestack. Lifeboat #1 has been lowered, with the davits still swung out. Boat #1A remains in place. *Courtesy of Louis Netherland*

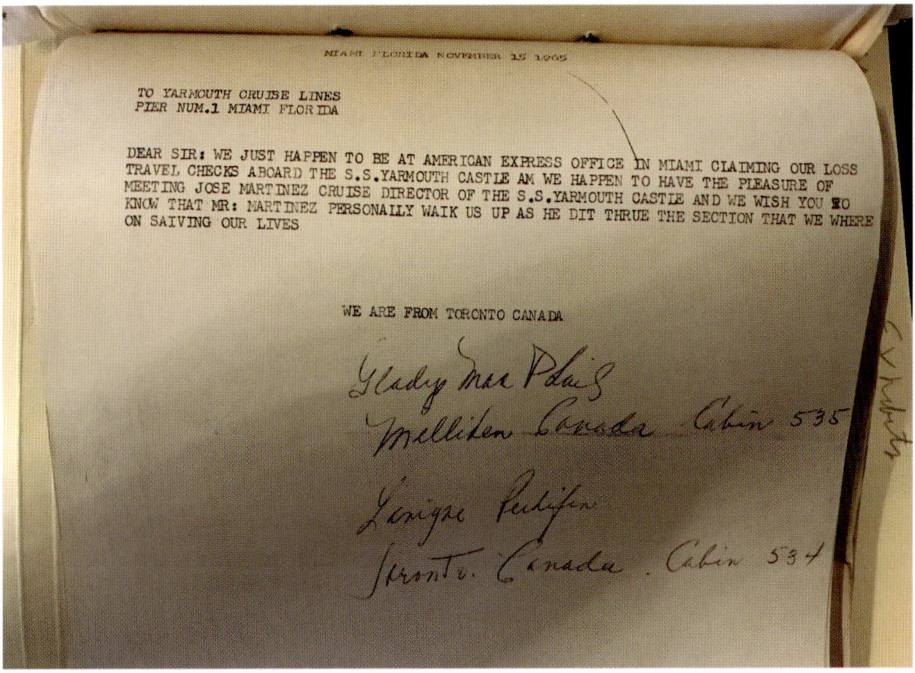

MIAMI FLORIDA NOVEMBER 15 1965

TO YARMOUTH CRUISE LINES
PIER NUM.1 MIAMI FLORIDA

DEAR SIR: WE JUST HAPPEN TO BE AT AMERICAN EXPRESS OFFICE IN MIAMI CLAIMING OUR LOSS TRAVEL CHECKS ABOARD THE S.S.YARMOUTH CASTLE AM WE HAPPEN TO HAVE THE PLEASURE OF MEETING JOSE MARTINEZ CRUISE DIRECTOR OF THE S.S.YARMOUTH CASTLE AND WE WISH YOU TO KNOW THAT MR: MARTINEZ PERSONALLY WAIK US UP AS HE DIT THRUE THE SECTION THAT WE WHERE ON SAIVING OUR LIVES

WE ARE FROM TORONTO CANADA

[illegible]
Milliken Canada Cabin 535
[illegible]
Toronto Canada Cabin 534

A letter from two Canadians thanking cruise director José Martinez for saving their lives. *Courtesy of National Archives and Records Administration, College Park, Maryland*

Bahama Star conducting a lifeboat drill. *Courtesy of Jeff Macklin collection*

Port bridge wing of *Bahama Star*, where Captain Brown directed his rescue operations. The engine order telegraph is visible just inside the bridge door. *Courtesy of Jeff Macklin collection*

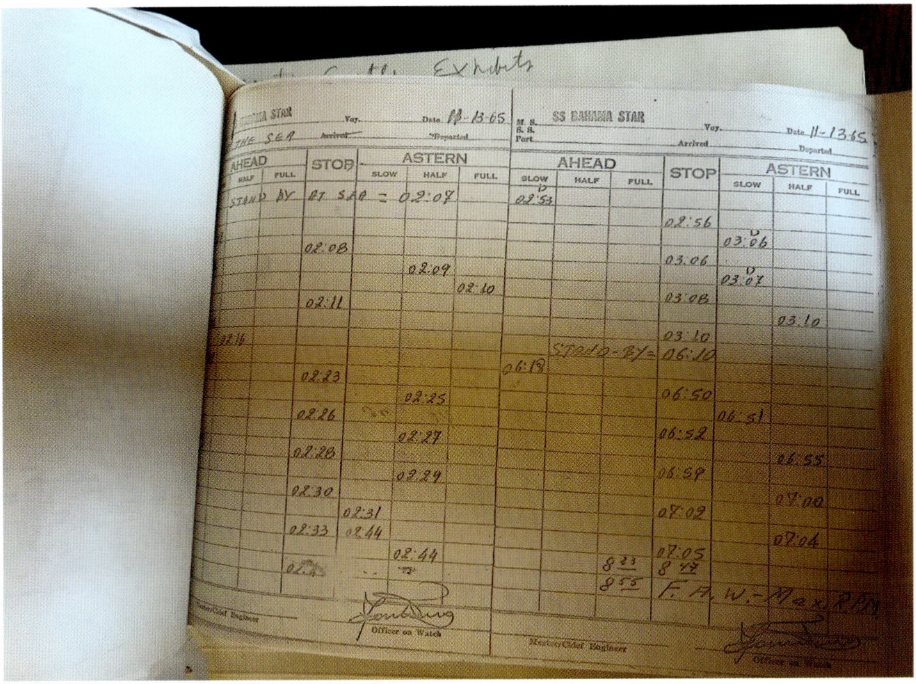

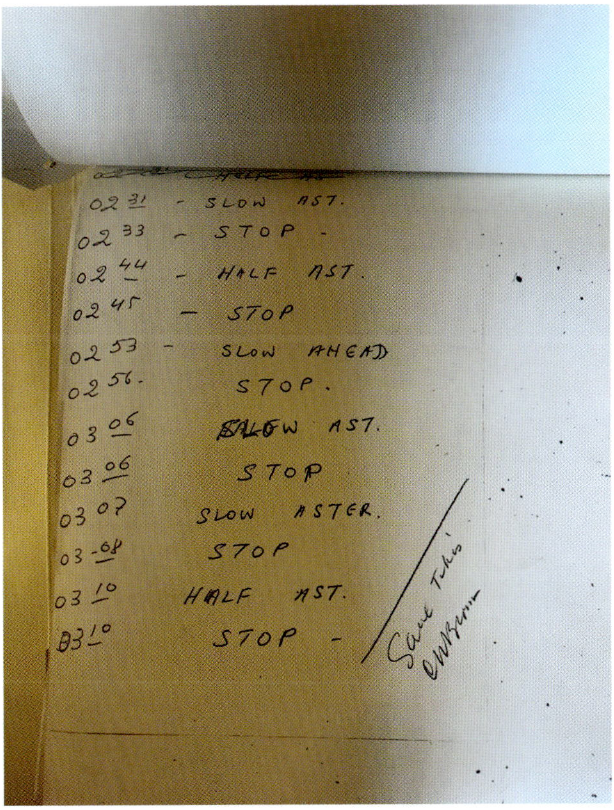

Bell book log page and engineers notes from *Bahama Star*'s engine room from the night of the rescue. *Courtesy of National Archives and Records Administration, College Park, Maryland*

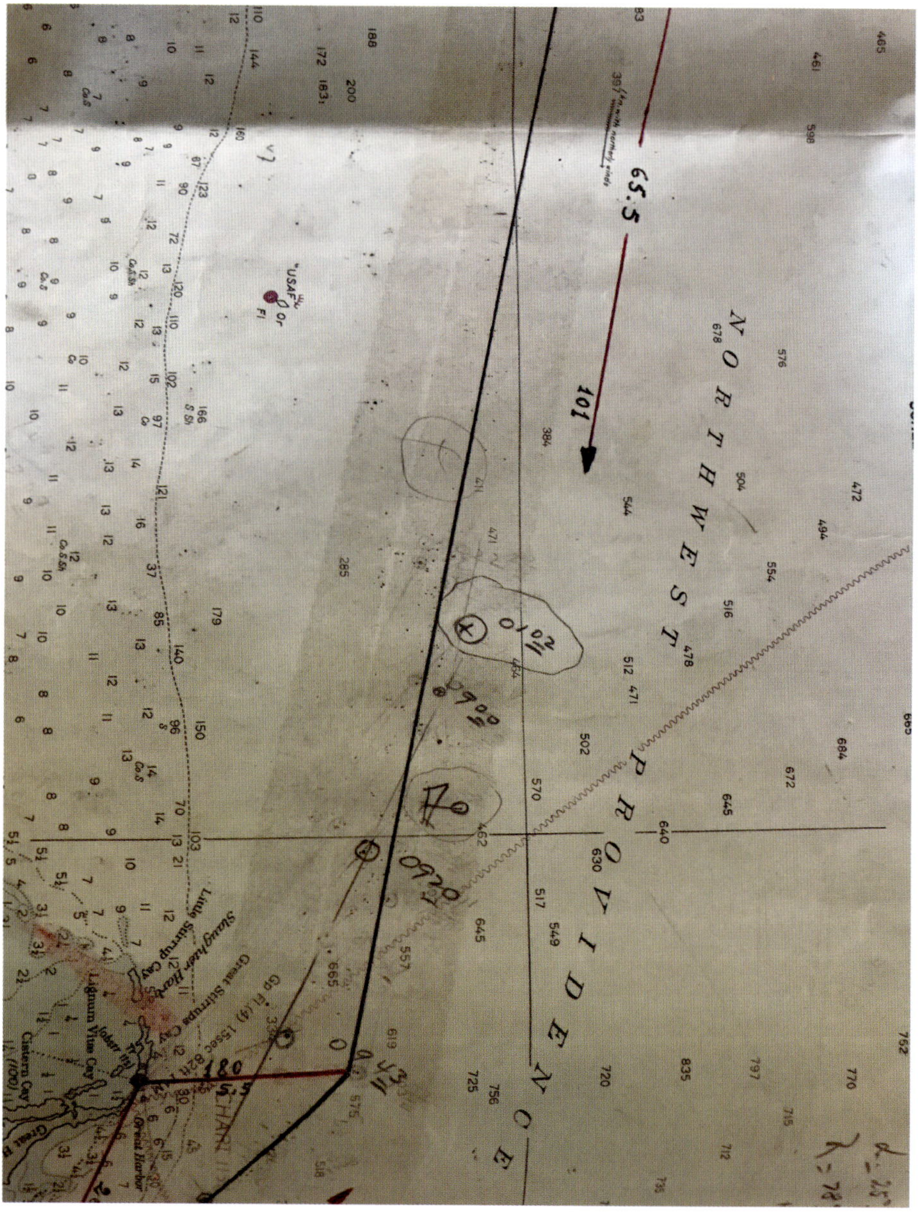

Bahama Star's chart indicating ship's position during the rescue and the location where *Yarmouth Castle* sank. *Courtesy of National Archives and Records Administration, College Park, Maryland*

Captain Byron Voutsinas speaking at the Coast Guard inquiry. Edwin Stephan is seated to Voutsinas's right. *Courtesy of Associated Press*

Finnpulp and *Bahama Star* standing by at the disaster site just after sunrise. *Courtesy of the Mariners Museum and Park, Newport News, Virginia*

US Coast Guard helicopters hovering over the stern of *Bahama Star* while lifting burn victims to safety. *Courtesy of the Mariners Museum and Park, Newport News, Virginia*

Coast Guard HH-52 hovering over the stern of *Bahama Star*. *Courtesy of Jeff Macklin collection*

Bahama Star on scene just after *Yarmouth Castle* sank, with smoke still visible on the sea surface. *Courtesy of the Mariners Museum and Park, Newport News, Virginia*

Bahama Star arriving in Nassau with survivors on board. *Courtesy of Jeff Macklin collection*

Above: Captain Johan Lehto and Second Mate Pekke Lavikka of the *Finnpulp* examining the *Yarmouth Castle* lifeboats they recovered the night before.
Authors' collection

Left: Survivors Mr. and Mrs. Kenneth Schler, who had been in the lifeboat with Captain Voutsinas, disembarking from the *Finnpulp* in Nassau.
Authors' collection

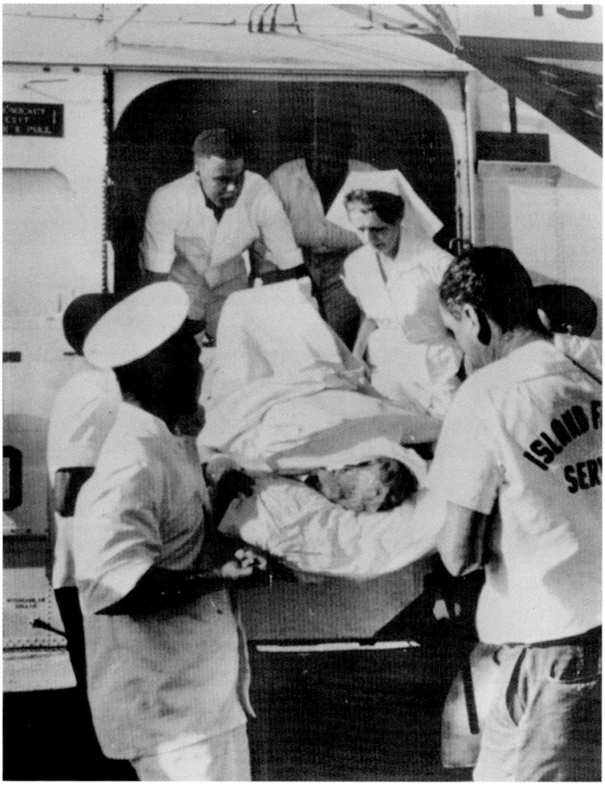

Woman survivor being unloaded from Coast Guard helicopter in Nassau. *Authors' collection*

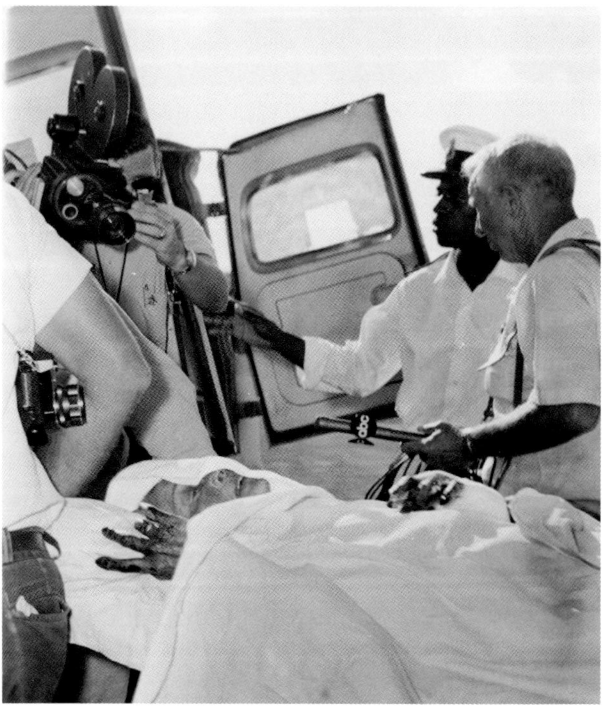

Woman survivor being loaded into ambulance in Nassau. *Authors' collection*

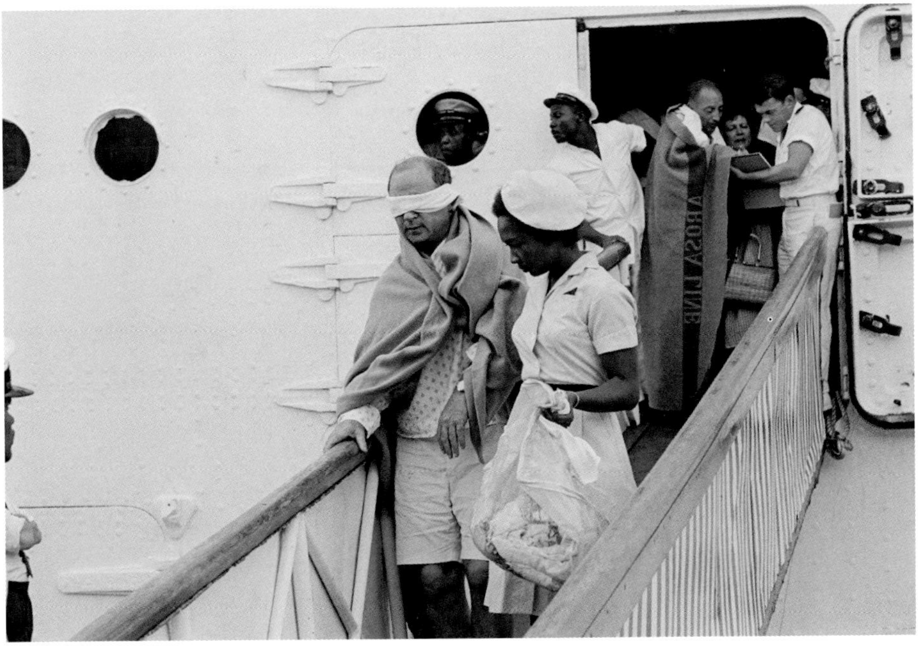

Man with eyes bandaged being led down *Bahama Star*'s gangway by a Bahamian nurse. *Courtesy of Associated Press*

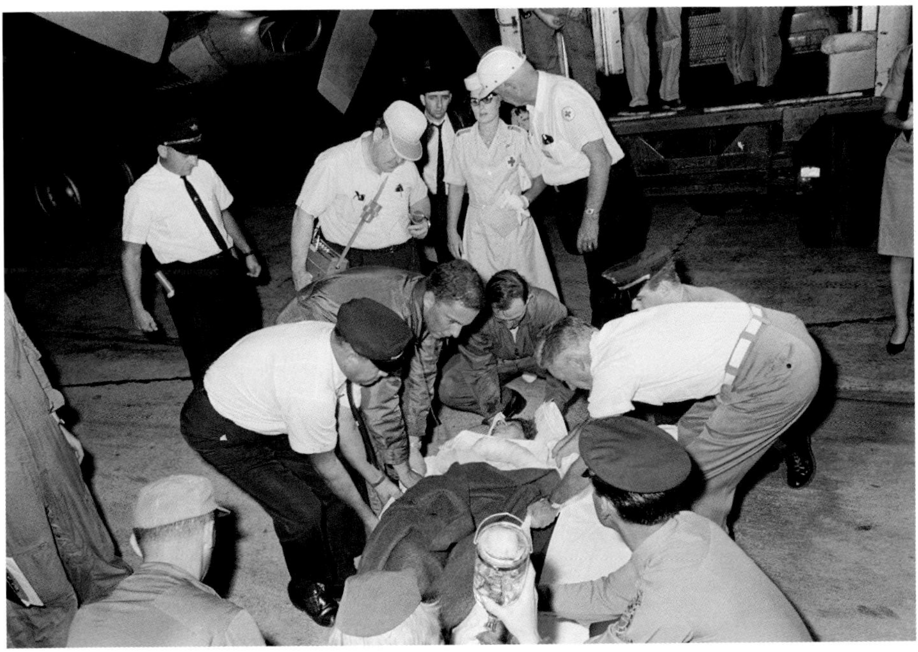

An Air Force flight crew transfers Mrs. Betty Barkin from an Air Force cargo plane to a waiting ambulance at Miami airport. *Courtesy of Associated Press*

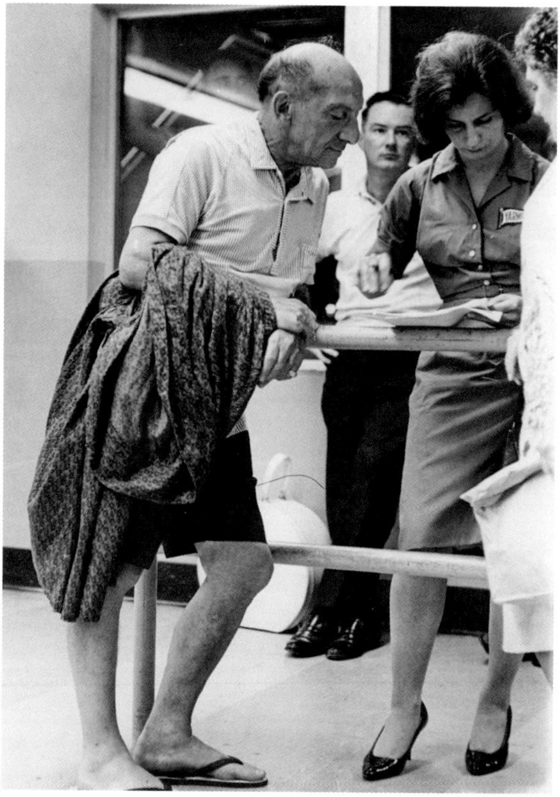

Survivors Mr. and Mrs. Cy Zymbol assisted by a Yarmouth Cruise Lines employee outside the company office in Miami. *Authors' collection*

Yarmouth Castle crew members outside company office, seeking wages and compensation for lost effects. *From* the *Miami Herald @1965 McClatchy, all rights reserved, used under license*

US Coast Guard investigation team boards *Yarmouth Castle*'s sister ship *SS Yarmouth* in Miami, on Friday, November 26. Rear Admiral Louis B. Thayer leads, followed by Captain Vitus G. Niebergall and Commander William Kesler. *From* the *Miami Herald* *@1965 McClatchy, all rights reserved, used under license*

Captain Carl Brown and Chief Engineer William Dagner accepting an award from Miami mayor Robert King High. *Courtesy of Louis Netherland collection*

Captain Carl Brown and Chief Engineer William Dagner, with an unidentified officer and Lovett company official, walking into the Nassau Customs House. *Courtesy of Louis Netherland collection*

Captain Carl Brown receiving an award from the Bahamian government. *Courtesy of Louis Netherland collection*

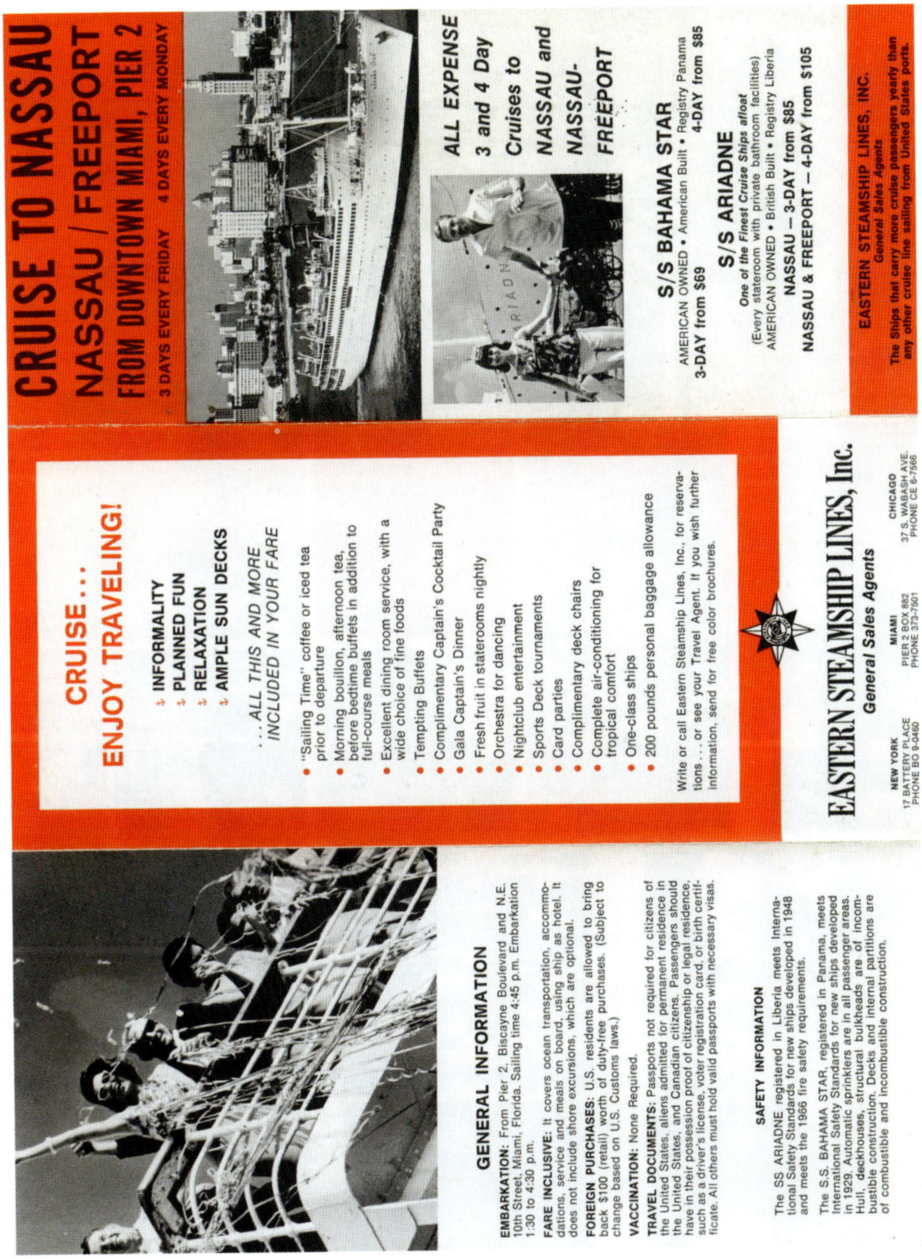

CRUISE TO NASSAU

NASSAU / FREEPORT

FROM DOWNTOWN MIAMI, PIER 2

3 DAYS EVERY FRIDAY 4 DAYS EVERY MONDAY

ALL EXPENSE 3 and 4 Day Cruises to NASSAU and NASSAU-FREEPORT

S/S BAHAMA STAR

AMERICAN OWNED • American Built • Registry Panama

3-DAY from $69 **4-DAY from $85**

S/S ARIADNE

One of the Finest Cruise Ships afloat

(Every stateroom with private bathroom facilities)

AMERICAN OWNED • British Built • Registry Liberia

NASSAU — 3-DAY from $85

NASSAU & FREEPORT — 4-DAY from $105

EASTERN STEAMSHIP LINES, INC.

General Sales Agents

The Ships that carry more cruise passengers yearly than any other cruise line sailing from United States ports.

CRUISE . . . ENJOY TRAVELING!

- **INFORMALITY**
- **PLANNED FUN**
- **RELAXATION**
- **AMPLE SUN DECKS**

. . . ALL THIS AND MORE INCLUDED IN YOUR FARE

- "Sailing Time" coffee or iced tea prior to departure
- Morning bouillon, afternoon tea, before bedtime buffets in addition to full-course meals
- Excellent dining room service, with a wide choice of fine foods
- Tempting Buffets
- Complimentary Captain's Cocktail Party
- Gala Captain's Dinner
- Fresh fruit in staterooms nightly
- Orchestra for dancing
- Nightclub entertainment
- Sports Deck tournaments
- Card parties
- Complimentary deck chairs
- Complete air-conditioning for tropical comfort
- One-class ships
- 200 pounds personal baggage allowance

Write or call Eastern Steamship Lines, Inc., for reservations . . . or see your Travel Agent. If you wish further information, send for free color brochures.

EASTERN STEAMSHIP LINES, Inc.

General Sales Agents

NEW YORK	MIAMI	CHICAGO
17 BATTERY PLACE	PIER 2 BOX 882	37 S. WABASH AVE.
PHONE BO 9-0460	PHONE 373-7501	PHONE CE 6-7566

GENERAL INFORMATION

EMBARKATION: From Pier 2, Biscayne Boulevard and N.E. 10th Street, Miami, Florida. Sailing time 4:45 p.m. Embarkation 1:30 to 4:30 p.m.

FARE INCLUSIVE: It covers ocean transportation, accommodations, service and meals on board, using ship as hotel. It does not include shore excursions, which are optional.

FOREIGN PURCHASES: U.S. residents are allowed to bring back $100 (retail) worth of duty-free purchases. (Subject to change based on U.S. Customs laws.)

VACCINATION: None Required.

TRAVEL DOCUMENTS: Passports not required for citizens of the United States, aliens admitted for permanent residence in the United States, and Canadian citizens. Passengers should have in their possession proof of citizenship or legal residence, such as a driver's license, voter registration card, or birth certificate. All others must hold valid passports with necessary visas.

SAFETY INFORMATION

The SS ARIADNE registered in Liberia meets International Safety Standards for new ships developed in 1948 and meets the 1966 fire safety requirements.

The S.S. BAHAMA STAR, registered in Panama, meets International Safety Standards for new ships developed in 1929. Automatic sprinklers are in all passenger areas. Hull, deckhouses, structural bulkheads are of incombustible construction. Decks and internal partitions are of combustible and incombustible construction.

Eastern Steamship Lines postfire brochure for *Bahama Star* and *Ariadne*, stating country of build, registry, and safety equipment information. *Courtesy of Jeff Macklin collection*

Evangeline moored in Port Antonio, Jamaica. *Authors' collection*

Yarmouth Castle postcard listing ports of call. *Courtesy of Jeff Macklin collection*

THE AUTHORS

Eric Takakjian and Randall Peffer are the coauthors of *Dangerous Shallows: In Search of the Ghost Ships of Cape Cod* (Lyons, 2020).

Eric Takakjian is the master of the *Chincoteague*, an oceangoing, 504-foot, articulated tug-and-barge unit engaged in the coastwise petroleum transportation trade. He has been sailing ships and oceangoing tugboats to various corners of the world since 1978. He holds a 1,600/3,000-ton oceans master's license, with first-class pilotage endorsements for vessels of any gross tons, as well as a "master of towing vessels upon oceans" endorsement. He is a US Coast Guard Designated Examiner for applicants engaged in the Towing Officer Assessment Record (TOAR) requirement process. Takakjian and his wife, Lori, owned and operated the oceanographic research vessel *Quest* for seventeen years, conducting oceanographic and shipwreck research in the northeastern United States. He has conducted extensive historical research on the maritime history of the North Atlantic and related shipwrecks. An avid shipwreck diver since 1975, Takakjian has been a National Fellow of the Explorers Club since 1997. He has been a member of the Steamship Historical Society of America since 1989 and has served on their board of directors since 2016.

Randall Peffer is the author of twelve nonfiction books as well as twelve crime and romantic suspense novels. His book *Watermen* is a documentary of the lives of the Chesapeake's fishermen. It won the *Baltimore Sun*'s Critic's Choice award and was Maryland Book of the Year. His crime novel *Provincetown Follies*, *Bangkok Blues* was a Lambda Award finalist and has been optioned for film. His recent book *Where Divers Dare: The Hunt for the Last U-boat* debuted as an Amazon "Hot New Read," with strong reviews in *Kirkus* and *Publishers Weekly*. Peffer has published over 350 travel-lifestyle features for *National Geographic*, *National Geographic Traveler*, the *New York Times*, *Smithsonian*, *Sail*, *Wooden Boat*, and most of the US major metro dailies. He holds a 100-ton master's license and has logged over 100,000 miles at sea. He taught literature and writing for thirty-seven years at Phillips Academy, Andover, Massachusetts.